THE
PHOTOGRAPHY BIBLE

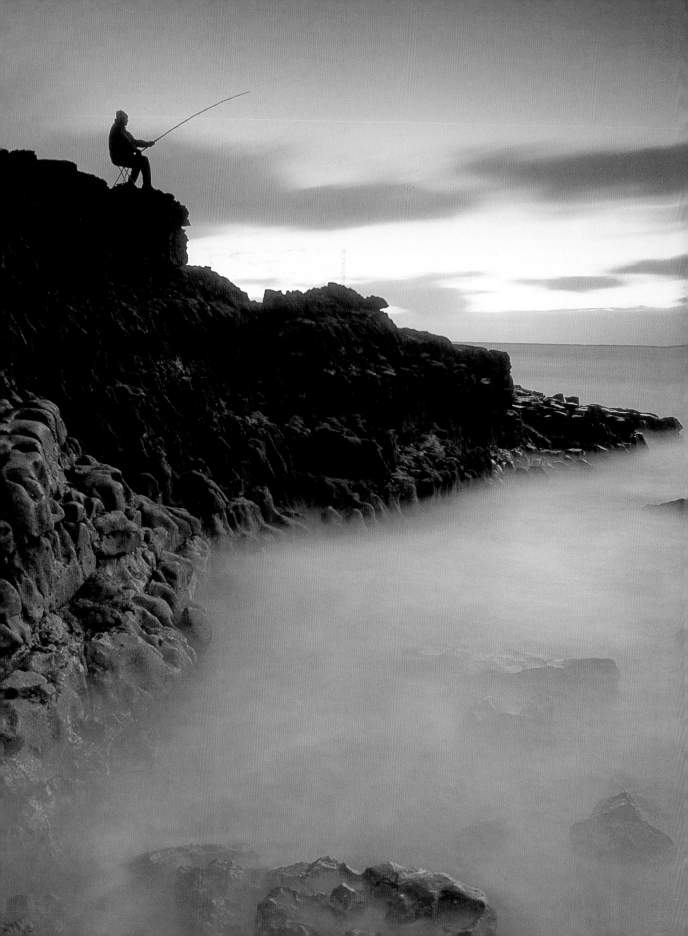

THE PHOTOGRAPHY BIBLE

DANIEL LEZANO

A COMPLETE GUIDE FOR THE 21ST CENTURY PHOTOGRAPHER

David & Charles

Dedication

This book is dedicated to my daughter Ellie, who has transformed my life, and to Jo and Max, who complete our perfect home. To my parents and my brother Adrian, I hope you enjoy the book.

A DAVID & CHARLES BOOK

David & Charles is a subsidiary of F+W (UK) Ltd.,
an F+W Publications Inc. company

First published in the UK in 2004
Reprinted 2005

Copyright © Daniel Lezano 2004

Distributed in North America
by F+W Publications, Inc.
4700 East Galbraith Road
Cincinnati, OH 45236
1-800-289-0963

Daniel Lezano has asserted his right to be identified as author of this work in accordance with the Copyright, Designs and Patents Act, 1988.

A catalogue record for this book is available from the British Library.

ISBN 0 7153 1806 3

Printed in China by Hong Kong Graphics & Printing Ltd.
for David & Charles
Brunel House   Newton Abbot   Devon

Commissioning Editor Neil Baber
Senior Editor Freya Dangerfield
Desk Editor Ame Verso
Executive Art Editor Ali Myer
Designers Lisa Forrester and Sarah Underhill
Production Controller Kelly Smith

Visit our website at www.davidandcharles.co.uk

David & Charles books are available from all good book-shops; alternatively you can contact our Orderline on (0)1626 334555 or write to us at FREEPOST EX2110, David & Charles Direct, Newton Abbot, TQ12 4ZZ (no stamp required UK mainland).

PHOTO CREDITS

© DANIEL LEZANO: 7 bottom, 29 bottom, 31 top and bottom, 35, 37 top, 49 all, 51 all, 53, 56, 57 all, 68-69, 77, 83 bottom, 87 top left, 87 bottom, 88, 90 top, 91 bottom, 92 bottom left and right, 93 bottom, 94 all, 95 bottom, 102 middle, 105 bottom, 109 middle, 111 bottom left, 119, 121 all, 122 bottom, 123, 124, 125 all, 132 bottom, 143 all, 145 middle and bottom, 148, 150 all, 151 all, 153 bottom, 156, 157 all, 162 all, 163 all, 166, 167
© BILLY STOCK: 2, 7 top, 29 right, 37 bottom, 87 top right, 98 top, 100 top, 101 all, 103, 104 bottom, 107 top, 111 bottom right, 116 bottom, 127 top, 128, 129 all, 130 all, 132 top, 133 all, 134 top, 135 top, 139 middle, 147 bottom, 158 right × 3, 159 top
© BJORN THOMASSEN: 6 top left, 40, 81 all, 108, 112 all, 113 bottom, 140 left, 141
© CHRIS ROUT: 6 bottom left, 52 all, 92 top, 93 top, 96 all, 97 all, 98 bottom, 99 all, 105 top, 109 bottom, 111 middle right, 113 top, 115 top, 120 all, 122 top, 134 bottom, 135 bottom left, 138 top right, 139 top, 140 right, 144 bottom × 3, 158 left
© SIMON STAFFORD: 7 middle right, 82, 83 top, 85 top and bottom, 86, 90 bottom, 106 all, 110, 114 all, 115 bottom, 136, 137 all, 138 left, 142 all, 145 top, 149 all, 152, 159 bottom, 161 all
© JON HICKS: 83 middle, 84 all, 89 all, 91 top, 100 bottom, 102 top and bottom, 104 top, 111 top, 117 top, 118, 126, 127 bottom, 131 bottom, 133 top, 135 right × 2, 144 top, 146 all, 147 top, 153 top, 154, 155 all
© LEE PENGELLY: (6 in total) 85 middle, 95 top, 109 top, 117 bottom, 131 top, 139 bottom
© DEREK HORLOCK: 107 middle, 160.

Contents

Introduction

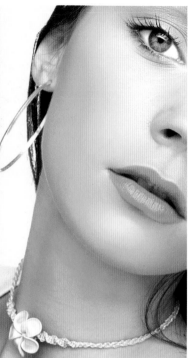

In photographic terms, the end of the 20th century marked the end of the film era, while the beginning of the 21st spelled the start of the digital age. The quality on offer from digital products has reached a level where it matches what is available from film. This, along with the many other advantages that digital photography has to offer, such as reusable media, instant review of images and so on, means that shooting digitally has become ever more tempting.

Photography is currently going through its most exciting and evolutionary time, with rapidly advancing technology marking a major change not only in how we take photographs, but also in how we can use and share them. It is a very exciting period for photography, but also a very confusing time for photographers, regardless of their level of experience. The purpose of this book is to provide essential information on the equipment available for the modern photographer, as well as the techniques needed to create the best possible images.

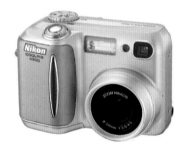

The first main section of the book provides a comprehensive overview of the many types of camera available. As well as providing clear descriptions of the various models, there are plenty of explanations of the terminology. With terms such as 'megapixel' and 'JPEG' becoming as commonplace in photography as 'aperture' or 'shutter speed', this book has been written to provide you with essential information in a jargon-free and crystal-clear format.

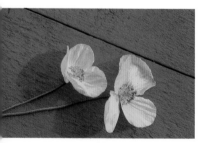

As you will discover, there is great similarity in the appearance of film and digital cameras, because of a conscious effort by manufacturers to make the transition from film to digital as painless as possible for photographers. The SLR (single-lens reflex) camera remains at the core of photography in both the film and digital worlds – its versatility, in particular its interchangeable lens capability, ensures that it remains the number one choice of photographers looking for high-quality results. For the more casual photographer, the rapid drop in price and increase in resolution of digital compact cameras is particularly exciting. It is generally accepted by most people in the photographic industry (myself included) that it is in the compact camera market that will see the most immediate shift from film to digital, although it is becoming increasingly obvious that a similar shift will soon occur in other areas, in particular SLR sales.

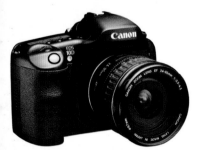

Despite using very different technologies, film and digital cameras are operated in very similar ways, so the actual technique for shooting images with either system is almost identical. *The Photography Bible* features a major section dedicated to picture-taking techniques to ensure that you make the most of your camera, regardless of what type you own. The technique guide has been divided into three main areas – basic techniques, equipment techniques and subject techniques – so whatever your level of photography or type of equipment, you'll find plenty of techniques to digest and try out.

For the new generation of digital photographers, the camera is where the scene is captured, but it is the computer where the image is created. The advent of image-manipulation software, in particular Adobe Photoshop, has led to the creation of the lightroom, a digital alternative to the traditional darkroom. The home computer offers a far more convenient and user-friendly option for the general photographer to create images than a chemical darkroom ever did. With personal computers found in the majority of homes, the chance to alter and enhance images has never been greater.

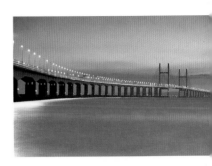

While only a very small percentage of conventional (film) photographers have ever produced their own prints, the advent of the photo-quality inkjet printer has meant that anyone can produce high-quality prints from the comfort of their home. While in the past having an enlargement – say, an 10 x 8in print – made from an image was relatively rare due to the effort and expense needed, producing 10 x 8in and larger prints from home is now easy. With peripherals such as scanners allowing images shot originally on film to be transferred to computer, even traditional photographers can become involved in the digital age.

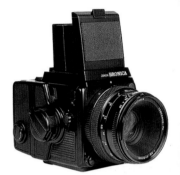

The Internet should not be forgotten for its major role in the rapid growth in popularity of digital photography. The chance to exhibit your images to a worldwide audience via a website, as well as being able to email images to anyone with Internet access, is something that should not be underestimated.

So, what of the future of film? Perhaps considering the subtle yet notable shift in the statuses of digital and film will address this. A couple of years ago, the biggest

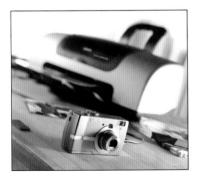

question raging among photographers was whether digital could ever replace film; the question now is how long it will be before digital replaces film. The future for film in the long-term therefore appears bleak, particularly in the general amateur and enthusiast arena, although it's worth pointing out that it still has a good few years left. While many professionals with medium-format equipment still prefer the higher quality available from film, it is surely only a

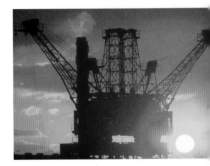

matter of time until the digital tide sweeps over them too. Is a filmless future ten years from now such a crazy prospect as it would have sounded five years ago? Certainly not. While film usage may not be completely eliminated for some time, its use will become increasingly marginalized. A good analogy can be found in the music industry: the digital CD is the dominant force, but vinyl still survives, although its appeal is to a niche market.

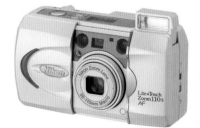

While some will rue the relatively sudden demise of film, the majority will appreciate the wide-reaching benefits that digital has to offer. Photography is going through a very exciting stage of its evolution at the moment. I hope that you will enjoy taking pictures (or should that be creating images?), and will find The Photography Bible an invaluable aid.

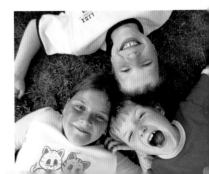

Cameras in the 21st century
The range

It is extraordinary to think that photography has only been around for about 160 years. In this time, things have moved at an astounding rate. From the first black-and-white plate cameras, we have moved on to the mass-produced Box Brownie, then the 35mm camera, on to colour, and now into the digital age. The diversity of equipment available today, and the quality of imagery that it produces, could only have been dreamed about back in the 1830s and 1840s, when photography was born.

35mm AF SLRs

The 35mm autofocus single-lens reflex, or AF SLR, is by far the most popular type of camera produced for the enthusiast photographer. Its versatility for use in a variety of photographic applications has made it the first choice of camera for many photographers, both amateur and professional.

There is a wealth of facilities on a 35mm AF SLR. Here are the main features on a typical mid-range model, the Nikon F75.

Anatomy of 35mm AF SLR

Lens
The zoom lens is the most popular choice for today's photographer, offering versatility and convenience. Choosing the right lens is vital – see page 50 for advice on which lens is best for different types of picture

Shutter button
This button does more than just take the picture: press it halfway, and it activates the autofocus and metering systems; press it fully and it fires the shutter

Custom functions
Many cameras offer the user the opportunity to customize certain functions to their own preferences

LCD panel
The liquid crystal display is the camera's information centre. Although its position has traditionally been on the camera's top-plate, it is now more frequently placed on the rear of the camera, where it can be made larger in size

Film transport selector
Depending on what you are shooting, you can set the camera to advance a single frame with each press of the shutter button, or to fire continuously until you release it. This control usually allows you to set the self-timer

Exposure mode dial
This provides fast and easy access to the camera's main exposure modes and often handles other functions

Hotshoe
Regardless of whether or not the camera has an integral flashgun, it will offer a facility to add an external flashgun. The central metal pin of the hotshoe triggers the flashgun when the shutter button is depressed

Viewfinder

This is the eyepiece through which you view the image. SLRs allow you to view through the lens, giving very good accuracy for composition

Dioptre correction

Spectacle wearers can have trouble looking through a viewfinder, so many models now offer a correction facility that allows the user to factor in their eyesight prescription, allowing them to view a clear image while not wearing their glasses

Input dial

You'll find one (and sometimes two) of these on the camera, usually located close to the shutter button for use by the index finger, or on the rear close to where the thumb rests. These serve to change variables, such as shutter speeds and apertures

Autofocus point selector

The majority of models boast an autofocus system with several autofocus points. This control allows you to select how the camera uses them (see page 26)

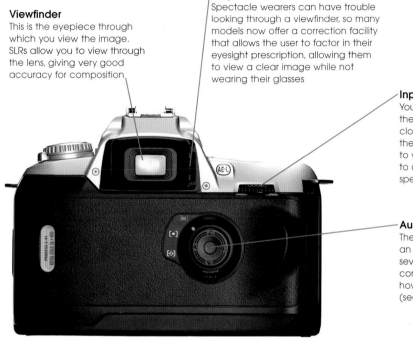

AF assist beam

As good as it is, a modern camera's autofocus system can have problems shooting in certain conditions, especially low contrast and dim lighting situations. The AF assist beam, located on the front or in some cases in the integral flash housing, provides a patterned light beam to help the camera lock on the subject

Integral flash

A built-in flash is now found on the majority of SLRs. Its power is limited, but it is useful for shooting subjects within a few metres' range. Depending on the camera, it offers a variety of modes, including automatic (see page 55)

Depth of field preview

Also known as the stopdown lever, this is a very useful and often underused feature. It allows you to close down the aperture to the working aperture so that you can gauge the depth of field in a scene through the viewfinder

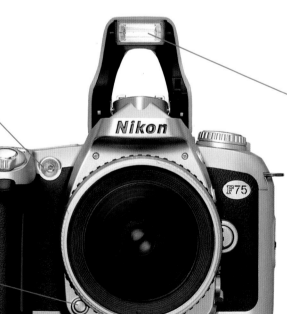

Digital AF SLRs

The beginning of the 21st century heralded the dawn of a new generation of digital autofocus SLRs – cameras boasting a very high level of features and performance and, above all, a price tag that offered widespread appeal. The rapid pace of increased digital performance and fall in price mean that it is no longer a question of 'if' or 'when' digital SLRs become the number one type of camera for the enthusiast, but how soon.

At first glance, the digital AF SLR looks very much like a 35mm AF SLR. This is what the manufacturers intend, as it makes the transition from using film to digital cameras that much easier for photographers. The main differences between the two are found on the rear of the camera, where the LCD monitor and controls for the digital functions are found.

Anatomy of digital AF SLR

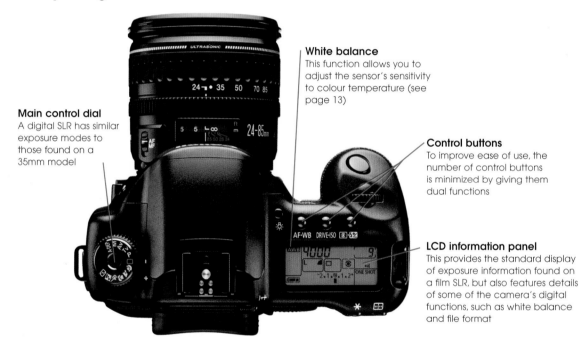

White balance
This function allows you to adjust the sensor's sensitivity to colour temperature (see page 13)

Main control dial
A digital SLR has similar exposure modes to those found on a 35mm model

Control buttons
To improve ease of use, the number of control buttons is minimized by giving them dual functions

LCD information panel
This provides the standard display of exposure information found on a film SLR, but also features details of some of the camera's digital functions, such as white balance and file format

Wi-Fi
A recent digital innovation is Wi-Fi, a technology that allows high-speed transfer of images from the camera to the computer without the need of any leads. This has particular applications for press and sports photography.

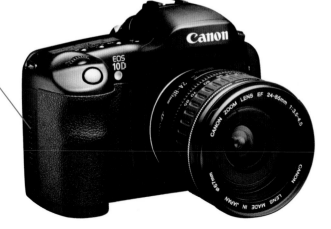

Card slot
Most models of digital SLR accept CompactFlash cards, although some models accept a choice of two types of card (see page 46)

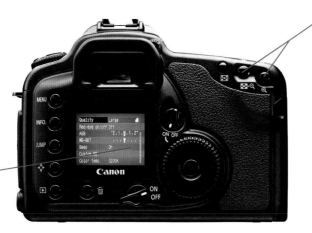

Review tools

A couple of tools are available to help when reviewing images. The multi-tool allows you to view small thumbnails of up to nine images at once on the screen, making it easier to search through multiple images to find a particular shot. The magnifying tool allows you to 'zoom' into an image to check its sharpness

LCD monitor

An on-screen menu allows you to select and change a wide range of functions, such as choosing what format to save the image in, adjusting flash modes and so on. The screen also allows you to review, protect or delete images from a memory card

TOP TIP

Try to restrict how much you use the LCD monitor, as it is one of the biggest drains on battery power.

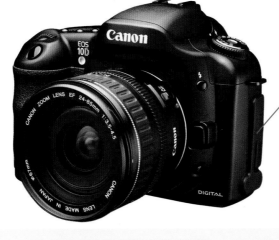

Interface

Connecting the camera directly to a computer via the appropriate lead allows images to be downloaded from the memory card. Most cameras use USB or FireWire connectivity, as well as a video-out socket

The four-thirds system

This digital system, developed by Olympus and Kodak, is unique in that it is not based on an existing film system, but has been developed from scratch as a digital system. The first camera in the four-thirds system was the Olympus Camedia E-1, a highly specified 5-megapixel camera.

The lens mount has been developed for various manufacturers to design cameras around it, in order that their lenses are cross-compatible. Because the lens system has been designed specifically for the four-thirds system, manufacturers promise a higher performance than that gained from lenses made for film SLRs.

Effective focal length

With interchangeable-lens SLRs, the effective focal length of the lens depends on the size of the chip used in the camera. There are only a couple of SLRs with sensors that match the size of the 35mm film format. These full-frame models do not magnify the effective focal length of a lens as cameras using smaller size sensors do. In most cases, the effective focal length is increased by 1.5x or 1.6x. This is good news if you use mainly telephoto lenses, as it increases the pulling power. However, it's a disadvantage for photographers who prefer to work at wider focal lengths.

Inside an AF SLR

The modern SLR has more processing power than NASA put into the first mission to land men on the Moon. This high level of computing power is required to control the various functions undertaken by the camera. From the materials used in the body shell to the sophisticated computer circuitry, every part of a modern camera is a marvel of technology, performing complex functions that were impossible to imagine only a couple of decades ago.

Mirror
The semi-silvered mirror reflects light passing through the lens up to the pentaprism and into the viewfinder

Body frame
Magnesium alloy is a popular frame choice due to its combination of strength and light weight. Polycarbonate, a very strong and robust plastic, is used for most outer housings

Pentaprism
Light travelling through the lens is viewed through the viewfinder via a mirror in the camera body and a prism, housed in the pentaprism

Power source
Lithium batteries are normally the main source of power, offering longer life and faster flash recycling times over more traditional alkaline cells

Shutter blind
This light-tight blind prevents light from reaching the film until an exposure is taken. Shutter speeds can vary from hours up to extremely fast speeds: a top shutter speed of 1/8000sec is commonplace today

DX-coding
This series of pins provides information on the film that is loaded in the film chamber. The most important data is the film speed, but the pins also identify what type of film it is

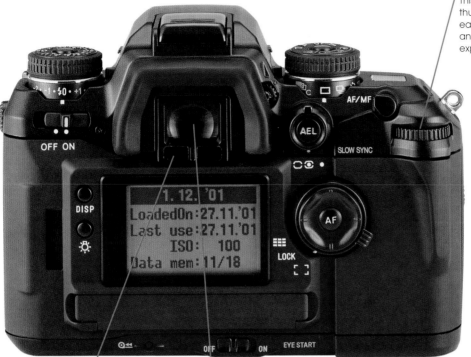

Rear control dial
This falls where the right thumb rests, making it easy and quick to make any adjustments such as exposure compensation

Eye-start system
Featured on some Minoltas, these sensors on the viewfinder or on the handgrip, activate the autofocus and metering systems when covered

Viewfinder
When you look through the camera's viewfinder, you will see the autofocus points and often a metering area in the screen. With many systems, the AF points light up in red when they are activated. A comprehensive readout is often located beside or below the viewfinder screen

Common features

Metering sensors
In SLRs, most sensors are found beneath the semi-silvered mirror, in the pentaprism, or positioned so that they measure the light reflecting off a pattern on the shutter blind or even off the film surface itself.

Focusing screens
Top-end models will allow the user to change focusing screens to suit a particular type of photography or an individual preference.

White balance
Digital sensors can be set to work under different forms of light source by adjusting the white balance. In the auto setting, the camera automatically calculates the appropriate white balance setting.

Camera innovations

Eye-control focusing
This allows the camera to focus based on where the photographer looks in the viewfinder by bouncing weak infrared beams from transmitters in the viewfinder off the photographer's eyeball.

Pellicle mirror
The pellicle mirror remains fixed during the exposure. This allows for very fast frame rates, as there is no delay related to the mirror swinging out of the light path.

Dot matrix LCD
This system aids the photographer in a unique fashion and offers a high level of information, such as calculating the depth of field of a scene based on current lens settings.

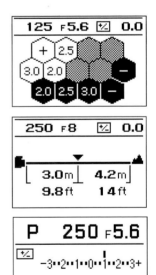

DOT MATRIX LCD
Although it is still rare on cameras, this is extremely versatile, as these three examples show. As well as exposure information, the display can provide details such as depth of field and focusing distance, or the difference in brightness of various segments of the frame.

Film compacts

The compact camera has for decades remained the most popular choice of camera for most people. Its fully automatic operation has made it the perfect choice for point-and-shoot photography for the mass market. The 35mm compact has always remained the number one type, with APS (Advanced Photo System) cameras taking a large chunk of the market since the system's launch in 1996. The future dominance of the film compact is now under threat, following the emergence and popularity of the digital compact.

Main types of film compact

There is a compact camera to suit every budget and level of photographer, from very simple point-and-shoots to high-quality models from prestigious brands. The two main types are fixed-lens and zoom compacts. The fixed-lens models fit into two main categories, the budget end of the market and the premium models. The latter compacts feature very high-quality wide-angle lenses that can rival SLR lenses for sharpness.

Zoom compacts are more versatile than their fixed-lens counterparts and are found throughout the price range, with the exception of the cheapest budget models. The zoom range varies from camera to camera, with more expensive models boasting more powerful zoom lenses. Again, premium models are available, although these tend to have a relatively short zoom range of around 35–70mm.

Anatomy of a film compact

Exposure/focus sensors
These sensors measure the amount of light for the exposure system and calculate the camera-to-subject distance for the lens focus. They are normally found above the lens

Built-in flash
This fires automatically when required and usually offers a number of mode options, in particular fill-in and red-eye reduction

Viewfinder
This is used to compose the picture. Because it does not offer through-the-lens viewing, it provides only an approximate guide to the scene the lens will capture. This isn't an issue for normal shooting situations, but presents the problem of parallax error for close-ups (see Parallax correction, opposite). With most compacts, a pair of indicator lamps give the status of the autofocus and flash systems

Lens cover
Most compacts have a sliding lens cover, which protects the optics when closed and switches the camera on when opened

Zoom lens
The majority of compacts now feature a zoom lens. The zoom range has increased from the 35–70mm zoom of the first generation compacts to the current standard of around 38–105mm

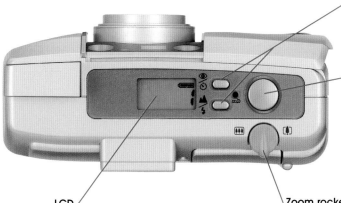

Function buttons
These handle a variety of the camera's functions, including self-timer, flash modes and focusing options

Shutter button
This works in two stages: slight pressure activates the exposure and focusing systems, and full pressure fires the shutter. Compact cameras feature a shutter within the lens, which handles the work of both an aperture and a shutter blind

LCD
A series of icons indicates current settings for the main camera functions, such as flash mode and battery status. Only the most expensive models provide exposure information such as shutter speed or aperture

Zoom rocker
This control allows you to change the focal length of the lens. A 'W' or a symbol with three trees indicates wide-angle, while a 'T' or a single tree symbol indicates telephoto

Parallax correction
The camera viewfinder does not offer through-the-lens (TTL) viewing, so it can only offer an accurate but approximate framing of the scene. Normally this works well, but with close-up photography, the short distances involved lead to a problem known as parallax error, where what the viewfinder shows and what the lens records are slightly different. Parallax correction lines in the viewfinder provide a guide to composing close-ups to prevent this problem from occurring.

Compact camera types

35mm and APS compact cameras come in various forms. As well as the mainstream zoom compact, there are other types worth investigating.

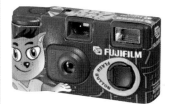

Single-use camera
Extremely popular due to their low cost, these basic cameras, loaded with colour print film, are used once, then handed in for processing. They are available in 35mm and APS, and come in many versions – with or without flash, underwater versions and panoramic types.

Luxury compacts
These models offer lens quality on a par with an SLR. They usually sport a wide-angle lens, although some have a zoom. The build quality is excellent, and many cameras offer control over the exposure and focusing systems. These come at a high price, but are popular with enthusiasts who want a pocketable camera capable of excellent results.

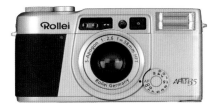

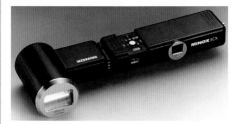

Spy cameras
For discreet photography, there is nothing to touch the Minox range of spy cameras, which use an unusual 8 x 11mm film to keep their size very small.

Digital compacts

Although digital compacts haven't been around for very long, they are already the dominant force in point-and-shoot photography, and are effectively ensuring a less than rosy future for film compacts. Digital compacts look similar to film-based models from the front, but the rear gives away their digital origins.

Because these cameras are aimed at the mass market, ease of use is of the utmost importance, both for designing and using them; because of this, controls are kept to a minimum and are clearly labelled. The variety of models is amazing, with budget models for web use and models with 1–5 megapixels to cater for all levels of photographer.

Choosing the right model of digital compact is discussed on pages 24–25, but here's a rundown of the main features.

Anatomy of a digital compact

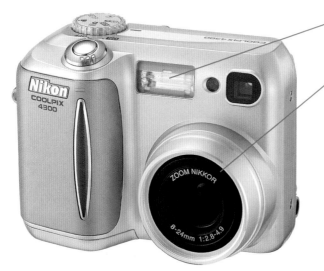

Built-in flash
All but the very cheapest models offer integral flash for taking pictures in low-lit or indoor situations

Lens
A zoom lens is standard on all but the most budget models. Most zooms offer a wider focal length and a faster maximum aperture than film compacts

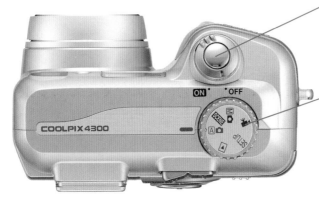

Shutter button
As on other types of camera, the shutter button has a two-step action – light pressure activates the autofocus and exposure system, while full pressure takes the picture

Mode selector
Some cameras have a dial that allows you to choose which mode you'd like to use, and others have a switch. Most cameras have two main types of mode – camera mode is for taking pictures; playback mode is for viewing images. Many models now sport a movie mode, which allows you to shoot short clips of video (usually, but not always, with sound)

Interface
Most models feature at least one socket for downloading images from the camera – usually USB. Many models also feature a video-out mini-jack socket that lets you view your images on a television screen.

Microphone
Depending on the model, the microphone serves two purposes: the first as a voice memo for still images; the second to record sound during a video sequence.

Battery
The high power consumption of a digital camera means that AA alkaline batteries aren't recommended. Instead, models are increasingly using rechargeable batteries (see page 18).

Card slot
There's no need for a film chamber, so instead of the camera's rear behaving like a large door, only a small compartment is required to store the card. Some cameras have the battery enclosed in the same chamber as the card, others don't. Generally, the smaller the type of card used, the smaller the camera.

Viewfinder
This isn't found on all models, as in some cases the LCD monitor is used for composing the frame. Models sporting a traditional viewfinder (known as an optical viewfinder) have the advantage of saving battery power. They are very similar to the type found on film compacts, and often have an autofocus and flash indicator light

Zoom control
As with film compacts, changing the focal length of the lens is via a simple zoom rocker switch

LCD monitor
This is relatively large compared to the size of the camera. In camera mode, the LCD can be used as a large electronic colour viewfinder, while in playback mode, it allows images to be reviewed. An on-screen menu provides the user with a wealth of options for adjusting the camera's settings

Macro facility
The flower icon signifies that the camera has a macro facility. Digital compacts boast much better close-focusing capability than film compacts, allowing high magnification images to be taken at extremely short focusing distances – in some instances, less than 25mm (1in)

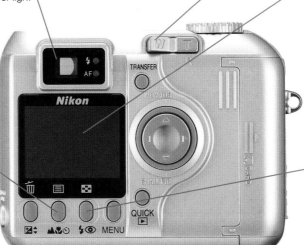

Flash button
Most digital cameras work in auto-flash mode unless you specify otherwise and set the flash to fill-in, flash-off, red-eye reduction or slow-sync flash. If you do turn the flash off, the camera not only changes the shutter speed and aperture to compensate, but also increases the ISO speed rating if necessary

Digital compact accessories

There are many useful add-ons available for digital compacts.

Lens attachments

Some models allow attachments to be fitted to the lens. A wide-angle converter increases the angle of view, while a teleconverter provides a stronger telephoto effect.

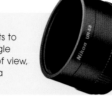

Cradle

Also known as a docking station, this is a very useful accessory that allows for the fast and fuss-free transfer of images from the camera, without having to connect any leads. The camera then simply sits inside the cradle and connects automatically. The cradle also acts as a power source, charging the camera's battery to full power.

Underwater housing

Fancy trying your camera beneath the waves? You'll find that most manufacturers make dedicated underwater housings, with independent brands also offering housings for many models.

Filters

Many models feature a thread for screwing filters in front of the lens element.

Flashgun

A few top-end models sport a hotshoe for fitting an external flashgun.

Remote control

Infrared remote controls are fairly commonplace on digital compacts as an option to the self-timer.

Optical/digital zoom

It's worth noting that cameras often boast two types of zoom – optical and digital zooms. The optical zoom refers to the actual zoom lens, while the digital zoom refers to an electronic process where the camera magnifies the central portion of the frame. You should be aware that digital zooms degrade the image the further they extend, and so are to be avoided whenever possible.

Battery options

Some cameras use AA batteries and are supplied with rechargeable Ni-Mh (nickel metal hydride) cells, which provide a better performance than alkaline and Ni-Cd (nickel cadmium) batteries. Long-life batteries offer a higher capacity than normal ones, which is useful if you use the camera in remote areas that prevent recharging.

More and more cameras are using lithium-ion batteries, which have a much higher capacity and faster recycling times than conventional rechargeables. These are often smaller than a pair of AAs, allowing the camera's size to be reduced.

Direct printing

Many cameras now sport a facility that allows them to work directly with a printer. The Pict Bridge system works with various camera and printer brands, such as Pentax and Epson.

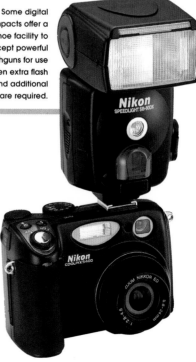

Some digital compacts offer a hotshoe facility to accept powerful flashguns for use when extra flash range and additional features are required.

Digital compact innovation

Porro lens
Minolta's X-series cameras are very thin (around 20mm/¾in thick), yet manage to incorporate an internal zoom lens. This is because they use an internal prism within the lens design, which means that the lens does not need to extend from the body as it zooms through its range.

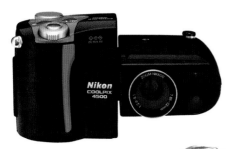

Swivel lens housing
Some models have the lens built in a swivel-action housing, which allows the lens to be pointed at unusual angles, yet still enables the LCD monitor to be seen by the user, such as for waist-level shooting. Several models in Nikon's Coolpix range offer this facility.

Bluetooth
This innovative feature is becoming increasingly popular on gadgets, including cameras and imaging phones. It allows pictures to be transferred from a Bluetooth-enabled camera to another product, such as a computer, that is also Bluetooth-compliant. As well as being easier to use, as there's no need to connect leads, the transfer speed is faster.

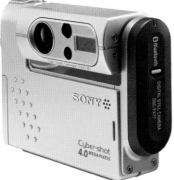

RTUNE technology
Kyocera Yashica were the first to use RTUNE technology in the Finecam S5R. This system allows for very fast frame capture by writing data to the card at a rate of around 10Mb per second. This is particularly useful for capturing action sequences.

Main types of digital compact

Budget
These cheap and cheerful models sport a fixed lens and 1-megapixel or less resolution. Their relatively low resolution makes them suitable mainly for web use or cataloguing images on computer.

Low-end
Boasting a resolution of around 2 megapixels and usually sporting a fixed lens or short zoom, these models look to cater for the snapshot user, delivering images of quality suitable for enprint size.

Mid-range
These models offer a relatively high resolution of 3–4 megapixels and a decent zoom range. A good range of options allows the user control of many of the camera's main functions.

Premium
The resolution of at least 4 or 5 megapixels makes these cameras capable of very high-quality results. Many have SLR styling and features, a powerful zoom lens and a range of dedicated accessories.

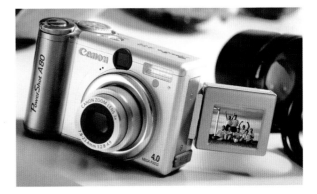

Medium-format SLRs

The benefits of the larger film frame of medium-format cameras have made it the choice of photographers looking for better quality than 35mm can muster. Images are recorded on roll film, which is wound from one spool to another. It appears an archaic system by today's standards, but the quality of results is first-rate, and many professionals working in the studio, as well as outdoors, still see it as their number one choice. Modern technology hasn't passed medium format by, with the latest models sporting autofocus and metering systems that are similar to 35mm and digital systems. As with other camera systems, there is a wide variety of medium-format camera types, although the SLR remains the most popular.

Anatomy of a medium-format SLR

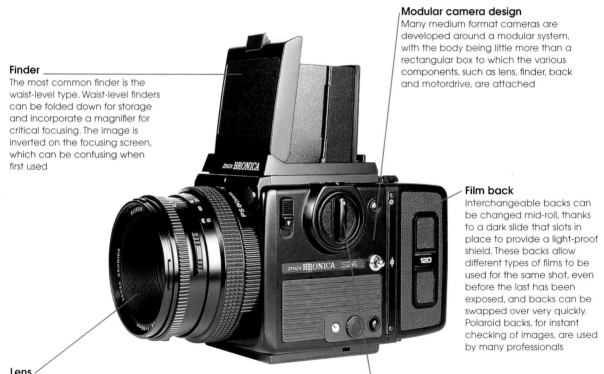

Finder
The most common finder is the waist-level type. Waist-level finders can be folded down for storage and incorporate a magnifier for critical focusing. The image is inverted on the focusing screen, which can be confusing when first used

Modular camera design
Many medium format cameras are developed around a modular system, with the body being little more than a rectangular box to which the various components, such as lens, finder, back and motordrive, are attached

Film back
Interchangeable backs can be changed mid-roll, thanks to a dark slide that slots in place to provide a light-proof shield. These backs allow different types of films to be used for the same shot, even before the last has been exposed, and backs can be swapped over very quickly. Polaroid backs, for instant checking of images, are used by many professionals

Lens
Most medium-format cameras offer interchangeable lenses. The majority of these are fixed, as opposed to zoom, as they provide best quality and a relatively wide maximum aperture. With some systems, the shutter is incorporated in the lens, as opposed to the camera body, allowing flash synchronization at all shutter speeds

Shutter speed dial
A large shutter speed dial with the numerals facing upwards, means it is easy to check and change when using the finder. Some models feature the shutter speed dial on the lens rather than the camera body

Main film formats

Despite using the same type of film, different medium-format cameras produce images of different sizes. The most popular are listed here:

6 x 4.5cm

This is the most popular entry point for first-time medium-format users, as it's the next step up from 35mm and is also the most inexpensive type. Its relatively small size and light weight make it a particularly good choice for outdoor and travel photographers.

Number of frames per 120 film: 15

6 x 6cm

The square format has been dominated by Hasselblad for decades. This format is particularly suited to portrait, wedding and fashion work, although some landscape photographers also use it.

Number of frames per 120 film: 12

6 x 7cm

Favoured by those looking for a rectangular format of superior quality than 6 x 4.5cm, and ideally suited for work in the studio, 6 x 7cm cameras are about as big as you want to go with a camera you plan to carry around.

Number of frames per 120 film: 10

6 x 8cm and 6 x 9cm

These two formats are becoming less and less popular, as only a handful of cameras are available, supported almost exclusively by Fujifilm.

Panoramic: 6 x 12cm and 6 x 17cm

Images from panoramic cameras need to be seen to be believed – the quality is outstanding, and the format shape works extremely well for landscapes. It's an expensive format in terms of running costs: a 6 x 12cm produces six shots per 120 roll, while a 6 x 17cm camera only manages four frames!

Digital backs

Many of the latest medium-format SLRs are fully compatible with high-resolution digital backs. This allows them to record images digitally rather than on film, with resolutions of up to 25 megapixels.

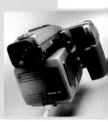

Other medium-format models

As well as SLRs, there are two main types of medium-format camera.

Rangefinder

Rangefinder models are available in formats from 6 x 4.5cm to 6 x 9cm and offer the advantage of being compact and lightweight. With the Bronica RF645 and Mamiya 7II, interchangeable lenses are available too.

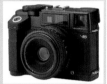

Twin-lens reflex

This classic design is still available. A twin-lens reflex uses the top lens for viewing the scene, and the bottom lens for capturing the image. The classic twin-lens reflex from the likes of Rolleiflex is capable of superb results.

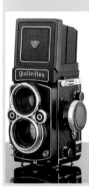

Focal length comparison

The following table indicates how the focal length of medium-format lenses of the three most popular formats relates approximately to the 35mm format.

6 x 4.5cm

6 x 4.5cm format	35mm	45mm	55mm	80mm	150mm	210mm	300mm
35mm format	22mm	28mm	34mm	50mm	93mm	130mm	185mm

6 x 6cm

6 x 6cm format	40mm	50mm	65mm	80mm	135mm	150mm	200mm
35mm format	23mm	28mm	35mm	45mm	76mm	85mm	110mm

6 x 7cm

6 x 7cm format	50mm	65mm	75mm	90mm	150mm	180mm	210mm
35mm format	24mm	32mm	37mm	44mm	74mm	87mm	102mm

Metering prisms

Many cameras do not feature integral metering, so taking an exposure reading requires a handheld meter. A metering prism provides a more conventional form of viewfinder, as well as offering integral metering.

Direct-vision cameras

In direct vision, the image is composed through a non-through-the-lens viewfinder, a similar system to compact cameras.

In terms of camera design, direct-vision cameras are relatively simple devices. But this functionality should not deceive you into believing image quality will prove sub-

standard. Brands such as Leica, which manufactures one type of direct-vision camera, the Rangefinder, are renowned for superb image quality. These types of cameras are also famed for their whisper-quiet operation, making them ideal tools for candid photography.

Anatomy of a 35mm direct-vision camera

Rangefinder
The rangefinder is used to create an image that is superimposed on the centre of the viewfinder

Rewind crank/rewind button
The wind mechanism is manually disengaged by pressing the rewind button, and the film is rewound into the canister by the crank

Battery compartment
On most rangefinders, the shutter is mechanical. However, some require power for electronic shutter speeds or an integral meter

PC socket
This cover hides a PC socket for connection to studio flash

Hotshoe
Most direct-vision cameras have a hotshoe with a single pin. More advanced models feature a multi-pin hotshoe. On some models, the hotshoe can also hold an optical viewfinder for particular lenses

Wind-on lever
Film wind-on is via a manual lever. Optional motorized winders are available for some models

Viewfinder
Frame lines around the edge provide a guide for composition (and change according to which lens is fitted), while a ghosted image at its centre is used for focusing. With some lenses, a separate viewfinder is attached to the hotshoe

Self-timer
A ten-second self-timer is found on many models, operated by a mechanical lever

Lens
The majority of interchangeable lenses on direct-vision cameras offer a fixed focal length, in the main offering wide-angle and short telephoto coverage. The aperture ring is set manually by the user

Film speed dial
The film speed is manually set, otherwise the integral meter will provide the wrong exposure

Shutter speed dial
The clean, uncluttered dial is designed to be very simple to use

Frame counter
This indicates the number of shots that have been taken

Shutter release button
The two-stage shutter release is usually very light and the shutter operation is extremely quiet

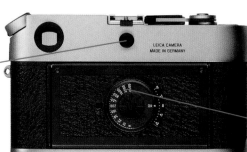
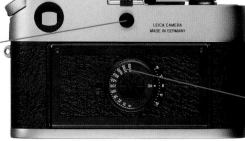
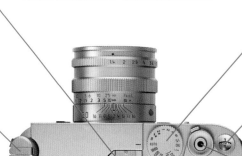

Other types of camera

In addition to the types of camera covered over the last few pages, the following are other popular formats.

Large format

As the name suggests, these cameras are big. The most popular type uses 5 x 4in film, available in sheets, rather than rolls, due to their size. These cameras are cumbersome, slow to use, and the running cost per image is high, but the quality is superb. These types of cameras allow movements, which can be used to achieve unparalleled image control, such as adjusting the plane of focus or correcting for converging verticals.

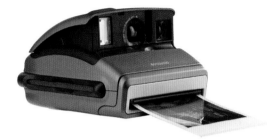

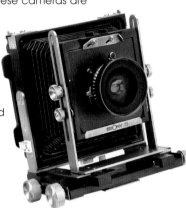

Instant

For many decades, Polaroid ruled the roost when it came to instant cameras. In recent years, Fuji has come onto the scene with its Instax range. Most models are aimed at the consumer market, but Polaroid also produces a high-end camera aimed at professionals.

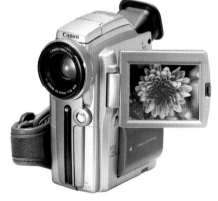

Megapixel camcorder

Many new camcorder models offer a digital stills facility for capturing images as well as movies. The quality isn't as good as with a digital camera, but with resolutions of 1–2 megapixels, they are a viable option for some applications, such as images for web use.

Imaging phone

Picture messaging on mobile phones has become increasingly popular, and with each generation of phones the quality improves, although imaging phones remain a fun gadget rather than a serious photographic tool. Wireless technology such as Bluetooth (see page 19) allows images to be transferred to a computer or a dedicated print station.

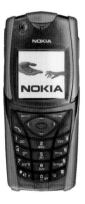

Hasselblad XPan II

This unique rangefinder camera, developed by Fuji and Hasselblad, is now in its second generation. It uses 35mm film but is able to shoot panoramic images. A switch moves a pair of blinds on the film plane, allowing panoramic 24 x 65mm, as well as standard 24 x 36mm images, to be recorded.

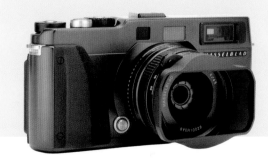

Choosing the right camera

With so many varieties of cameras on the market, deciding which type – let alone which model – is the right one for you can be extremely difficult. The easiest way to determine which best suits your needs is by answering a few questions and exploring the options.

What type of photography do you plan to do?

This is possibly the biggest consideration to make, as deciding what you will photograph is the biggest single factor in choosing a particular camera. While the following text provides guidelines, there will always be exceptions to the rule, as, ultimately, personal preference has the final say.

If you're not planning on anything too serious or demanding, a compact or low-end SLR delivers adequate results. For documentary and candid photography, where you almost always use a wide-angle lens, consider a rangefinder. However, if you wish to cover more specialist topics, such as close-ups or sports, an interchangeable-lens SLR becomes the first choice. This is because the versatility of an SLR system is unrivalled, with lenses, flashguns, filters and other accessories to suit almost every photographic application.

If you're after the ultimate in quality, look for a medium-format SLR system. Whether you use a film or digital back, the larger size of the frame area means that quality will be exceptional.

Digital or film?

Whether to use a digital or film camera represents an enormous decision. Film is available in a variety of types, from saturated colours to grainy black and white, but digital images can be manipulated to mimic any film's characteristics. The cost of a film SLR is still less than that of an equivalent digital SLR, but the price gap is closing every year. It's also worth bearing in mind that the running costs of a film SLR , in particular buying film and having it processed, aren't applicable to digital SLRs, making the latter a cheaper long-term investment.

Both have advantages and disadvantages, but the pendulum is swinging towards digital and, at some point in the near future – be it five, ten or twenty years – the demand for film will be too low for manufacturers to sustain production. So while film has its merits, digital will dominate in the not-too-distant future.

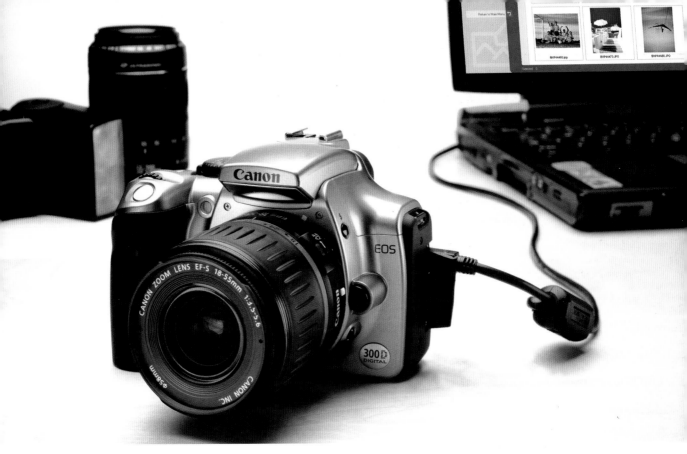

Other factors to consider

Cost
In general, you get what you pay for. Expensive cameras offer better build quality and far more sophisticated features. But do you need these, or would a more basic camera be just as adequate, freeing up more of the budget for lenses and other accessories?

New or used?
Getting the latest camera guarantees cutting-edge technology, but the used market is now so large that you can pick up relatively recent cameras at a fraction of their original cost.

System compatibility
With only a few exceptions, lenses and other accessories from a particular brand will not work on another one. If you already own a camera system, opting for a camera that can use items from your current outfit makes sense. Choose one of the big brands, and you'll usually find a wide range of products available, both new and used.

Summary

- For snapshots and general picture-taking, a compact or low-end SLR is the best choice.

- Enthusiasts looking to make the most of their creativity should use an SLR.

- If you want pictures quickly, go for digital.

- If you never use a computer or don't plan to manipulate images, use film.

- For the ultimate in quality, look to medium format.

How cameras work

Autofocus

Most cameras use an autofocus (AF) system to ensure sharp pictures. The last few years have seen major advances in autofocus technology to give faster, more accurate and more sophisticated focusing than ever before.

Main types of autofocus system

There are two main types of autofocus system: active and passive. The active system is found most commonly in compact cameras. It works by emitting an infrared beam, which bounces back from the subject and is detected by a sensor on the front of the camera. This determines the camera-to-subject distance by measuring the angle or strength of the beam or the time difference between it being emitted and received.

This system is fast and works in almost all lighting conditions, including total darkness. Its main disadvantage is that it has a limited range of a few metres. Many cameras link the active AF point with the metering system to ensure accurate exposures.

The passive system is used in more sophisticated cameras, including SLRs, and works by detecting subject contrast to aid autofocus. Also known as the phase-detection system, this is a very reliable and precise system for focusing from close-ups to distant or moving objects. It can struggle in low light or with subjects lacking any contrast, such as a plain wall, but in these instances, many cameras boast an AF-assist beam, which fires a patterned beam on to the subject and allows the autofocus system to focus.

Wide-area autofocus
Some cameras offer wide-area autofocus. This usually refers to three active AF sensors being used, one at the centre and one to either side. The user normally cannot select either of the two outer sensors, but can opt for Spot AF, which uses the central point only.

TOP TIP
AF sensors require light to work correctly. A good way of noting the sensitivity of an AF sensor is to find out the smallest aperture it can work with to provide effective AF. Most sensors require a lens with a maximum aperture of at least f/5.6, while some very sensitive systems can work well at f/8 (see page 30).

Focus points and AF sensors

The focus point is the area of the frame where the autofocus sensor is located. Traditionally, autofocus cameras used a single AF point at the centre of the frame. This system is still found on many cameras, particularly those at the lower end of the price range.

Far more common today are multipoint autofocus systems, which boast a number of autofocus sensors arranged in a pattern in the frame. The benefit of this system is that the increased area of coverage makes it easier for the AF system to lock on the subject, in particular if it is off-centre. With a single-point AF system, focusing on an off-centre subject involves locking the focus, usually by pressing the shutter partway down, then recomposing the frame. Multipoint AF allows for a far easier and faster system, as all the sensors are active, with the AF point corresponding to the closest subject. Most multipoint systems allow the photographer to choose between leaving all the AF sensors active or selecting individual points.

There are two main types of AF sensor: cross and line. Cross sensors are the most sensitive, as they have vertical and horizontal sensors, which allow for faster and more accurate AF. Line sensors measure in one plane only, and, while suitable for most situations, do not match the accuracy of a cross sensor in low light or with moving subjects.

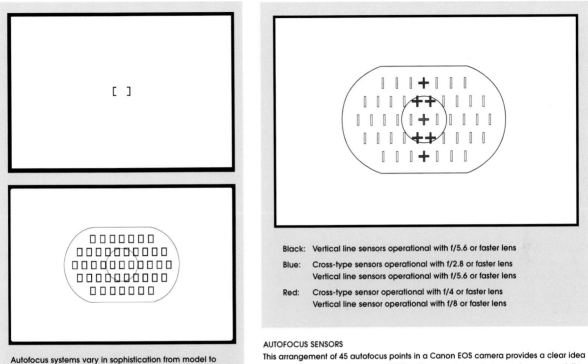

Black: Vertical line sensors operational with f/5.6 or faster lens

Blue: Cross-type sensors operational with f/2.8 or faster lens
Vertical line sensors operational with f/5.6 or faster lens

Red: Cross-type sensor operational with f/4 or faster lens
Vertical line sensor operational with f/8 or faster lens

AUTOFOCUS SENSORS
This arrangement of 45 autofocus points in a Canon EOS camera provides a clear idea of a modern SLR's autofocus capabilities. There are two main types of sensor used: the most common is the vertical line sensor, while at the centre of the arrangement is the cross sensor, which is far more sensitive.

Autofocus systems vary in sophistication from model to model. The most basic have a single AF point at the centre, while advanced systems have multiple AF points covering a large area of the frame.

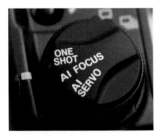

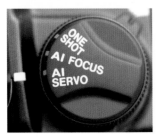

Autofocus modes

Most cameras offer a choice of autofocus modes, which are optimized for particular shooting situations.

Single-shot AF (also termed S or one-shot AF) is the standard autofocus mode. This system locks onto the subject until you take the picture or release the shutter button. If the subject moves, the autofocus will not compensate for the change in distance. This is where the Servo AF, or AI servo, mode comes into play.

Servo AF constantly monitors and tracks the subject and is therefore the choice when photographing moving objects. The more advanced servo-AF systems offer predictive autofocus, where the camera constantly monitors the rate of change in the subject distance, so that when the shutter is finally released, the camera predicts where the subject will be. This system works particularly well with multipoint-AF systems, which can track a subject as it moves across the frame.

AI focus is a combination of the two modes, with the AF starting off in single-shot mode, then automatically switching to Servo AF when movement of the subject is detected.

Exposure

Exposure can be defined as the duration and amount of light needed to create an image. Getting the correct exposure requires calculating how much light reaches the film or image sensor to an incredible accuracy. Too little exposure and the image is dark; too much and it is too light. The exposure is controlled by a combination of two factors: the lens aperture and the shutter speed. By controlling both of these and setting the right balance between them, the correct exposure can be calculated.

The fundamentals of exposure

The two main factors in determining the exposure are the aperture and the shutter speed. It is worth mentioning an important point before explaining what these two terms mean and how they affect the exposure. The basic unit of exposure is usually referred to as a stop. One stop is equivalent to a doubling or halving of an exposure. So the difference between an exposure of 1sec and 2sec is one stop; 1sec to 4sec is two stops, and so on. This will become clearer when shutter speeds and apertures are explored in greater detail later on.

Shutter speeds

Understanding how shutter speeds work is easier for most people than apertures. Most exposures require shutter speeds that only last a fraction of a second, although some long exposures can take seconds, minutes, or even hours!

Shutter speeds are generally quoted in stops. Below is a list of shutter speeds from ½sec to ¼₀₀₀sec in ½-stop increments.

½sec ⅓sec ¼sec ⅙sec ⅛sec ¹⁄₁₀sec ¹⁄₁₅sec ¹⁄₂₀sec ¹⁄₃₀sec ¹⁄₄₅sec ¹⁄₆₀sec ¹⁄₉₀sec ¹⁄₁₂₅sec ¹⁄₁₈₀sec ¹⁄₂₅₀sec ¹⁄₃₅₀sec ¹⁄₅₀₀sec ¹⁄₇₅₀sec ¹⁄₁₀₀₀sec ¹⁄₁₅₀₀sec ¹⁄₂₀₀₀sec ¹⁄₃₀₀₀sec ¹⁄₄₀₀₀sec

On most cameras the shutter speeds are displayed on the LCD or dial without the ¹⁄, so ¹⁄₆₀ will be shown as 60, ¹⁄₁₂₅ as 125, and so on. On dials, full seconds are usually shown in a different colour to avoid confusion. With most modern SLRs, all these shutter speeds are displayed on the LCD and in the viewfinder.

There is no hard and fast rule that determines what shutter speed is applicable to particular subjects. See Which shutter speed when? opposite for recommended settings.

Handholding

There is a general rule to remember about shutter speeds when you are taking handheld pictures: always keep the shutter speed to above whatever the reciprocal of the lens's focal length is. So when you are shooting with a 300mm lens, make sure that the shutter speed is always above ¹⁄₃₀₀sec.

ISO ratings

All exposure systems use the ISO (International Standards Organization) rating as the basis for its calculations. The ISO rating is used on all cameras, even though it was originally developed to be a universal guide for film speeds. A film's ISO rating indicates its sensitivity to light, or what is generally termed the film speed. The higher the ISO rating, the more sensitive it is to light. This is covered in more detail on page 41. Digital cameras follow the same rating, as it is understood by all photographers.

Changes in ISO ratings are measured in stops in the same way as apertures and shutter speeds, which simplifies exposure calculations. For instance, changing the ISO rating from ISO 100 to ISO 200 is an increase of one stop.

Mechanical shutter speed

A few cameras have what is known as mechanical shutter speed (some offer a range of mechanical speeds). This relates to the shutter speed that the camera will fire at, even if the batteries fail.

Is there such a thing as a correct exposure?

This isn't as odd a question as it might sound. There's an argument to say that there is no such thing as a correct exposure, let alone a perfect one. Some people prefer more detail in the highlights, while others prefer more emphasis on the shadows and therefore expose an image in line with their personal tastes. In this way, the same scene may be recorded at slightly different exposures, with some people preferring the lighter image and others the darker.

Exposure values

A correct exposure can be achieved by a variety of combinations of aperture and shutter speed. For instance, if $\frac{1}{60}$sec at f/4 gives the correct exposure, it is possible to use $\frac{1}{125}$ at f/2.8 or $\frac{1}{30}$sec at f/5.6 and have the same amount of light reaching the film/sensor. All combinations of aperture and shutter speed have what is known as an Exposure Value, or EV.

Which shutter speed when?

So when should you use a slow, medium or fast shutter speed? The choice really depends on factors such as the light level, but the following gives a rough guide.

Slow shutter speed: slower than $\frac{1}{30}$sec
Use this at night when a long exposure is required to record the scene. Use it during the day with a small aperture to blur moving subjects.

Medium shutter speed: $\frac{1}{60}$-$\frac{1}{200}$sec
Ideal for general photography. Use when handholding the camera with a standard lens to avoid camera shake. Suitable for slow-moving subjects, such as a jogger.

Fast shutter speed: $\frac{1}{250}$sec and faster
The choice for freezing the motion of fast-moving subjects such as galloping horses, or cars on a motorway.

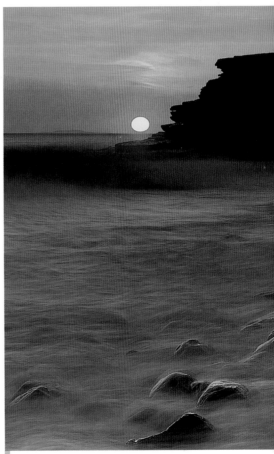

COASTLINE
A slow shutter speed is required in low light, and also acts to blur moving subjects, such as these waves.

MOTORBIKE
A fast shutter speed freezes the action of fast-moving subjects.

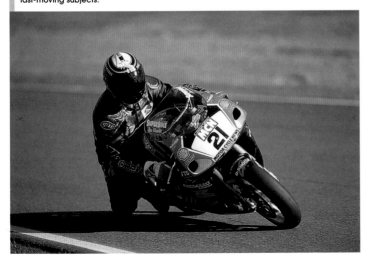

Aperture

The lens aperture controls the amount of light reaching the film/image sensor during a given exposure. The aperture is the common term relating to the iris in the lens. Like the pupil of the eye, controlling the size of the lens iris determines the amount of light entering the lens. A wide-open aperture allows more light through than an aperture that is closed down.

The lens aperture can be closed down in regular intervals. While the majority of cameras can only allow adjustments in ½ stops, some of the more sophisticated systems allow the aperture to be changed in ⅓-stop increments.

The maximum aperture relates to the widest setting of the lens iris, while closing it down to its smallest setting, in other words to allow the least amount of light through, is referred to as the minimum aperture.

On every lens there is an f/number, which is how aperture values are stated. This figure indicates how the aperture value relates to the lens focal length – see the panel opposite for details.

Aperture values can seem confusing at first, but once you start to use them, they become much easier to understand. A wide aperture has a low figure, for instance f/2, while a small aperture, in other words one that is closed down, has a higher figure, such as f/16.

Apertures are normally quoted in ½ or full stops – on the scale below, running from left to right, each full stop results in half the exposure, and vice versa.

f/1 f/1.2 f/1.4 f/1.8 f/2 f/2.4 f/2.8 f/4 f/4.5 f/5.6 f/6.7 f/8 f/9.5 f/11 f/13 f/16 f/19 f/22 f/27 f/32 f/38 f/45

How is an f/number measured?

This information isn't vital to taking a picture, but it's worth understanding, if only to impress fellow photographers with your knowledge of photography. The f/number corresponds to a fraction of the focal length. So f/2 means that the diameter of the aperture is half the focal length; f/4 is a quarter; f/8 is an eighth and so on. With a 50mm lens, the diameter at f/2 is 25mm; at f/4 it is 12.5mm, and so on.

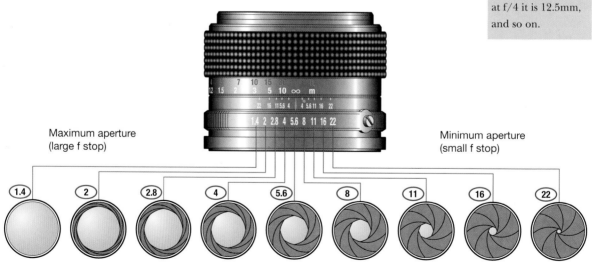

Maximum aperture (large f stop)

Minimum aperture (small f stop)

1.4 2 2.8 4 5.6 8 11 16 22

Which aperture when?

There is no set rule for when to use a particular aperture, but as a general guide, follow these rules:

Wide aperture

Use when shooting in low light and handholding the camera, as it reduces the risk of camera shake by increasing the shutter speed.

Use when you want a shallow depth of field, in other words an out-of-focus background.

Mid-aperture

Use when you want the best resolution from the lens – the sharpest is at f/8–11.

Small aperture

In extremely bright conditions, you may need to set a small aperture to give a usable shutter speed.

When you require the background to appear sharp, set a small aperture to increase depth of field.

Use when shooting macro or close-up photography, to give as much depth of field as possible.

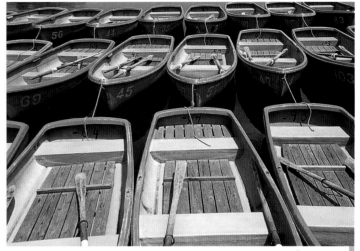

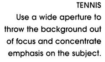

APERTURES AND DEPTH OF FIELD

By varying the aperture, it is possible to affect the depth of field. The general rule is that depth of field increases as you stop down the lens. In other words, the widest aperture gives the minimum depth of field, while the minimum aperture gives the most depth of field. For a far more comprehensive explanation of depth of field, see pages 86–89.

BOATS
Using a small aperture allows depth of field to extend from close distances to far away.

Why do some lenses have two maximum aperture values?

Most zoom lenses have two maximum apertures listed, for instance 80–200mm f/4.5–5.6. This means that the maximum aperture of the zoom changes as you change its focal length. Taking the example given, the maximum aperture at 80mm is f/4.5, while at 200mm it is f/5.6. If you have the zoom on a camera set to its widest focal length and maximum aperture, slowly zoom the lens: you can see on the LCD when the aperture changes from f/4.5 to f/5.6.

WHAT'S A FAST LENS?

Some lenses are referred to as fast. This means that their maximum aperture is wider than the norm, giving a corresponding faster shutter speed. For instance, a 70–200mm f/2.8 lens is deemed a fast lens, as a standard 70–200mm is more likely to have a maximum aperture of around f/4.

TENNIS
Use a wide aperture to throw the background out of focus and concentrate emphasis on the subject.

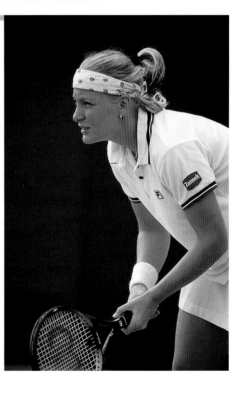

Exposure systems

Light is at the very heart of photography, and likewise, the exposure system is at the heart of a camera. Although you can find some models that lack any form of metering system, all must have control of the exposure of an image to successfully produce a photograph.

Exposure modes

An exposure is made up of two key elements: the amount of light passing through a lens (determined by the aperture), and the duration of light allowed to reach the film or image sensor (determined by the shutter speed). Most cameras offer a multitude of modes that all aim to give the same result – a perfect exposure – but each has its own bias towards particular creative goals, such as providing the fastest shutter speed or combining the flash with ambient light. You'll find the letters AE after most of the modes – this stands for Auto Exposure and signifies that the camera automatically tries to set the correct exposure for you. Below is an explanation of the most popular modes.

The core four

Most SLRs and many compacts will sport what is termed the core four exposure modes: program, aperture priority, shutter priority and manual. These are often termed as creative modes, as they offer the user varying levels of control over the exposure.

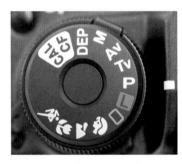

Program AE

Shown as P, program AE is a point-and-shoot mode where the camera sets the aperture and shutter speed for you. However, with most cameras you do have some creative control over the exposure in the form of program shift. This allows you to vary the combination of aperture and shutter speed without affecting the overall exposure. For instance, if the camera sets $\frac{1}{125}$sec at f/8, but you want a faster shutter speed, you can shift the combination along – in this case, to $\frac{1}{250}$sec at f/5.6, or $\frac{1}{500}$sec at f/4. The overall exposure remains unchanged, but you have biased the camera to your preference.

Most cameras also allow you to affect the exposure by selecting the flash or set exposure compensation.

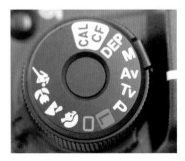

Aperture priority AE

Arguably the favourite mode among enthusiast photographers, this mode gives you control over the aperture, with the camera selecting the appropriate shutter speed. As well as being an ideal exposure mode for general photography, aperture priority AE is particularly favoured by landscape photographers, as it allows them full control of depth of field. Most cameras signify aperture priority AE as A or Av.

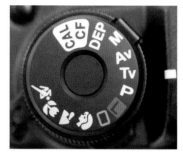

Shutter priority AE

Shutter-priority AE (S or Tv on most cameras), offers the opposite control over aperture priority AE; in other words, you select the shutter speed, and the camera sets the aperture. It is most used by people who want to set a shutter speed at the extremes of the shutter speed range – for instance, action and sports photographers who want a fast shutter speed to freeze action, or creative photographers who purposely want to choose a slow shutter speed to blur moving subjects.

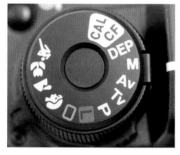

Manual

Manual, or M, is the favourite choice with professionals, who value their understanding of the scene over what the camera thinks. It allows full control of the exposure, so the user sets both the aperture and the shutter speed. With many cameras, a scale in the viewfinder indicates any deviance between what the camera believes is the correct exposure and what the photographer has set. Manual is the mode to use if you are taking an exposure reading with a handheld meter and need to set this on the camera, or if you are using the camera with studio flash.

More manual control

The Bulb (B) and Time (T) modes are two modes that are very similar and are used when very long exposures (from minutes to hours) are required. With both, you determine how long the exposure lasts. With a Bulb or B exposure, the shutter remains open as long as you keep the shutter button (or remote release) depressed. With a Time or T exposure, the shutter is triggered once, then remains open until triggered again. The Bulb facility is found on more cameras than Time, with the latter in the main found only on medium-format cameras.

On many cameras, battery power is consumed during the exposure, so be careful how long you use it for.

X-factor

The X mode, also known as X-sync, was once a common feature on cameras but is now found almost exclusively on medium-format cameras and older 35mm SLRs. Set the camera to X and it automatically switches to the camera's flash synchronization speed. It is selected when using the camera with an external flash source such as studio flash.

No more aperture rings

In the past, lenses featured an aperture ring for varying the size of the iris on the lens barrel. However, electronics now means that this feature is more or less defunct on a modern SLR. Instead, the selected aperture is selected and the camera closes the lens iris to the appropriate setting electronically.

Flashing numbers!

In some instances, particularly in very bright or very dark conditions, you may notice that the reading for the aperture or shutter speed flashes. This indicates that the current combination of aperture and shutter speed is not possible in that instance. For example, if you are using shutter priority and have selected a very fast shutter speed, the aperture value may blink, indicating that the camera cannot set the aperture required to give a correct exposure because it is wider than the lens's maximum aperture. When this happens, you should change your setting until the blinking stops. In this instance, you would need to lower the shutter speed until the lens is able to set an appropriate aperture.

Subject-biased programs

The core four on the previous pages have long been the most used modes. However, the development of modern electronics brought with it the opportunity to develop programs tailor-made for specific types of photography – the subject-biased programs.

Often termed picture modes or subject modes, these are program modes that bias the camera's exposure, focusing and frame transport facilities for specific subjects. These program modes are often a good choice for beginners unsure about how best to use the camera in specific shooting situations. Subject-biased programs are found on the majority of SLRs and compacts, and the pictures below show the symbols that are used for these programs on nearly all cameras.

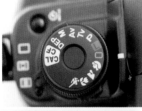

Full auto AE

This is similar to the standard program AE mode, but doesn't allow you any control over the exposure. Often termed the 'idiot mode', it's the one to use if you lack even a basic grasp of photographic knowledge, with the camera making all the necessary exposure calculations and even popping up the flash if required.

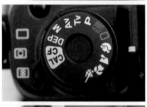

Portrait AE

As the name suggests, this is the perfect choice for taking pictures of people. The camera will select a wide aperture in order to throw the background out of focus, sets the autofocus to one-shot mode, and often uses a burst of fill-in flash as well.

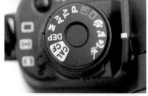

Landscape AE

In this instance, the camera tries to select an aperture that gives good depth of field while at the same time not dropping the shutter speed so low as to cause camera shake. The flash system is disabled, as the subject is presumed to be too far away for it to be any use, and the autofocus is set to one-shot AF, as the subject is static.

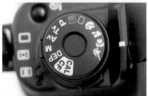

Close-up AE

If the camera has multipoint autofocus, it will activate the central AF sensor only as it presumes that is where the subject will be. Most cameras often use the integral flashgun and set an aperture with a mid-range combination of shutter speed and aperture.

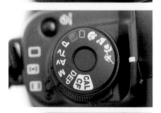

Action AE

The subject is presumed to be moving, so the autofocus is set to continuous AF. The camera also sets its transport system to continuous shooting to record an action sequence. The bias is towards a fast shutter speed and wide aperture.

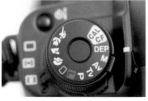

Depth AE

This mode is exclusive to the Canon EOS range of cameras. It allows you to specify the amount of depth of field in a scene by highlighting the nearest and furthest points in the scene that you want in focus, with the camera then determining the appropriate aperture and shutter speed settings. Some models feature the A-Depth AE mode, which is a simplified form of the Depth AE mode.

Camera settings for subject-biased programs

The following table gives an at-a-glance view of how a typical camera automatically adjusts its main systems to compensate for different shooting situations. Please note that some cameras will deviate from the settings shown – check your camera's instruction manual for details.

Mode	Autofocus	Exposure	Flash
Full auto	Set to AI Focus	Mid-range combination of aperture and shutter speed	Fires if required
Portrait	Set to one-shot AF	Wide aperture for minimal depth of field	Fill-in flash
Landscape	Set to one-shot AF	Mid-range combination of aperture and shutter speed	Disabled
Close-up	Set to continuous AF	Mid-range combination of aperture and shutter speed	Fires if required
Action	Set to continuous AF	Fast shutter speed Continuous frame advance	Disabled
Night portrait	Set to one-shot AF	Very slow shutter speed	Always fires

Night portrait AE

With this mode, the camera tries to create the right balance of flash and ambient light. It assumes the camera is mounted on a tripod (or set on a steady surface), and sets a long exposure time to record detail in the background. It also fires the flash with enough power to correctly expose the subject in the foreground.

Scene modes

Many digital cameras offer scene modes. These often include all the subject-biased programs listed opposite, along with many more modes, suitable for specific shooting situations or scenes. These could include a sunset mode, sand-and-ski or party modes. With each of these, the camera automatically sets its exposure and focusing systems to what it thinks best suits these scenes.

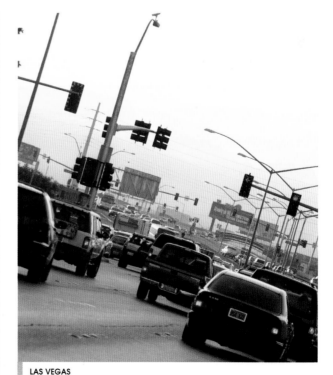

LAS VEGAS
General scenes such as this dusk image poses no problems for the standard AE program mode.

Metering systems

All camera meters assume that an average of all the tones in a scene equates to 18 per cent grey. For most scenes, this proves to be highly accurate. Where the meter system falters is if the scene is overly white, such as a winter landscape, or blacker than usual, say a close-up of a crow's head. In these situations, the meter will underexpose and overexpose respectively. However, although many shooting situations fit nicely into this assumption, there are times when this isn't the case. The metering patterns of today's cameras aim to keep exposure error to a minimum, and although they succeed to a large degree, the only true way to eliminate inaccurate exposures is to understand how a camera meters, and to know when to take things into your own hands.

Metering patterns

How a camera determines the exposure for a scene is determined by how it measures the light reaching the metering sensor. The term 'metering pattern' refers to how a camera's exposure system measures not only the amount of light in the scene, but how the light varies within the scene. Most cameras offer a choice of metering patterns, each of which measures the light in different ways.

Multizone metering

This has become the most common type of metering pattern, as it provides the highest ratio of success. It works by dividing the scene into a number of zones, with an individual reading taken from each. Some zones have a higher priority given to them by others, and the camera's microprocessor examines the various readings to determine the final exposure. Often the camera has its own library of thousands of scenes, and compares data from these to help assess what it believes is the correct exposure – all in the blink of an eye!

The number of metering zones varies from camera to camera. The minimum is two; some SLRs offer 35 zones, while some digital compacts boast 256 individual zones.

Selective metering

As the name suggests, this type of pattern takes a reading from a selective part of the frame, usually the central 7–9 per cent of the frame. It is used in tricky lighting situations where the photographer believes the multizone meter may be ineffective, such as strong backlighting. By taking a selective reading from a mid-tone, achieving the correct exposure is far more likely.

Spot metering

A spot meter is essentially a far more refined version of a selective meter, allowing a reading to be taken from a very small part of the frame – usually 1–3 per cent. It is extremely accurate when used correctly. Some cameras offer a multispot facility, which allows you to take several spot readings and use the average one.

Centre-weighted average metering

The oldest metering pattern, this system takes an average reading of the scene, with emphasis given to the central 70 per cent of the frame. It is relatively basic, giving underexposure in scenes with plenty of sky in the frame or in backlit conditions. However, it is consistent, and photographers who know how it works are reluctant to move to newer, more sophisticated patterns. Therefore, this pattern is found on many cameras, in particular SLRs.

Reflected and incident light readings

A camera's integral meter takes what is known as reflected readings. In other words, it takes a reading of the light being reflected from the subject. As reliable as these systems are, they are prone to inaccuracy when the subject is very dark or very light: dark subjects are overexposed, while light subjects are underexposed.

Incident light readings do not suffer from this problem, as they measure the light falling off the subject, rather than reflecting off it. The tonal characteristics of the subject do not influence the meter reading. This is why handheld meters, which take incident light readings, are used by experienced photographers.

What is a mid-tone?

If you imagine a scale from pure white to pure black, a mid-tone is an area in between that represents a mid-tone of grey. In the real world, finding this colour is unlikely, unless you're in the middle of a concrete jungle. However, if you are looking to take a spot or selective reading off a mid-tone, suitable subjects include the skin tones of a Caucasian person, grass or brickwork.

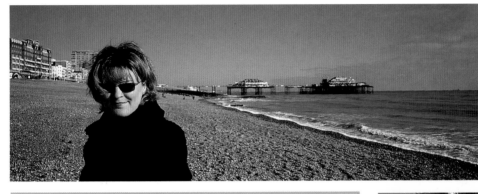

BEACH PORTRAIT
Strong sidelighting and an off-centre subject can cause metering problems. AE-L from the face ensured a perfect exposure.

PALM TREE
In this sequence, the camera's metered exposure is at the centre, with +1 stop above and −1 stop below.

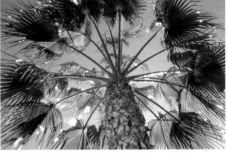

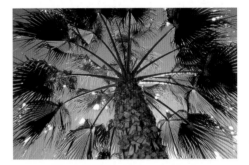

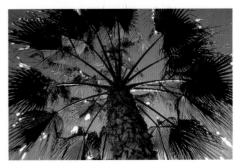

Exposure overrides

As reliable as a camera's autoexposure system is, there are times when a photographer requires some control over the final exposure. Almost all cameras offer this option in one form or another. The three most common types of control are shown below.

Exposure compensation

Using this facility, you can give a little more or less than the indicated exposure. Set a '+' value and you add some exposure, set a '-' value and you reduce the exposure. Most cameras allow you to set ½-stop increments, some offer ⅓-stop increments, while some can select either.

Depending on what mode you select, the camera will make this compensation by altering the aperture or the shutter speed. Shooting a series of images at slightly different exposures times is known as bracketing your exposure.

Autoexposure bracketing

This function allows you to shoot a bracketed series of exposures. Set autoexposure bracketing (AEB) to ½ stop and the camera shoots at the normal exposure, then ½ a stop under and ½ a stop over (although not necessarily in that order).

Autoexposure lock

More commonly referred to as AE-L, this facility allows you to lock an exposure value independently of the focus. This feature is particularly useful if you are shooting in tricky lighting conditions, or when the scene is markedly bright or dark.

Image capture

Film

Photographic film is now in its third century, so you'd expect the quality to be good! Modern film emulsion is a robust, versatile material that is capable of extremely detailed image capture. The emergence of digital threatens its long-term future, but it has a good few years left in it yet.

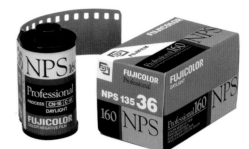

Main types of film

Film comes in many different forms. Choosing the best type for your photography is vital if you are going to get the very best from your subject. There are no right and wrong choices: the type of film that you use should be dictated by what type of image that you are trying to create.

The three main types of film are colour negative, colour transparency and black-and-white negative.

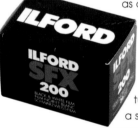

Colour negative film, more commonly known as colour print film, is by far the most popular choice with amateur photographers. The quality is excellent, and it is a relatively easy film to use, thanks to its wide exposure latitude. Because the actual print is a second-generation image (the negative is the original), print films have generally not been used by professionals, who, looking to achieve the highest quality possible, have used slide film. However, as digital scanning has come to the forefront, this attitude has changed, as scanners can scan negatives as well as slides.

Colour slide film, also known as transparency or reversal film, has been the first choice with professionals for many years. Because the slide is the first-generation image, it offers higher sharpness, better contrast and more accurate colour rendition and saturation than print film.

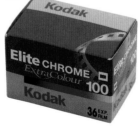

However, it has a very narrow exposure latitude compared to print film, and so is not recommended for use in film compacts (with the exception of premium models) and requires a more experienced photographer to expose it correctly. Another drawback is that a slide is far more difficult to view than a print, requiring a viewer or projector to see it at a decent size.

Black-and-white print film is the oldest type of the bunch. Its appeal is more limited, as it is not the best choice for general amateur photography such as holiday or family snaps. However, it is very popular with the enthusiast and professional photographer, who see black and white as a more creative medium than colour.

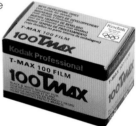

If you want to shoot slides in black and white, there's only one choice – Agfa Scala. This ISO 200 film offers good quality, medium-contrast black-and-white slides, but is difficult to find and requires specialist processing.

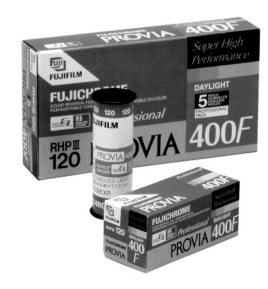

Specialist films

As well as mainstream films, there are a number of specialist emulsions available.

Infrared film is sensitive to infrared light and is capable of surreal results – see pages 156–7 for more information.

Tungsten-balanced film is sensitized to give natural colours under tungsten lighting, as opposed to being daylight-balanced, like the majority of films.

Duplicating film is a low-contrast emulsion developed for high-quality slide duplication.

Polaroid instant film allows a photographer to check a scene for lighting, props, composition and so on before committing to capturing the shot on film.

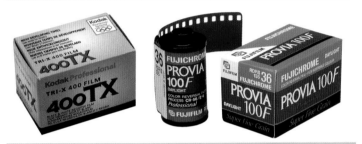

Chromogenic films

For years, a large number of amateur photographers were put off using black-and-white film because having the film developed and printed was seen as a long, expensive process. Film manufacturers realized this and developed chromogenic black-and-white films, which could be processed in standard C-41 colour chemistry, making them as affordable and fast to process as colour print film. Examples include Ilford XP2 Super, Kodak TMAX T400CN and Fuji Neopan 400CN.

Exposure latitude

This term refers to how well a film can handle over- or underexposure. Print films are said to have a wide exposure latitude, as they can be underexposed by at least one stop and overexposed by four stops without any significant loss in quality.

Slide film, on the other hand, has a narrow exposure latitude – usually underexposing more than ½ stop produces a very dark image, while overexposing more than one stop creates a very bleached slide.

This is why it is recommended to bracket print film in one-stop increments and slide film in ⅓- or ½-stop increments.

How colour film works

A colour negative film is made up of several layers. The top layer provides protection from scratching, while the celluloid base has an anti-halation layer to prevent light from bouncing back into the emulsion and fogging the image. This base also supports the light-sensitive material, separated into layers that respond to different wavelengths of light. The layers are arranged to provide the optimum colour reproduction – the blue-sensitive layer is found at the top, the red-sensitive layer at the bottom and the green-sensitive layer between them.

When a colour negative film is exposed, the light-sensitive silver halide crystals react to create microscopic clumps of silver ions. When the film is developed, the silver particles are triggered to release colour dyes, and during the processing the silver particles are expelled to leave behind three layers of colour dyes, which, when exposed, create the final colour image.

Colour slide film works in a slightly different way – at the first development stage, the exposed silver halides are transformed into silver crystals. But the film is then chemically fogged to expose the unused silver halides, and a colour developer triggers dyes to be created around them. During the final processing stages, the silver and unused dyes are removed to leave a colour slide.

Film speed

Understanding a film's speed rating, which indicates how sensitive it is to light, is crucial when deciding what film is best for a particular shooting situation. Film speeds vary enormously, with films that are less sensitive to light being termed 'slow', and those with heightened sensitivity being described as 'fast'.

Film speeds are indicated by an ISO (International Standards Organization) rating, which is marked on the film box and the canister. Each doubling of the figure relates to a one-stop increase in sensitivity, and vice versa. So an ISO 100 film is twice as sensitive as an ISO 50 emulsion, while an ISO 200 film is half as sensitive as ISO 400. General photographer's parlance is that ISO 100 is twice as fast, or double, the speed of ISO 50, while ISO 200 is half the speed or a stop slower, than ISO 400.

Almost all cameras feature a system called DX-coding, which sets the film speed automatically when the canister is loaded – see the box opposite for more details.

DX-coding

If you look on the side of almost any 35mm film, you will see a silver and black pattern of 12 squares. This is the film's DX code, which, when placed in a camera, aligns with silver pins in the film chamber to provide information, including the film speed and the film type (whether it is colour or black and white, print or slide, and so on).

Own-brand films

Among the films from big-name brands like Agfa, Fuji and Kodak, supermarkets and other retailers have their own ranges of films. These own-brand films are usually manufactured by one of the major brands, but are a slightly older generation of film. You can thus expect very good quality results and, although they may not match the branded films, they usually cost much less. Incidentally, looking at the country of origin is a major clue as to who makes own-brand film.

Which film speed to use?

The choice of film speed dictates what apertures and shutter speeds are selectable to the camera for a given exposure, so it is important to match the speed to the shooting conditions. While using a faster speed offers the most options, you should also take into consideration that it has its consequent disadvantages, such as more evident grain and a loss in sharpness. Each film speed has its own advantages and disadvantages that make it ideal for particular shooting situations, which are listed opposite.

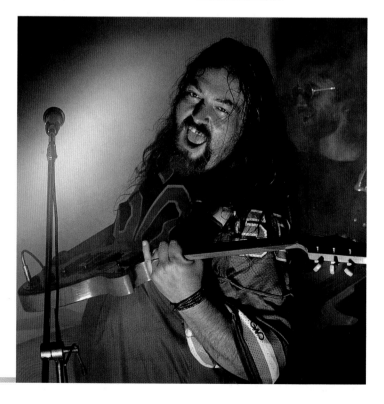

ROCKER
A fast film is the best choice when shooting in low light. With black-and-white photography, you will find the grain often adds to the atmosphere and mood of the image.

Slow film
(ISO 25–64)

Main advantages:
Boasts the best quality, as grain is extremely fine, giving very sharp, detailed results. In terms of colour reproduction, slow film provides the richest saturation.

Main disadvantages:
Slow speed brings slower exposure times, making it unsuitable for use in handheld photography in low light.
Using filters, such as polarizers, effectively reduces the exposure by two stops.

When to use slow film:
● You want to make big enlargements and want optimum quality
● Rich, saturated colours are required
● You are photographing static subjects and can place the camera on a tripod

Recommended films:
Colour slide: Fuji Velvia 50, Agfa RSX II 50
Colour print: Konica Impresa 50
Black and white: Ilford Pan F Plus

Medium-speed film
(ISO 100–200)

Main advantages:
Huge number of films available, so you're spoilt for choice.
Ideal for general photography, as it offers a good balance of quality and convenience.
Extra speed makes it suitable for handheld photography in most daylight conditions.
Portrait photographers have a wide choice of films that offer realistic skin tones.

Main disadvantages:
No real minus marks, other than not offering the same level of detail as slower films.

When to use medium-speed film:
● General use
● Good choice of portrait films
● You want the best image quality and are shooting handheld
● You need a little extra speed than slower films can offer

Recommended films:
Colour slide: Fuji Velvia 100F, Kodak Elite Chrome Extra Colour 100, Fuji Astia
Colour print: Agfa Ultra 100, Fuji Reala, Kodak High Definition 200
Black and white: Ilford Delta 100, Ilford FP4 Plus, Fuji Neopan 100

Fast film
(ISO 400+)

Main advantages:
Allows handheld photography in low-light situations.
Lets you freeze moving subjects by allowing faster shutter speeds.
Grain can be used to add mood.
Good choice of black-and-white emulsions.

Main disadvantages:
Evident grain, especially with ISO 800+ films.
Colours aren't as accurate or saturated as slower emulsions.
Sharpness isn't always as high.

When to use fast film:
● Low-light work
● Action work
● When using flash for distant subjects
● Deliberately grainy images with mood

Recommended films:
Colour slide: Fuji Provia 400F
Colour print: Fuji Superia 400, Kodak Portra 400VC, Kodak Royal 400
Black and white: Ilford HP5 Plus, Ilford Delta 400, Fuji Neopan 1600

Uprating film

It is possible to use a film at a faster speed than it is rated at, and then compensate for this later at the processing stage. For instance, if you have an ISO 100 film and need some extra speed, you can uprate it to ISO 400, in effect underexposing it by two stops. This can be addressed at the processing stage, when the film is 'push-processed' to compensate. Although it is not always recommended, due to an increase in grain and contrast, uprating film is generally a better option than not capturing an image at all. Push-processing works best with colour slide and black-and-white print film, but does not produce very good results with colour negative film.

Using a film at a slower speed is known as downrating, and the shorter development time is referred to as pull-processing. This process is fairly uncommon.

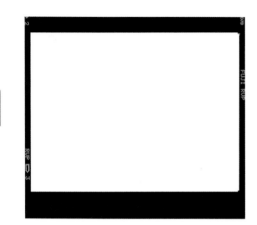

Medium Format 6 x 7cm

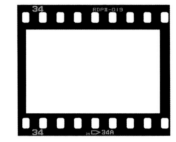

35mm

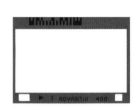

APS

Main film formats

After the various types of films available and their speed rating, the next consideration is the formats that they are available in. Different cameras use different film formats, and these come in a wide variety of shapes and sizes.

35mm is the most popular film format, thanks to its combination of versatility and image quality. APS (Advanced Photo System) is the newest system; despite various innovations, its life looks as though it will be a short one, thanks to the rise of digital.

Medium-format roll film offers a better quality than the smaller formats, and provides various image formats, ranging from 6 x 4.5cm to panoramic 6 x 17cm images, with those up to 6 x 7cm being generally the most popular.

Finally, sheet film, which is used in large-format cameras, offers film originals measuring 5 x 4in, 10 x 8in and bigger, but its expense and the large size of the cameras make it a format for only the keenest of enthusiasts and professionals.

Size matters

The general rule is that the larger the film format, the better the quality of the final image, all else being equal. This is because to produce, say a 10 x 8in print, an APS frame requires an enlargement of around 12x, a 35mm film 8.5x, a 6 x 4.5cm 5x, and a 5 x 4in sheet just over 2x.

Obviously, the bigger you blow up the original frame, the more the quality suffers. In truth, other factors come into play, in particular the lens optics, but in working practice, this rule works well.

Print sizes

Note that the sizes of film and format are still referred to in either metric or imperial measurements; this is the industry standard, so no comparative measurements have been provided, as for lenses elsewhere in the book.

APS (Advanced Photo System)

1996 saw the launch of the Advanced Photo System, developed by five of the biggest film and camera manufacturers – Canon, Fuji, Kodak, Minolta and Nikon. This new system offered a real alternative to 35mm, in particular to compact camera users. The key benefits of APS are:

- **Smaller film size:** The actual film cassette is smaller than a 35mm film, so cameras can also be smaller.
- **Information Exchange (IX):** A magnetic strip along the edge of the film allows exposure information to be recorded. This data is used by the processor to ensure premium print quality.
- **Drop-in loading:** Statistics showed that the cause of a majority of unexposed 35mm films was incorrectly loaded film. Drop-in loading aimed to remove this problem.
- **Mid-roll change (MRC):** This facility allows a partly used film to be reloaded and then automatically wound on to the first unexposed frame.

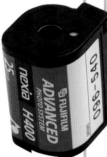

- **Index print:** Supplied with prints is an index print; this is a sheet of thumbnail images of all the pictures on the film.
- **Print formats:** APS users are given the option of choosing from three print formats – C (Classic); H (HDTV); and P (Panoramic). Classic is the standard enprint size of 6 x 4in; HDTV is a slightly wider print (7 x 4in); Panoramic is much wider, at 10 x 4in. The image is actually always recorded in H format, which is only the type of print format that you select, so it is always possible to get further reprints in any format.
- **Film status indicator:** The top end of the film cassette has four indicators, which show the status of the film:
  - ○: film is unused
  - D: film is partly used
  - ✕: film is used but has not yet been processed
  - □: film has been used and processed.

Colour temperature

During the course of the day, the colour temperature of light changes, although we hardly notice this, as our brain constantly adapts our vision to compensate. The same fact applies to artificial light sources, which work at different colour temperatures to daylight.

Film cannot adapt as our vision does, and because it is daylight-balanced, in certain lighting conditions a colour cast will be recorded unless colour-compensating filters are used.

The table below indicates the colour temperature (measured in degrees Kelvin) of various light sources and the result of using daylight-balanced film in these conditions.

Light source	Colour temperature	Colours on film
Candlelight	1000K	Very strong orange/red cast
Sunset	2000–3000K	Very warm orange cast
Tungsten	3000K	Warm orange cast
Average noon light	5500K	Accurate colours
Flashgun	6000K	Accurate colours
Cloud/haze	6500–8000K	Blue cast

Digital image sensors

The image sensor is the light-sensitive device at the heart of the digital camera. Different camera manufacturers use different types, so it's important to be clear how each works.

The basic workings of an image sensor

An image sensor is essentially a silicon chip featuring an array of tiny light-sensitive diodes, often referred to as picture elements, or pixels. These are arranged in rows on the chip. When they receive light, they create a charge; the charges are processed row by row, with the information used to create the image. Because the information from the rows is joined together, or coupled, these sensors became known as charge-coupled devices, or CCDs.

Individual sensors are sensitive to monochromatic light, so to create colour images, colour filters must be placed over them to allow the sensor to record only a particular colour. By using green, red and blue filters placed in a particular arrangement, colour images are formed. There are normally twice as many green sensors as red or blue in an array, as the sensitivity of the chip to light varies, depending on its wavelength.

Main types of image sensor

Although all image sensors have the same purpose – to capture light and convert it into electronic form – the basic principle of how they work varies from one brand to another.

While the CCD remains the most popular, CMOS (complementary metal oxide semiconductor) has become increasingly common on SLRs. Fuji has its own unique variant, the Super CCD; Nikon has its LBCAST; and Sigma has the Foveon.

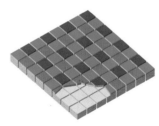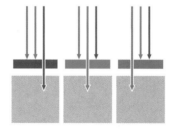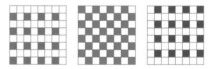

MOSAIC CAPTURE
This is the general basis of how most image sensors capture the image (Foveon and Super CCD are alternative systems). From left to right: In conventional systems, colour filters are applied to a single layer of photodetectors in a mosaic pattern; the filters let only one wavelength of light – red, green or blue – pass through to any given pixel, allowing it to record only one colour; as a result, mosaic sensors capture only 25 per cent of the red and blue light, and just 50 per cent of the green.

Super CCD

Fujifilm's Super CCD is in its fourth generation and offers a major departure from the normal CCD. For a start, the sensors are honeycombed in shape, rather than square, allowing them to be more tightly packed together. By using special processing technology, the output from the sensor doubles the resolution of the chip: for example, a 3.1-million pixel sensor gives a 6.2-million pixel image.

There are two types of Super CCD: HR and SR. HR is designed to give optimum sharpness, while SR provides a wider exposure latitude and tonal range than conventional CCDs. It does this by featuring a primary sensor with high sensitivity and a secondary sensor with low sensitivity, which, when the information from each is combined, effectively produces results more in common with colour negative films than a standard CCD image.

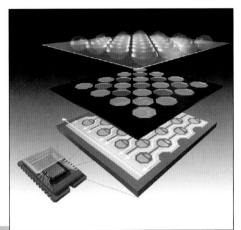

Foveon

This is another variant of the CCD, most commonly found in the Sigma range of digital SLRs. The principle behind it closely resembles how a film emulsion works, with three separate layers of photodetectors: blue, green and red. Because all three colours lie above each pixel, the sensor captures red, green and blue light at every pixel. In theory, this system has the greatest potential to deliver the closest possible quality to film. Because there are three colours per pixel, the resolution is normally rated x3, so a 3.4-megapixel Foveon sensor will be depicted as 3.4 (x3) megapixel, or 10.2-megapixel CCD. In reality, the resolution from a 3-megapixel Foveon sensor is similar to that from a 6-megapixel CCD or CMOS.

CMOS

The CMOS sensor has gained increasing popularity over recent years, and is most commonly found in the Canon EOS range of digital SLRs. It offers several benefits over CCD, the most important being that it consumes less power, is cheaper to produce and has an amplifier linked to each pixel, offering benefits for transferring the data to the processor. A negative point of CMOS sensors was that it produced more noise than CCD, but this is no longer the case. CMOS is likely to become the dominant type of sensor found in digital SLRs and, quite possibly, digital compacts in the near future.

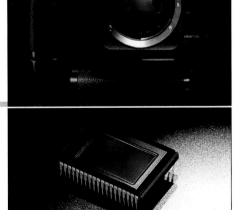

LBCAST JEFT

The lateral buried charge accumulator and sensing transistor array, or LBCAST, is the very latest type of sensor. First used in Nikon's D2H, launched in 2003, it uses similar principles to a CMOS sensor, but has a different type of amplifier, known as a JFET (junction field effect transistor). Although Nikon claims it offers better performance than CMOS, in particular in terms of power consumption and image quality, it is still too early to tell.

Image storage

Digital images need to be stored in a safe and reliable way that is also easy to access. Digital cameras store the images on removable storage cards. These images are usually transferred to a computer's hard disk and from there to CD or some other form of digital storage.

Storage cards

MultiMedia Card (MMC)

MMC is small at 24 x 37 x 1.4mm (1 x 1½ x ¹⁄₁₆in), and has a current maximum capacity of 128Mb. It has struggled to make its mark, and doubts remain on how long it will remain viable.

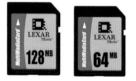

Secure Digital (SD)

This format was developed from MMC but offers a write-protect facility to prevent accidental erasure of images, and a higher maximum capacity of 512Mb. Although it has already gained a larger following than MMC, it has yet to establish itself as a major player.

xD-Picture Card

xD (eXtreme Digital) is the latest type of card format, and offers the key advantages of an extremely small size of 20 x 25 x 1.7mm (¾ x 1 x ¹⁄₁₆in) and high capacities (up to 8Gb is claimed, although the current highest capacity is 512Mb). Developed by Olympus and Fujifilm, xD is increasingly popular and may develop into a leading format.

CompactFlash

Although CompactFlash has been around for over ten years, it has stood the test of time extremely

well and remains the most popular choice of card format. It's larger than most, but at 43 x 36 x 3.3mm (1¾ x 1⅜ x ⅛in) is still relatively tiny – and has been proven to be robust and reliable. It has very high capacities (up to 8Gb) and, thanks to its popularity, additional cards are quite inexpensive to acquire.

SmartMedia

This was a popular choice when digital cameras were in their earlier generations, due to its wafer-thin size of 45 x 37 x 0.76mm (1¾ x ½ x ¹⁄₃₂in) and relatively inexpensive cost. However, newer types of card, such as SD and MMC are even smaller and offer a higher capacity than the SmartMedia's maximum capacity of 128Mb. Also not in its favour, SmartMedia was known for being easy to damage. A card format of the past.

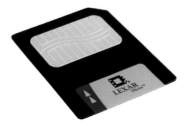

MemoryStick

This was developed by Sony as a small, portable storage system that could be used not only in its cameras, but in MP3 players, camcorders and so on. At 50 x 21.5 x 2.8mm (2 x ⅞ x ⅛in), it's relatively large, although a smaller type, the Memory Stick Duo (31 x 20 x 1.6mm/1¼ x ¾ x ¹⁄₁₆in) has been released. The 128Mb capacity is not as large as rival formats, and it has only been adopted by a handful of manufacturers.

IBM Microdrive

When CompactFlash cards were first introduced, their memory capacity was very limited. The IBM Microdrive worked in most cameras that accepted CompactFlash, and offered a much higher capacity (currently up to 4Gb). However, CompactFlash now has a similarly high capacity so the Microdrive is not in such demand, although its very low cost has meant it is still available. Microdrives are easier to damage and are less reliable than CompactFlash.

Long-term image storage

The first place you are most likely to transfer your images to is your computer's hard disk, which has a high capacity, is easy to get to and allows you to edit, manipulate and print your image – it also makes great sense. However, as you take more and more images, you will slowly fill up your hard disk space. And having all the images in one place may sound ideal, but should your computer be stolen or irreparably damaged, your images will also disappear. It thus makes sense to copy and store images on a alternative medium – thankfully, there are various options to consider.

Card adapters

Many of the card formats offer adapters that allow them to be slotted into a laptop, adding to their versatility and making it easier to free up memory on the card.

CDs

The recordable CD, or CD-R, is the most popular and cost-effective method for storing images, with a capacity of around 650Mb. Most personal computers are now supplied with an integral CD-writer, while external units are available for computers without this facility. For most photographers, a CD-R represents the best option. A CD-RW is similar, but has the advantage that it can be rewritten; it is more expensive, however.

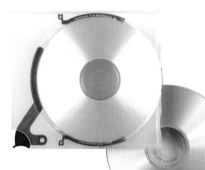

Other forms of image storage

Several novel devices have appeared dedicated to making image storage easier.

Apacer disk steno CD writer

This works much like a typical CD writer, but has card slots on its side that allow you to transfer images directly to a CD-R without a computer. It runs off batteries as well as mains power.

Portable hard disks

These self-contained hard disks connect to computers and allow you to store enormous amounts of data – 250Gb is not uncommon.

Portable storage device

Similar to portable hard disks, portable storage devices also allow you to view and work with images. They feature an LCD monitor to select and view images, delete or protect them. The playback options allow them to be used independently of a computer.

USB Flash hard drive

These keyring-sized devices plug straight into USB sockets and provide a simple and very portable form of memory storage. The capacities are impressive, ranging between 128Mb and 256Mb.

DVDs

The higher capacity of DVDs and the falling price of DVD burners means this format is gaining popularity. It's a great way of storing images for yourself, but because you need a DVD drive to view them, it hasn't the universal appeal of CDs, which can be played on all computers.

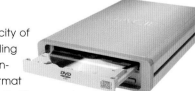

Zip disks

At one time, the Zip disk (which is available in 100Mb, 250Mb and 750Mb capacities) was one of the most popular ways of storing and transferring. However, the arrival of the CD-R has made the Zip disk a specialized medium.

File formats

Digital images can be stored in a variety of file formats, each of which has its own advantages and disadvantages.

The importance of file formats

The format of the digital image plays a vital role in the image quality and how much memory space each takes up on a storage card or computer hard disk. With most cameras, the options are JPEG, TIFF or RAW, while working on computers also allows images to be saved as PSD, GIF and a number of other formats.

The most important fact to remember is that when images are stored, they are usually compressed. There are two forms of compression: lossy and lossless. Formats that use the lossy format compress the image by losing some information from it. This degrades the image, with the greater compression resulting in increased loss of information. However, the lossy format is a useful format when storage space may be at a premium.

Lossless compression, often referred to as LZW, stores images without losing any information, therefore maintaining optimum quality, although file sizes are larger than lossy, to compensate.

JPEG

The Joint Photographic Expert Group format, or JPEG, is the most common file format used by photographers. It is a lossy system (see above), so there is some image-quality loss, although you can usually adjust the level of compression to offset this. Most cameras offer the option of capturing images as a JPEG in three sizes, which relate to the level of compression. When working on a computer, you usually have the option of using a slider scale to vary the level of compression.

TIFF

The Tagged Image File Format, or TIFF, is the most popular lossless file format. Only the more expensive cameras offer this option, although most software allows digital images, such as those made on a scanner, to also be recorded as a TIFF. The compromise for retaining quality is that the file size remains relatively large compared to JPEGs.

RAW

For the ultimate quality, some cameras allow images to be saved in the RAW, unaltered format. This has the advantage of retaining a great deal of information, but viewing images requires specific software, so it's not a universal format. In reality, the difference between a RAW and a TIFF file is only marginal.

OTHER MAIN FILE FORMATS

GIF

The Graphics Interchange Format is predominantly used on the web, as the small file size offers relatively low quality and a maximum of 256 colours.

PSD

This Photoshop file format retains information on how the image has been manipulated, such as Layers and other features.

TOP TIP
Always try to save the original as a TIFF format. Make a JPEG copy of it if you want to quickly view images or send them via email.

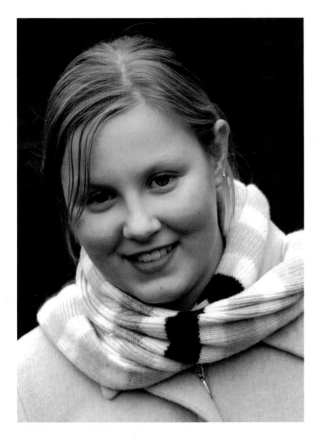 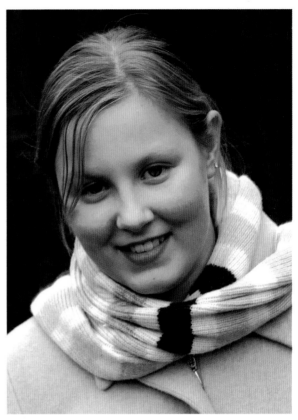

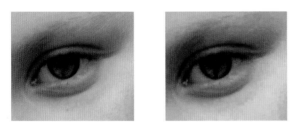

COMPARISON OF FILE FORMATS

This set of images illustrates the difference in quality between file formats. Both images are the same size – 13.7Mb (2536 x 1893 pixels) – but the image on the left is a TIFF file, while the one on the right is a high-compression JPEG. Both images look similar in quality when the image as a whole is viewed at relatively low magnification, but zoom into the image and the difference in quality is obvious. A close crop of the eye reveals the difference in detail, with the JPEG providing far less quality.

System accessories
Lenses

Choosing the right lens is just as important as deciding which camera to use. The choice on offer is enormous, from general-purpose lenses to specialist optics, so it is worth knowing what's available and the advantages and disadvantages of each type.

Main types of lenses

Considering the large number of lenses available to the modern photographer, it is best to start by classifying the main types of lens available and the pros and cons of each.

Fixed lenses

Today's modern zooms offer such good quality that most amateurs rarely consider a fixed lens, let alone use one. This is a shame, because fixed lenses still have much to offer. In terms of optical quality, fixed lenses still have the edge over zooms, in particular at very wide apertures. Also, a fixed lens normally has a wider maximum aperture, which gives it an advantage in low light and provides a brighter viewfinder image. The obvious disadvantage of a fixed lens is its single focal length.

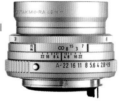

Zoom lenses

The modern zoom is a marvel of modern optics. We now have lenses covering all sorts of focal lengths, from ultra wide-angle zoom to super-telephoto zooms. This means photographers can choose from a range of focal lengths at a fraction of the cost of buying individual fixed lenses covering the same range.

The professional-class zooms provide a much closer contest in terms of optical quality, and often boast a fast maximum aperture. Zooms are also more likely to exhibit lens aberrations, especially those covering a very wide range – see opposite.

Wide-angle

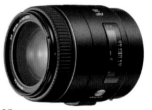

This lens gives a wider angle of view than the human eye. The most common types range from 21–35mm, with 28mm being the most popular. Ultra wide-angle lenses cover a focal length of 15–20mm and have a very wide angle of view, useful for providing unusual perspectives. The ultra wide-angle zoom offers a versatile choice of focal lengths, usually in the region of 16–35mm. This type of lens has found appeal with travel and architectural photographers.

Standard

The traditional standard lens is the 50mm lens. This type of lens gives a similar angle of view to that of the human eye. Standard zooms cover a range of around 28–80mm.

Telephoto

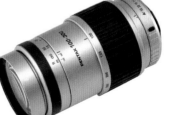

Any lens with a focal length greater than 50mm is termed a telephoto, and has a narrower angle of view, making it useful for distant subjects.

The 70–200mm has been the most popular telephoto zoom until recent years, when the 70–300mm has taken over. More powerful telezooms include the 135–400mm and the 170–500mm. Fixed telephoto lenses include the 300mm, 400mm, 500mm and 600mm.

Superzooms

The most versatile zoom ever, superzoom lenses offer an all-in-one package, boasting a range of 28–200mm and later 28–300mm. The latest generation are small and light, offering a decent optical quality. However, they still cannot match a two-lens combination covering a similar range for overall quality, and also suffer from having a relatively small maximum aperture.

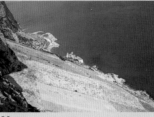

Focal lengths

Now we've established the main types of lenses, the next step is to see how the focal length of the lens determines how a scene is captured.

Focal length comparison

The series of images shown right illustrates how changing the focal length of a lens completely transforms the scene that is captured. Here, the images range from 8mm full-frame fish-eye through to 400mm.

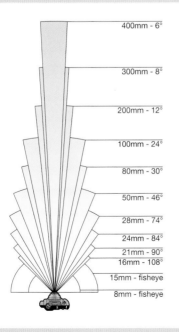

ANGLE OF VIEW
This diagram shows how the angle of view varies according to the focal lengths in use.

400mm - 6°
300mm - 8°
200mm - 12°
100mm - 24°
80mm - 30°
50mm - 46°
28mm - 74°
24mm - 84°
21mm - 90°
16mm - 108°
15mm - fisheye
8mm - fisheye

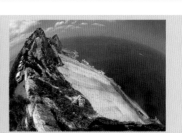

8mm fish-eye

15mm fish-eye

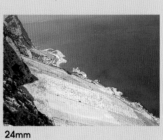

18mm

24mm

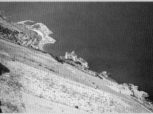

28mm

35mm

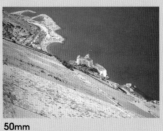

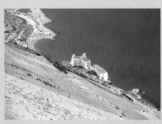

50mm

70mm

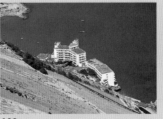

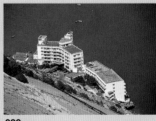

100mm

200mm

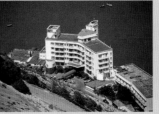

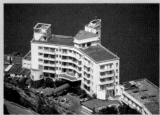

300mm

400mm

Specialist lenses

As well as the more popular lens choices, there are a number of specialized lenses that deserve consideration. As the name suggests, these are designed for a specific use. This is not only their greatest selling point, but also their biggest drawback, as they are often not suitable for other types of photography. However, for their chosen application, there is nothing to touch them.

Macro lenses

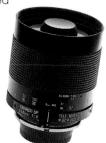

The macro lens is the most useful specialist optic. Most record a life-size image (1:1) on the film/sensor, while some only manage half life-size (1:2). There are macro lenses at various focal lengths, 50mm, 105mm and 180mm being the most common. Go for the longest focal length you can afford, as it allows you a longer working distance from the subject. A 105mm or 180mm macro lens can also be used as a telephoto lens or as a very good portrait lens.

Perspective-control lenses

These lenses are very useful in architectural photography, as they allow tilt-and-shift movements, which allow you to manipulate the plane of focus, control depth of field in unusual ways and correct converging verticals when shooting buildings. The focal length is usually between 45mm and 90mm.

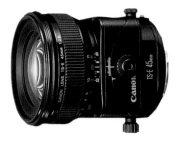

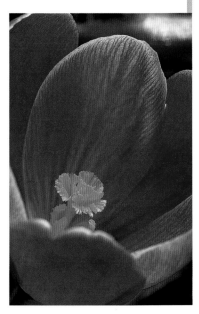

FLOWER
A macro lens allows you to fill the frame with small objects, usually giving life-size reproduction.

Mirror lens

A mirror lens (usually around 500mm or 600mm) uses mirrors in its construction, allowing the lens to be far more compact compared to conventional telephotos. The lenses are ideal for when you want to travel light but need a lens with strong pulling power. Mirror lenses work with a fixed aperture (normally f/8), so you cannot change apertures or control depth of field.

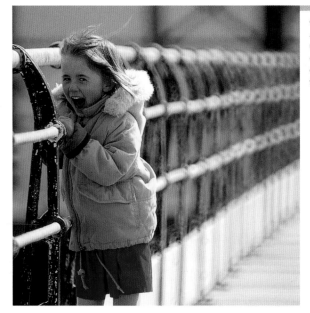

GIRL BY RAILINGS
A mirror lens has the unique effect of creating 'doughnuts' around out-of-focus highlights.

Fish-eye lens

Fish-eye lenses offer a 180-degree field of view, and are available in two forms, circular and full-frame. The focal length of a circular fish-eye is usually 8mm, while the full-frame fish-eye is around 15mm.

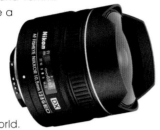

Circular fish-eyes create a circular image in the centre of the frame, with black edges around it, while full-frame fish-eyes fill the frame with a very distorted look on the world.

DOORWAY
Distortion, a characteristic of a fish-eye lens, was used deliberately to curve the straight lines of this frame.

Image stabilization

Image stabilization, also known as vibration reduction, is found on an increasing number of lenses, in particular telephotos. As its name suggests, the lens incorporates a system of gyro sensors that work to reduce camera shake. Shots taken at slow shutter speeds have proven that the system works, making a difference equivalent to a shutter speed two to three stops faster. Some lenses even offer an image-stabiliz-ing facility that caters for panning shots, as well as standard shooting.

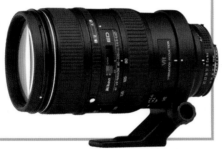

Types of lens elements

A lens is made up of several elements arranged in specific groups. Zoom lenses generally tend to have more elements and groups than a fixed lens. When choosing a lens, it is worth getting a brochure from the manufacturer to find out exactly how the lens is made up.

The elements vary from lens to lens. While most use optical glass, some are made from plastic, while others are made from glass and plastic. Many lenses incorporate aspherical elements, designed to reduce distortion, and some telephoto lenses incorporate fluorite, apochromatic or low-dispersion glass to counter lens aberration.

Lens aberration

Not all lenses are perfect. Some, in particular those at the cheaper end of the scale or those offering the widest zoom range, are prone to one or more of a number of lens faults, or aberrations.

Aberration describes an image that suffers a number of problems caused by the lens. This includes chromatic aberration, when different wavelengths of light focus at different points, leading to loss of sharpness.

Distortion relates to the shape of the subject on the image not corresponding to the real thing because of straight lines appearing to be curved. Zoom lenses typically produce barrel distortion at the wide-angle end and pincushion distortion at the telephoto end. Barrel distortion causes straight lines to bulge outwards, while pincushion distortion sees straight lines curve inwards.

Other aberrations include astigmatism, where off-centre points of light record as a line, and spherical aberration, where light at the edges of the lens cause flare to spill over the image, causing the image to appear soft and exhibit low contrast.

The 'speed' of a lens

A lens may be termed slow or fast. This relates not to its focusing speed, but to its maximum aperture. It is in fact an indirect reference to how the maximum aperture affects the shutter speed.

A fast lens is one that has a faster aperture than is the norm for its particular focal length. For instance, a 70–200mm f/2.8 is a fast telephoto zoom, because its maximum aperture is better than the average, in this case f/3.5–4.5. A slow lens is the reference given to lenses with a smaller than average maximum aperture. For instance, a 28–300mm f/4.5–6.3 is slow, as a 28mm lens normally has an aperture of f/2.8, while a 300mm is more often around f/4.5 or f/5.6.

Flashguns

When available light isn't good enough, the trusty flash can be relied upon to rescue the shot. This highly sophisticated piece of equipment does far more than simply fire off a burst of light.

How does a flash unit work?

In very simple terms, a flash unit is a gas-filled chamber. Pressing the shutter release triggers an electrical current to pass through the chamber and charge the gas, which produces the flash burst. The actual flash exposure is controlled by the camera, ensuring that the correct amount of light is provided to give a nicely balanced image. Many cameras use a TTL (through the lens) system to do this, while others have sensors close to the lens that measure and control the flash output.

Anatomy of a flashgun

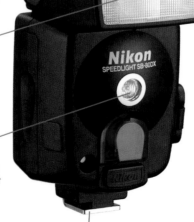

Control buttons
These controls allow you to set the various flash modes. The chosen settings appear on the LCD for ease of use

Flash head
This can swivel from side to side and be raised or lowered for bounce flash. The flash head often has a zoom facility (usually 28–80mm), so that flash coverage is optimized for use with particular lenses

Diffuser panel
Some flashguns have an integral diffuser panel that can be pulled down in front of the flash head to diffuse the light when shooting subjects in a relatively close range

Focus assist lamp
Some flashguns feature an AF assist lamp, which is activated in low light to project a patterned beam that aids the autofocus system to lock on the subject

LCD
As with cameras, the LCD provides information on the flashgun's settings

Ready lamp
This provides a visual indication of when the flash is charged up and ready to be used

Test button
Press this to test the flash exposure or when you want to fire the flashgun off-camera – for instance, when painting with light (see page160)

Hotshoe mount
This attaches the flashgun to the camera and has metal contacts for transmitting information electronically between the flash and camera – the more metal contacts, the greater the sophistication of information

Flash modes

Most flashguns boast a variety of modes. The most common are listed below.

Automatic

This is the most common mode, and its operation is fairly straightforward. If the camera detects that the ambient light level is high enough, it doesn't activate the flashgun. Once the light level has fallen below a certain threshold, it triggers the flash to fire automatically.

Fill-in

Set the camera to fill-in (also called forced-on) mode and the flash fires, even though light levels are high. It's a useful mode when shooting portraits, to remove shadows from the face and add a catchlight to eyes.

Forced-off

This mode switches off the automatic flash and forces the camera to set a longer exposure time to compensate. It is used in situations where a flash isn't allowed (for instance, museums) or when you want to purposely set a long exposure for creative reasons.

Second-curtain sync

Here, the flash fires at the end of the exposure rather than at the start (see Flash synchronization below).

Red-eye reduction

This mode fires either a series of short flash bursts or a beam of light before the actual flash exposure to reduce the risk of red eye (see Red eye below).

Slow sync

This mode is found on increasingly more cameras – on some models it is often termed the night-portrait mode. Slow sync (short for slow synchronization) mode mixes a long exposure with a burst of flash. It's a useful mode when you want to illuminate a subject with flash and record background detail as well.

Flash compensation

This is similar to exposure compensation, but it works by altering the power of the flash in relation to the ambient exposure.

High-speed flash

Some models allow the camera to synchronize the flash at any shutter speed in the camera's range. This offers up more creative options than just being restricted to a particular speed.

Flash synchronization

The duration of a flash burst is extremely short – on average around $\frac{1}{40000}$sec. With a normal flash exposure, the flash fires at the start of the exposure and is termed first-curtain synchronization.

With second-curtain synchronization, the flash fires at the end of the exposure. The advantage of using this is that any light trails that appear in the frame will appear natural.

With high-speed synchronization, the flash burst takes a longer period of time (often around $\frac{1}{1000}$sec), which allows a far faster shutter speed than normal to be set.

LCD INFORMATION
This is the LCD panel from a Canon Speedlite flashgun, with all icons active. It reveals not only the number of features that are available to photographers, but the level of information provided to aid the user.

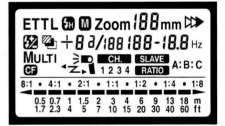

Red eye

Red eye is the term given to the phenomenon of the pupils of people's or animals' eyes appearing red due to the flash reflecting off blood vessels at the back of the subject's retina; this is the unfortunate 'demon eyes' effect that often mars portraits. Red eye is more likely to occur the closer the flash is to the camera and the longer the lens's focal length. To reduce the problem with an integral flash, move closer to the subject and use the lens at a wider setting – and, where possible, use a hotshoe-mounted flashgun.

Guide number

The power output of a flashgun is indicated by its guide number (GN), usually stated in metres at ISO 100. The higher the stated guide number, the more powerful the unit. Before cameras did the calculations automatically, photographers used the following formula to calculate the flash exposure:

Aperture = guide number/flash-to-subject distance (metres)

Filter systems

One of the first accessories many photographers add to their camera kits is a filter system. Filters can transform your photography, and are a great addition to any photo outfit. Although they are modest in cost at the start, building up a comprehensive collection can be expensive, so it's important to make sure you invest in the system that's best suited to your needs.

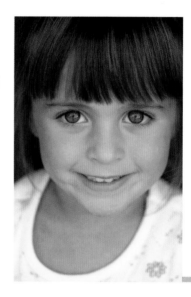

Screw-in filters come in various sizes to fit most lenses.

Main types of filter system

There are two main types of filter system to consider: screw-in and slot-in filters. Each has their own advantages and disadvantages, so it's important to weigh up all factors before investing.

Screw-in filters

These filters attach directly to the front of the lens. Because various lenses have different diameters, a screw-in filter must be a particular size to fit the lens, referred to as the filter thread size. The most common sizes for SLR lenses range from 52mm to 77mm, although sizes as small as 22.5mm and as large as 95mm are available. If you own a number of lenses all with different thread sizes, you will need multiple filters of the same type to fit them all. For this reason, screw-in filters make most sense if you only have one or two lenses, or if they all use the same thread size.

TOP TIP

For screw-in filters, Hoya offer a good mix of quality and price. For optimum quality at a premium cost, consider B+W filters.

EMMA
A warm-up filter is ideal for enhancing natural skin tones.

Slot-in filters

Slot-in filters, often called square filters, are a far better option if you use several lenses. The actual filter slots into a holder, which is fixed to the lens via an adapter ring. Because you only need to buy different sizes of adapter ring to fit different lenses, the cost of building up a comprehensive filter system is far less.

Another advantage of slot-in filters is that more than one can be used in combination without causing any problems. While this can be done with screw-in filters by screwing one into another, there is the risk of vignetting, which results in the corners of the image appearing black because they are obscured by the filter ring.

Slot-in sizes

Slot-in filters come in a range of sizes. Smaller ones are aimed at 35mm and digital SLR users; larger ones are suited to medium-format lenses, and large-diameter ultra wide-angle zooms for 35mm and digital SLRs.

The smallest systems are based around filters with a width of 67mm – these can be used safely with wide-angle lenses as wide as 28mm. This is a relatively cheap option, but you are limited in what lenses you can use the system with.

The next size up is 85mm filters, which cost more but are far more versatile, as they can be used with wide-angle lenses for 35mm or digital SLRs of up to around 21mm, as well as medium-format lenses.

The next step up is to 100mm filters. Unless you are a professional, you are unlikely to want to go up to this size, especially as these filters are relatively expensive.

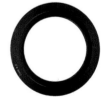

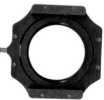

System filters require the use of an adaptor ring and filter holder.

Step-up and step-down rings

These are rings that allow you to attach a screw-in filter to a lens with a wider or narrower filter thread. A step-down ring allows you to use a filter with a lens offering a smaller filter thread. For instance, a 72–82mm ring allows an 82mm filter to be used on a filter with a 72mm thread. A step-up ring has the opposite purpose, but should be used with great care as vignetting is very likely to occur.

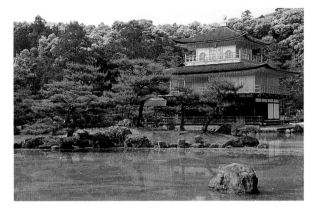

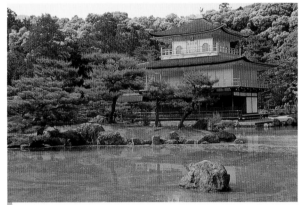

Filters for compacts

Some premium compacts (film and digital) feature a filter thread that accepts small screw-in filters. The Ricoh GR-series of 35mm compacts, for instance, has its own dedicated range of filters. For compacts without a filter thread on the lens, a system from Cokin allows slot-in filters to be used.

BELL
A polarizer delivers richly saturated skies.

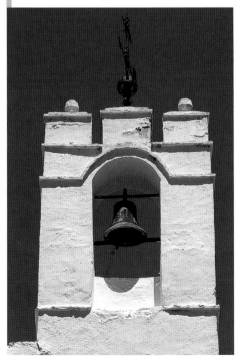

JAPANESE TEMPLE
Don't be afraid to experiment with filters. These images show a scene photographed with no filter (top) and then with a sepia filter.

The square slot-in filter cannot be beaten for versatility.

Rear-element filters

Large telephoto lenses and some ultra wide-angle zooms do not feature a filter thread on the front of the barrel due to the diameter of the lens. Instead, the rear of the barrel has a holder that accepts a very small filter.

TOP TIP

With slot-in filters, you can't go far wrong with the Cokin A (67mm) or Cokin P (85mm) systems. Another 85mm system to look at is Hitech, while for 100mm filters, Lee Filters and Hitech are both excellent. The biggest system is Cokin's X-Pro range, which use 130mm filters.

Studio lighting

For the ultimate in controllable light, there is nothing to beat a studio flash outfit, as this versatile system offers the photographer complete control over every aspect of lighting an image.

Anatomy of a studio flash head

Slave cell
In multiple flash set-ups, only one head is connected to the camera/meter. When this head is triggered, the slave cell on other heads detects the flash output and fires the other heads.

Ventilation
The heads generate heat and include a fan to prevent overheating. Be sure not to cover the ventilation slots

Carry handle
This useful feature allows you to handle the heads, which may be very hot if used for long periods

Sync lead socket
The sync lead connects the flash head to a camera or meter. Some heads allow various types of lead to be used

Accessory locking ring
Attachments such as a softbox or reflector dish are attached and removed using this ring

Audible beep
This sounds when the head has recharged and is ready for the next exposure

Flash output
This slider switch allows you to control the flash output. Controls are limited to steps, such as full-power, half-power and quarter-power. More sophisticated models allow stepless control

Modelling light
This is a tungsten bulb that provides a continuous light source, allowing you to adjust the lighting effect

Power socket
This is where you connect the flash head to the mains power

Modelling lamp
This links the output of the modelling lamp with the flash power output slider for an accurate representation of the flash output

Flash tube
This ring-shaped tube produces the flash exposure once the shutter is triggered

Main types of studio light

Although studio flash heads serve a similar purpose, there are quite a few variations available.

Monobloc

Monoblocs are studio flash heads that incorporate an integral power source and all controls, allowing fully independent usage. Because everything is built into the head, monoblocs are compact units that are easy to transport and store away. They're relatively cheap, making them particularly popular with amateur photographers.

Powerpack

More common than monoblocs in professional studios are studio heads powered by a large generator pack. This type of system has the advantage that it offers more power and faster recycling times than monoblocs, but is more expensive – and should the powerpack fail, there is no way of using the lights. Controls for the lights are usually found on the powerpack, so it's easy to make quick adjustments to several heads.

Portable studio flash

For studio flash on the move, there are a number of portable flash systems to choose from. These work in a similar fashion to standard powerpacks, but the generator includes a rechargeable battery, allowing it to be used where an electricity supply is unavailable. This is a very versatile system, but an expensive one.

Tungsten lighting

While the majority of professional photographers opt for daylight-balanced studio flash, there are a small number who use tungsten lighting. These have the advantage of providing a continuous light source, although the light output is much lower. Tungsten lights also generate high levels of heat, making them an uncomfortable choice for portrait subjects.

Flash lighting accessories

The type of attachment you fit to the front of the flash head determines the characteristics of the final lighting effect.

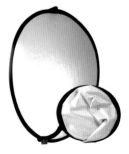

Softbox

This is a favourite with portrait photographers as it provides a very diffused light. It is basically a large fabric box with a white front panel, available in various sizes. Although the square type is the most popular choice, other shapes are available, including rectangular (known as strip light) and octagonal.

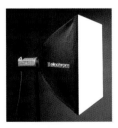

Reflector

Also called a dish, this is usually supplied as standard. Reflectors are used to provide direct illumination of a subject, and are available in different depths to vary the coverage of light.

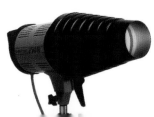

Snoot

This is a long, cone-shaped attachment that narrows the light into a narrow beam. The snoot is not normally used with the main light but as a secondary light, usually to create a highlight around a portrait subject's hair.

Umbrella

Often called a brolly, this comes in various effects. Silver brollies give a bright result, while gold adds a warm tone to the subject. White brollies provide the softest effect and are the most popular choice.

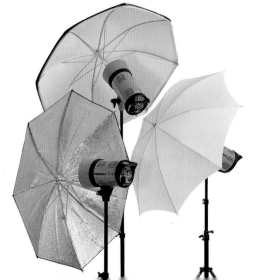

Studio and camera accessories

A vast number of accessories are available for the various types of camera on the market. Some of these can be classed as essential items, while others are useful but not always necessary. Optical attachments that aid close-up photography are covered in detail on page 149.

Sync lead
The humble sync lead connects the flash head to the meter or camera. Some cameras require use of what is termed a reversed-polarity lead, which looks identical, but has the positive and negative terminals in the lead set in the opposite way.

Backgrounds
Backgrounds can be divided into paper and fabric types. Paper backgrounds are plain in colour, with white and black the two most popular choices. They are relatively cheap, and can be rolled up for storage. Fabric backgrounds are available in a wide choice of plain and mottled colours. As well as large rolls of fabric, collapsible backgrounds, which fold away into a small bag, are also available.

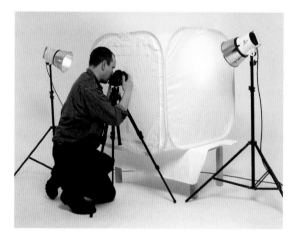

Cubelite
A relatively new product, this is portable light tent ideal for still-life photography. It provides an efficient means to photograph reflective subjects, such as silverware, without the normal problem of reflections appearing on the subject.

Camera storage
One of the first accessories to consider is also one of the most important – where you will store the camera when it's not in use. There are various options to consider, each with its own pros and cons.

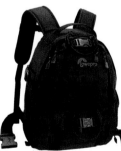

Gadget bags
The gadget bag, which hangs over the shoulder via a long strap, is the most popular type with enthusiast photographers. Available in various sizes, gadget bags can be found to suit all sizes and types of camera outfit. They are well protected, and thanks to features such as adjustable internal dividers, are very versatile for storage. A major advantage of these types of bags is their accessibility, allowing very fast access to your camera. One major disadvantage is that the weight of the outfit is taken by one shoulder, which can prove uncomfortable, especially when you are carrying a full, heavy bag.

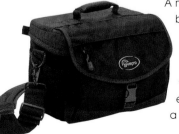

Photo rucksacks
Also called backpacks, these offer a far more comfortable option than the gadget bag, as the weight of all your gear is evenly distributed across the shoulders and back. The rucksack comes in various guises and sizes and is particularly popular with outdoor types. Its biggest disadvantage is that you can't get to your gear particularly quickly, as you need to take the pack off your back first.

Hard cases

For the ultimate in protection, look for a hard case that is tough enough to stand on. The two main types are metal and plastic, with the latter tending to be more popular. These are great for when you are transporting gear overseas, but aren't as practical as gadget bags or rucksacks.

Protective cases

This is the type that usually comes supplied with a compact camera. These cases are made from soft material, and provide protection from scratches and scuffs.

Zoomsters

These are designed to hold an SLR body with zoom lens attached. They are a good option if you are travelling light, but the storage space is restricted. The zoomster is the modern equivalent of the ever-ready case (ERC), which was the number one choice before zoom lenses became popular.

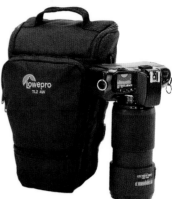

Pouches

These are designed to hold either a specific lens, or a particular type of lens, such as a telephoto. Pouches offer good protection, but are somewhat limited in their appeal.

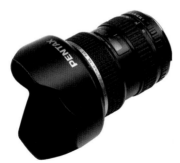

Lens accessories

As well as filters, various accessories are available for use with lenses.

Converters

These allow you to convert the focal length of the lens. A wide-angle converter increases the field of view, making it useful for shooting interiors or landscapes. A teleconverter increases the telephoto power of a lens, making it suitable for high-magnification shots of distant subjects.

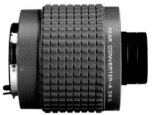

Lens hoods

Possibly one of the most overlooked accessories is also one of the most useful. A lens hood shields the optics from stray light that can create flare and reduce the overall contrast of the image. There is little reason not to leave a hood permanently attached. Although universal hoods to fit various lenses are available, wide-angle users should fit the appropriate hood to avoid vignetting.

Masks

These are black plastic accessories that fit in a filter holder in front of the lens. They have shaped windows cut away in the centre, to give an effect such as that of looking through a keyhole or binoculars. Masks were popular in the 1970s, but are not in particularly great demand today.

Power accessories

SLR power grips

Some SLRs allow for extra grips to be attached to the base of the camera, which aid handling. There are two main types.

Battery packs

These offer an alternative power source to those used in the camera. These are usually run on AA batteries, which are more readily available than lithium batteries.

Motordrives

Some of the top-end SLRs accept a motordrive, which not only offers an alternative power source, but adds a boost to the frame rate and offers alternative controls for vertical shooting.

Battery types

Alkaline AA batteries have long been the most common type used in cameras. However, with higher levels of power consumption, newer types of battery have now been developed.

With rechargeable AAs, the older Ni-Cd (nickel cadmium) types are gradually being replaced by Ni-Mh (nickel metal hydride) batteries,

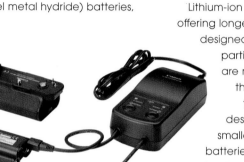

which last longer and do not suffer from memory problems.

Lithium-ion batteries are now also offering longer lifespans. They are designed specifically for particular cameras and are much more compact than a pair of AAs, thereby enabling designers to create ever smaller cameras. Long-life batteries offer extended running time.

Camera supports

Any photographer looking to take the sharpest possible pictures will sooner or later need to invest in one form or another of camera support.

Tripods

The tripod is by far the most popular type of camera support. Tripods are available in various sizes and are constructed from different materials to suit different applications.

Small table-top tripods are designed for film and digital compacts. Some offer movable heads, making them relatively versatile for snapshots and self-timer pictures.

SLR tripods

These are the most popular tripods. There are three main types.

Standard

The majority of amateur photographers are likely to need nothing more than a standard tripod. With extendable legs, a fitted head and good stability, all obtained at a fair price, this type is deservedly popular.

Studio-based

These tripods are far heavier than the standard types. They are made with far thicker legs, which are necessary to provide a stable support for larger and heavier studio-based cameras, such as a medium-format outfit.

Carbon-fibre

For outdoor photographers who are likely to have to carry a tripod around over long distances, a carbon-fibre model is hard to beat. It is 35 per cent lighter than equivalent aluminium models, and offers excellent stability. This comes at a higher price, but landscape photographers all around the world reckon that the initial investment is well worth it.

Anatomy of a tripod

It's worth knowing what to look for when considering which tripod to buy, to be sure you get a model suited to your type of photography.

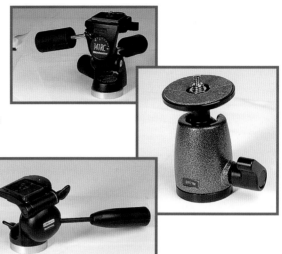

Head

Not all heads are the same. Pan and tilt, ball and socket and three-way heads all work in different ways to support the camera and adjust its alignment. When buying a tripod, check out the head and make sure you are happy with how it works. Some tripods come without a head, allowing you to fit your favourite type.

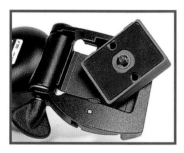

Quick-release plate

To make attaching and removing the camera easier, look for models with a quick-release plate, a removable platform that screws into the base.

Spirit level

Landscape photographers find a spirit level useful to ensure that the horizon is completely level for each shot.

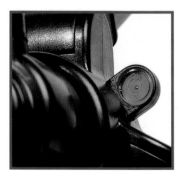

Centre column

This can be extended to increase the maximum height the camera can be used at. Some tripods allow the centre column to be removed and attached horizontally for shooting at odd angles – usually in close-up work.

Leg locks

Personal preference dictates whether you prefer hinged locks or twisting locks. Try before you buy.

Leg sections

The number of leg sections on a tripod varies from model to model, with three or four being the most popular. The general rule is the more leg sections a tripod has, the higher it extends. But don't overdo it, as stability is compromised the more legs are extended.

Feet

Rubber or plastic feet give a good grip on most surfaces, bar smooth or icy conditions. Spiked feet are great for outdoors on soft or slippery land, but can scratch wooden floors if used indoors. Look for feet that combine both types.

Monopods

Sometimes, one leg is better than three! The monopod is a good choice of support when a tripod is too cumbersome an option. It is particularly popular with sports photographers as support for their large telephoto lenses.

Beanbag

These small accessories can be kept in the boot of the car until needed. They feature a tripod bush that screws into the base of the camera, allowing a firm fitting on which to rest.

Suction clamp

An unusual accessory for attaching the camera to smooth surfaces like metal or glass. Used by some motorsports photographers to clamp the camera to a car bonnet and trigger it remotely.

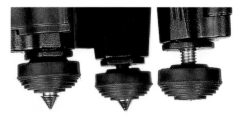

Remote releases

Optional accessories are available for firing the shutter when the shutter button isn't the best option, such as in low-light photography.

Cable releases

The traditional type screws into the shutter button (or appropriate terminal). When you press the plunger, a metal pin extends from the base of the release and triggers the shutter release.

Corded electronic releases

The majority of modern cameras use an electronic release to fire the shutter. These are corded (usually 60cm/2ft in length), and are specific to certain types of camera. Some feature a lock facility, which allows you to lock the shutter open during long exposures.

Short-range infrareds

These are very small units that fire the shutter from up to a range of around 5m (16ft).

Long-range transmitters/receivers

These are particularly favoured by wildlife photographers. A transmitter is positioned in direct line of a receiver, fitted to the camera's hotshoe. The shutter is triggered when an infrared beam between the two elements is broken.

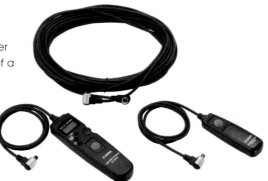

Lighting accessories

There are a number of accessories that allow you to control the characteristics and direction of light falling on your subject. They can be divided into two main types: reflectors and diffusers.

Reflectors

Reflectors work by bouncing light back on to the subject. The colour of the reflector is important – white provides a soft, diffused light; silver is more efficient but can look harsh; and gold adds warmth.

Collapsible reflectors

For convenience and practicability, there isn't much that can touch this type of reflector. They can be stored away neatly when not required and instantly pulled out when needed. The larger the size, the wider the area of reflected light, so small reflectors are only suitable for smaller subjects, such as close-up photography. Lastolite manufacture a huge range, available in various sizes and colours. The best models feature a handgrip that makes them very easy to use.

California Sunbounces

These huge reflectors are favoured by fashion and portrait photographers who want the ultimate in control. The large size of the panels means they can reflect light onto a full-length subject.

Triflectors

An unusual reflector that is growing in popularity, the triflector has three individual panels that allows for excellent control of reflected light. It is most commonly placed beneath the chin of a subject, but can also be used much like any other reflector.

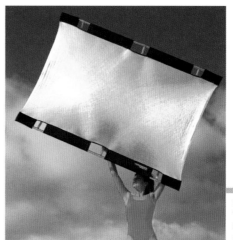

LARGER THAN LIFE
The California Sunbounce is the ultimate reflector.

Diffusers

The aim of a diffuser is to soften the light falling on a subject. It is used predominantly in portrait photography to reduce the harshness of sunlight. Because light travels through a diffuser to reach the subject, they must be white so as not to create a colour cast. The Sun Swatter is a large diffuser popular with professionals, while a diffuser panel is available for the California Sunbounce. If you want to save money, you can make your own diffuser from net curtains or muslin.

Exposure meters

Although the majority of cameras boast highly sophisticated forms of integral metering, the handheld exposure meter is still a popular accessory. There are three main types of meter: the light meter takes readings of ambient light only; the flash meter measures only a flash exposure; and a combined meter can take a reading of both. Considering the small variance in price between all three, the combined meter is the recommended choice.

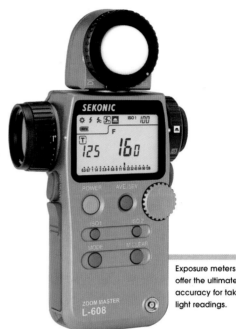

Exposure meters offer the ultimate accuracy for taking light readings.

Anatomy of an exposure meter

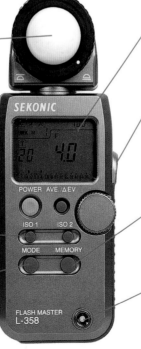

Invercone
This white dome, also known as a lumidisc, is used to take incident light readings. With most meters, a switch or dial raises or lowers the dome to adjust how it takes readings. In its raised position, it is ideal for general use outdoors. In its lowered position, it is better suited for metering for flat objects, such as paintings

ISO button
To meter correctly, you must ensure that it is set to the correct ISO rating

Mode button
Press to change between taking ambient or flash readings

LCD
The LCD is the information centre of the meter, providing information about the exposure reading

Meter button
This is usually located on the side of the meter for easy use. Press it to take a meter reading and, if connected to studio heads, to fire the flash

Memory
You can store set-ups using the memory function

Sync socket
This connects the meter to the studio flash via a sync lead

Image usage
Scanners

The advent of the digital darkroom has enabled photographers to control the whole process, from taking the image all the way through to the final print. The scanner is equivalent in some respects to an enlarger in a traditional darkroom.

What is a scanner?

A scanner is a device that uses light to convert an image or object into digital form. A strip of sensors work their way across an image during the scanning process, forming a digital image. Imagine an office photocopier capable of making high-resolution colour or black-and-white scans, and you can get an idea of what a scanner does. The scanner can be operated through image-manipulation software like Adobe Photoshop, or independently as a standalone.

TOP TIP
When considering which model of scanner to buy, check the scanning speed at maximum resolution – some models are much quicker than others.

The flatbed is the most versatile type of scanner.

Types of scanner

Some flatbed scanners, such as this model, incorporate a transparency hood for scanning negatives and slides. The film is placed on a holder on the glass plate, as shown.

The two main types of scanner are flatbeds and film scanners. Flatbed scanners are small, table-top devices that look like mini-photocopiers. Earlier models were designed to scan prints or documents – usually up to A4 (21 x 30cm/8½ x 11in) in size – although some current models boast a transparency hood, which allows scanning of negatives or slides.

Film scanners are more specialized, in that they are designed to work only with film. Most models offer a range of carriers, which hold mounted slides or strips of slides or negatives. Most are designed for use with 35mm and can often accept APS cartridges as well. There are a handful of models that can scan medium-format originals (up to 6 x 9cm).

Some film scanners, such as the Nikon Coolscan 8000ED, allow various film formats to be scanned, from 35mm to medium-format.

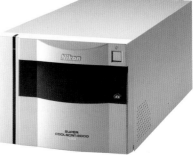

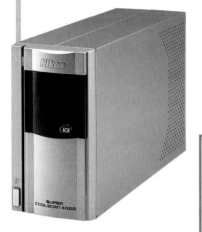

The most popular types of film scanner are those that accept 35mm film, such as this Nikon Coolscan 4000.

Scanner resolution

A scanned image is made up of hundreds of thousands of pixels, created as the sensor moves across the image. The number of pixels, stated as ppi (pixels per inch), or dpi (dots per inch), is called the scanner's resolution. The higher the resolution, the better the quality, although other factors, such as the sensor used in the scanner and the software, also determine the final quality of the scan. A decent film scanner has a resolution of 4000dpi, with flatbed scanners around 3200dpi.

Interpolation

It's worth noting that when determining the scanner resolution, the important figure is the optical resolution (stated in dpi or ppi), which is the maximum number of pixels that the scanner is capable of achieving. Many scanners offer the capability of scanning resolutions higher than the optical resolution, but these are not recommended, as the higher figures are created by using interpolation, an artificial process for adding pixels by guessing its characteristics based on neighbouring pixels.

Scanning 3D objects
If you are feeling imaginative, flatbed scanners can be used to scan 3D objects, such as flowers. The secret is to choose items that are thin. These provide the best scans because the scanner hood needs to be lowered as far as possible to achieve optimum results.

TOP TIP
If your system is TWAIN-compliant, you can use the scanner through an image-manipulation program, such as Adobe Photoshop. This offers the advantage of opening the image directly in the software.

Scanner software

The scanning software plays a vital role in the quality of the final scan. The following is a breakdown of the most important scanning features.

Document type

This is where you inform the scanner what type of image you are working with. 'Reflective' refers to a print (or document), while 'transparency' means slide. Some scanners allow you to specify whether the image is colour or black and white.

Resolution/image size

The resolution that you scan at is the most important parameter to consider, as it will determine how you can use the scanned image. For web use, you need only scan the image at 72dpi as that is screen resolution. For publication, 300dpi is the optimum setting.

Bear in mind how large you want to use the final image before determining the resolution to scan at. If you plan to make to make large prints, for instance, it's pointless scanning 35mm at 300dpi because once you set the scanned image to A4-print size (21 x 30cm/8½ x 11in), the resolution will be far less. The general rule is to always scan your image at the optical resolution of the scanner, as this gives you the maximum number of options on final picture use. For instance, if your scanner has an optical resolution of 4000dpi, always scan at this resolution. You will end up with large file sizes, but that's not a problem as you can always reduce the file size at a later date.

Mode/user setting

Most scanners allow you to make up particular settings, which allow you to optimize the parameters of the scanner to suit your preferences. For instance, if you often scan colour slides for use on the Internet, you can set up a user setting titled 'Web', which automatically sets the scanner to scan a colour slide at 72dpi.

Single or batch scanning

Film carriers can hold one or a number of images at one time. Selecting batch scanning allows scans to be made from multiple images on the carrier.

The sequence here demonstrates the basic capabilities of scanning software. The following is a series of adjustments made to a 10 x 8in colour print.

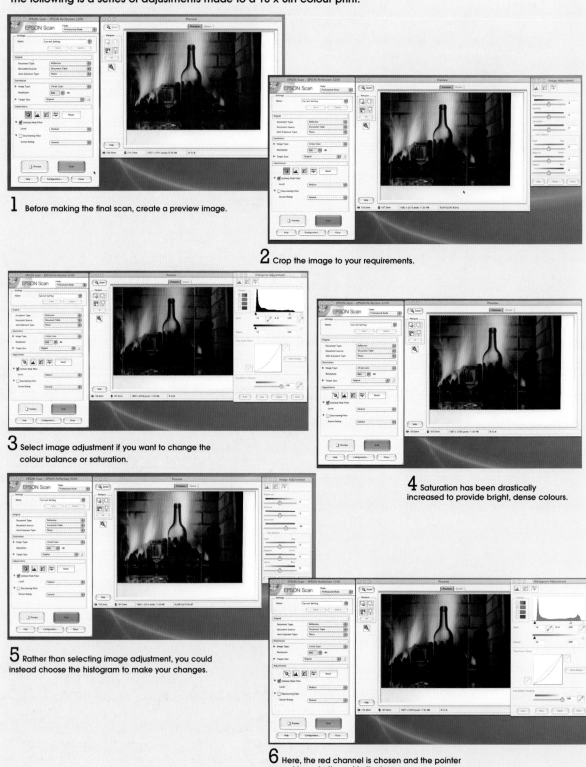

1 Before making the final scan, create a preview image.

2 Crop the image to your requirements.

3 Select image adjustment if you want to change the colour balance or saturation.

4 Saturation has been drastically increased to provide bright, dense colours.

5 Rather than selecting image adjustment, you could instead choose the histogram to make your changes.

6 Here, the red channel is chosen and the pointer moved to mute the red in the image.

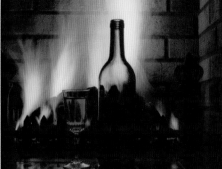

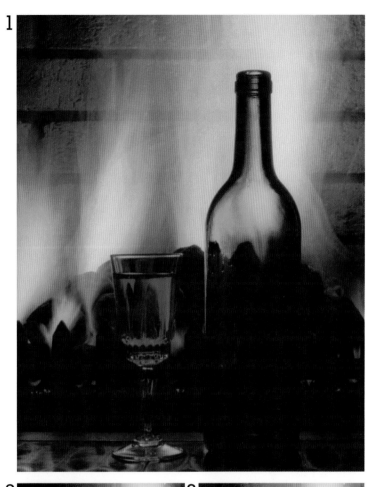

* Original
1 The cropped image, with no colour adjustments.
2 The image with +40 saturation.
3 The image following changes to the red channel in the histogram.

Image adjustments

There are various adjustments that you can make to an image:

Autoexposure allows the scanner to determine the exposure of the image.

Histogram allows you to adjust the highlights, shadows and mid-tones.

Brightness/contrast/saturation/colour controls are usually found in the same window and allow you to manipulate various elements of the final image.

Auto/manual focus Normally the scanner can be relied upon to give sharp results. However, you can usually specify what part of the image the scanner should focus on, should it have trouble.

Crop If you don't want to include the whole image in the scan, you can crop the image to however you prefer it.

Preview/scan

Making a scan is normally a two-stage process. The first is to take a preview – a fast, relatively low-resolution scan that provides an indication of how the final scan will look. It is at the preview stage that the various controls above can be selected.

Once you have cropped and manipulated the image to your liking, hit the scan button. Depending on the resolution you have selected and the model of scanner, the final scan can take from several seconds to several minutes.

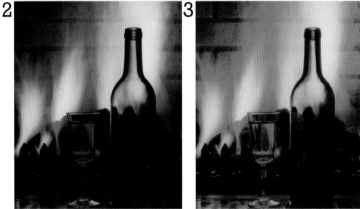

Correcting surface defects

Most scanners incorporate software that can remove surface defects such as scratches, dust or hair. The most popular types include Image Correction Enhancement (ICE). This usually works extremely well, and can be switched off when not required.

Home printers

The emergence of the photo-quality home printer is possibly one of the main factors behind the rapid advance of the digital era. Gone are the days of printing in a pitch-black room with chemicals – now you can print easily, cheaply and in daylight.

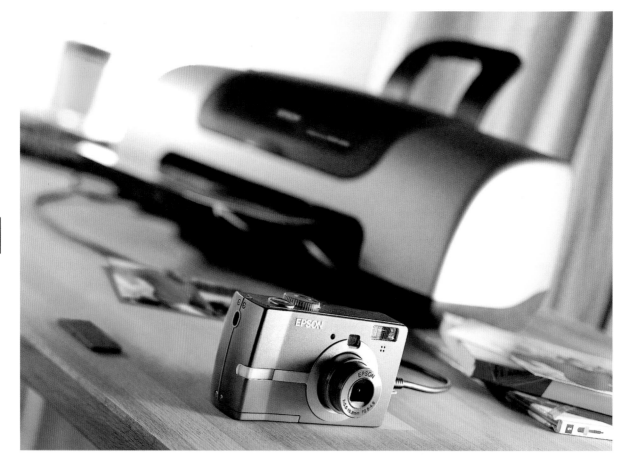

Main types of printer

There are two main types of printer for use in the home: inkjet and dye sublimation. Each produces a print using a different system.

Inkjet printers

These have the greatest variety of models, most offering prints up to A4 size (21 x 30cm/8½ x 11in), while some managing prints above A3 (29 x 41cm/11½ x 16in). Inkjets are capable of photo-quality results. The printers work by squirting very small droplets of ink onto the paper's surface. Each individual ink droplet is minute, resulting in dots with diameters a quarter that of a human hair. The inks are produced when nozzles in the printer's head are heated, causing the ink to vaporize and forcing it from the nozzle where, once cooled, it drops onto the paper. Like grain in film, the smaller the dots, the greater the amount of detail in the prints.

Direct printing

There are several printers that are available that allow prints to be made without the need of a computer. Some inkjet printers feature card slots, which accept the main types of cards from digital cameras. Also available are dye sublimation printers that connect with compatible cameras and allow prints to be made directly from the camera.

Dye sublimation printers

These can produce stunning results, but they are more costly to run and the maximum size of prints is limited – most models print up to 6 x 4in or 7 x 5in, with only a handful printing up to A4 (21 x 30cm/8½ x 11in). Dye sublimation printers work by heating inks on special ribbons, which are then transferred to the paper.

Dye sublimation printers, like this Olympus model, are capable of superb quality, but print size is limited.

Large format

Although still out of the price range of most consumers, large-format printers, which are capable of poster-sized prints, have started to creep into the studios of many professional photographers. These offer the potential for very large photography prints at a relatively affordable cost. Many photographers are looking at large-format printers to produce their exhibition prints.

The inkjet is the most popular type of home printer. The Canon Bubble Jet i9000 can produce photo-quality prints up to A3+ size (11½ x 16in/29 x 41cm).

Which printer?

When deciding on which printer is best for you, consider the following points.

Printing resolution: Printers state their resolution as dots per inch (dpi), with typical figures ranging from 1440dpi to 4800dpi and above. These figures can seem confusing, but as a rule, check that the printer offers photo-quality printing of at least 1440dpi.

Printing speed: How long it takes for a colour, photo-quality print to be produced. Some models, in particular those from Canon, are far quicker than others.

Printing inks: The number of colour ink cartridges can have a bearing on the quality (see page 73). Some models house all the colour inks in one cartridge, making it easy to change. Other printers have one cartridge per colour ink, offering the advantage that you only change the colour that has been depleted.

Many printers, like this Epson Stylus Photo 830U, feature card slots for direct printing from a digital camera's memory card.

Using home printers

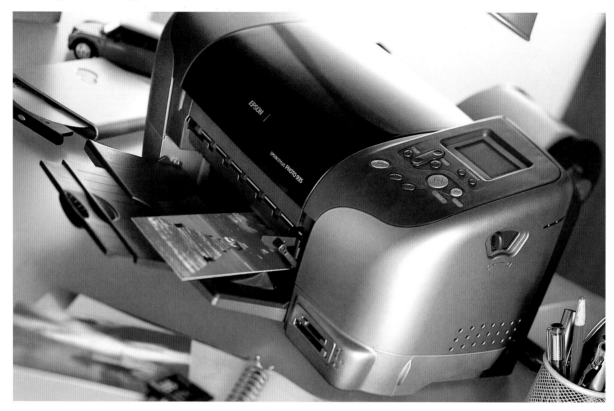

Printing software

Every printer comes with its own software program that allows you to control all aspects of the print, from its size to the type of paper you want to print on. The two areas to be particularly careful with are print resolution and paper type.

Print resolution

When making a photo-quality print, the optimum resolution to aim for is 300dpi. However, if setting this figure results in too small an image, you can reduce the resolution to around 200dpi without any obvious degradation in print quality. When changing resolution, it is important to ensure that the three measurements for document size (width, height and resolution) are all linked. This means that changing one figure automatically changes another, without affecting the size of the image. For instance, take the following example – you have an image that is 1.9Mb, with a width of 5.62cm, height of 8.47cm and resolution of 300dpi. Change the resolution to 200dpi and the height and width adjust automatically, to 8.43cm and 12.7cm respectively, while the actual image file size remains the same.

Clicking the resample image box removes the link and means that the image file size can be changed. This is fine when you want to reduce the file size but you should never use this option to increase the file size, as interpolation will be used and the overall quality will be degraded.

TOP TIP

Most printer software allows you to check the status of your inks, ensuring you are aware in advance when new cartridges are required.

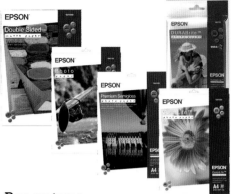

Paper type

It is important that you inform the printer of the paper type, as the amount of ink that the printer uses varies from one type to another. By selecting the wrong option, the print will suffer by receiving too much ink, exhibiting lines or various other problems.

Some printers incorporate a sensor in the paper tray that detects the type of paper loaded in the tray, making the necessary adjustments to the printer.

Printing troubleshooter

The following table lists the main printing problems and their solutions.

HORIZONTAL BANDING: This is when lines appear through part or all of a print.
Solution: Ensure the correct media type is selected and the correct side of the paper is facing up. Run the head-cleaning utility.

VERTICAL MISALIGNMENT: Ghosted double image, most apparent on edges.
Solution: Ensure the correct media type is selected and the correct side of the paper is facing up. Run the head-cleaning and print-head alignment utilities. Choose a slower print-ing speed if possible.

INCORRECT/MISSING COLOURS: Prints show incorrect colours or print in black and white.
Solution: Check ink setting is set to colour and not greyscale. Run the head-cleaning utility. Ensure the inks are fresh.

BLURRED/SMEARED PRINTS:
Solution: Ensure the correct media type is selected and the correct side of the paper is facing up.

ROLLER MARKS: Rollers leave marks on prints.
Solution: Ensure the correct side of the paper is facing up. Clean the rollers with a cleaning pad – see printer instructions for details.

Inkjet paper

A print is only as good as the paper that it has been printed on. Inkjet papers come in a variety of types – in fact, there is a wider choice of inkjet paper than there has ever been for darkroom-based prints.

For traditional-looking photo-quality prints, premium glossy paper is by far the most popular type. It has very similar characteristics to traditional photo paper in that it is thick and durable, and has a high-gloss finish. Other popular types of inkjet paper include photo-quality satin and matt finishes, while there are also various types of specialist paper available, including silver foil, art canvas and opaque film.

As well as the manufacturers' own-brand products, there are several independent paper manufacturers. Finding out which best suits your printer is a case of trial and error. A cheap way of sampling is to contact paper manufacturers and ask for a trial pack to experiment with.

Inkjet inks

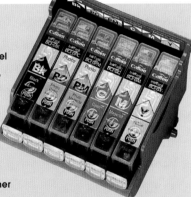

The number of inks used by a printer varies from model to model – four is the most common (cyan, yellow, magenta and black) but some also offer six-colour printing (four as before, but with the addition of light cyan and light magenta). With four-colour systems, dark colours are usually produced by using a higher density of dots, with lighter areas having a reduced number. This causes the problem that the dispersed dots can be noticeable in the lighter areas and reduce print sharpness. With the six-colour ink system, the extra colours mean that lighter areas in particular appear sharper and have a smoother tonal range.

The two main types of ink are dye-based and pigment inks. Dye-based inks are by far the most common type, and are capable of photo-realistic quality. Pigment inks are found on more expensive printers and offer the extra benefit of being more resistant to fading in light. DURABrite from Epson is a pigment-based ink that locks onto the surface of the paper, rather than being absorbed by it, and offers the benefit of being waterproof and offering fade-resistant colours for up to 80 years.

While colour inks are suitable for making black-and-white inkjet prints, monochrome specialists often use a range of ink cartridges that are made up of different shades of grey, as well as black, to give much more accurate monochrome prints.

Depending on the brand and the printer model, colour inks are supplied in individual cartridges or in one tank.

Software

If you're handling digital images, knowing the various types of software packages will ensure you are making the most of your pictures.

Software applications

There are two main types of software program: image-manipulation and cataloguing software. The former allows you to alter your images, while the latter is used to order them on your computer.

Image-manipulation software allows images to be enhanced and altered in more ways than you can possibly imagine!

Image-manipulation software

As the name suggests, this type of software allows you to manipulate images, from simple tweaks such as cropping the image to more wholesale changes such as converting a colour image to black and white.

Although it is possible to make a 'straight' print from an image taken on a digital camera or produced by a scanner, on almost every occasion manipulating the image to a lesser or greater extent will give a better result.

By far the most popular software package is Adobe Photoshop, an industry-standard package that offers an unrivalled level of power and versatility. It is used by a whole range of image manipulators, from amateur photographers on their home computer to various commercial and professional applications.

Photoshop is updated on an almost annual basis (at the time of printing, Photoshop CS is the latest full version). Because it is such an expensive package, Adobe has released a streamlined version, Photoshop Elements 2.0, which offers many of the major facilities of the full version that the amateur photographer will find useful, while leaving out the more professional elements of the package.

Despite Photoshop's dominance, there are a great number of other software packages offering similar features, usually at a more affordable price. Of these, Jasc Paint Shop Pro 8 is one of the most popular. Corel Photo-Paint 11 and Ulead Photo Impact XL are other options.

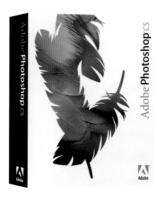

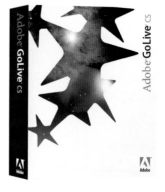

Cataloguing software

Cataloguing software, also termed image-management or album packages, does very much what it says on the tin. It allows you to arrange and order your images on your computer so that they are neatly filed and easy to find. An analogy is taking thousands of photos from shoeboxes and drawers and arranging them into a filing cabinet. To make them more attractive, these packages often offer image-manipulation tools, but these tend to lack the range and versatility of purpose-made packages.

Adobe again has a market-leader in this field, with Photoshop Album 2.0 offering an easy-to-use, versatile and affordable package.

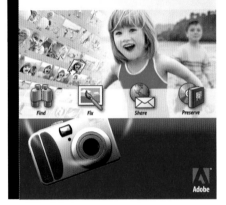

Other types of software

Although they do not deal specifically with images, there are many other types of program that the photographer should consider using.

Website creation

Creating your own website is an excellent way of exhibiting your images to a worldwide audience. Although the idea might seem daunting at first, there are various packages available that provide a relatively straightforward guide to setting up a website without necessitating specialist programming skills. Popular programs that offer such a facility include Microsoft Front Page and Adobe Go Live.

Specialist use

If you look in your local computer store, you are likely to find a multitude of low-cost software packages that allow you to use your image for various applications, such as creating calendars. These programs provide an inexpensive means of using your images for creating personalized projects.

Rescue software

There are a variety of packages available that can be used to rescue or salvage images from your computer hard disk or the image storage card. These are relatively inexpensive to buy, but can prove invaluable for retrieving images that would otherwise be lost. SanDisk's Image Recall and Lexar's Image Rescue are two such programs.

DVD viewer

As DVD burners become more popular on computers and DVD players are a common appliance in most people's homes, it is no surprise that there are a number of packages that allow images to be burned to DVD for viewing on a TV. Popular packages include Ulead DVD Pictureshow 2 and Jasc Paint Shop Pro Album 4, which also includes a digital album package.

Basic image-manipulation tools

The following are the most commonly used tools in image manipulation. Usually an image will have most if not all of these tools applied to it before the final version is produced.

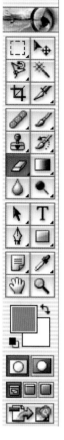

Crop

This is the most popular selection tool, allowing you to crop an image to remove any unwanted areas. It is usually the first tool used, as by cutting out a section of the image, you reduce the file size and speed up future stages. With most packages, the cropped area darkens to help you judge the correct crop.

Clone

This tool is used to remove unwanted elements from the image, which can range from tiny specks of dust to whole objects. It works by cloning an area of the frame and transferring it to another area. The size of area that is cloned is set by choosing the appropriate brush. It is mainly used to remove objects from a scene and replace them with a dominant backdrop.

Unsharp Mask

The final tool to be used before printing is Unsharp Mask. This gives a slight sharpening to the image, which results in prints having slightly better edge sharpness than when the feature is not applied.

Blur

Sometimes reducing the sharpness of an image can improve the creative result. There are various types of blur available, with Gaussian Blur being the most popular. Blur is useful when you want to isolate the main subject from the background – for instance, in a portrait taken at a small aperture, using blur can give the effect of shallow depth of field.

Layers

This is one of the most important tools in image manipulation. By creating layers, it is possible to have a copy of an original created as a layer, so that changes made do not appear unless you choose to show them. This means that effects you are not happy with can be scrapped without affecting the original version.

In addition, different images can be set as separate layers, much like layers of acetate on top of one another, allowing the photographer to merge the images as required.

Image-adjustment tools

Various tools can be used to change the fundamental elements of an image, such as saturation, colour balance, exposure and contrast. These are the most common options.

Exposure

The two most popular tools for manipulating exposure are Levels and Curves.

Levels is the easiest of the two options, with a histogram displaying the tonal range of the image. Below the histogram are three pointers, which can be moved to make adjustments to the highlights, shadows and all the tones in between.

The Curves tool is more difficult to use, but allows far more control. By changing the shape or angle of the diagonal line, it is possible to make infinite changes to the exposure, including making adjustments to one part of the tonal range, for instance shadows, without affecting the other parts.

Colour

Using the various colour controls, it is possible to make various changes to the colour characteristics of the image. This could include adding or subtracting a particular colour to remove a colour cast, or increasing or decreasing the saturation or brightness of the colours.

Desaturation

The biggest change you can make to a colour image is to convert it to black and white. By selecting the Desaturate tool, all the colour information is lost. Further adjustments can be made by selecting the colour channels. These offer a more sophisticated form of control than colour filters, such as controlling the red channel to increase contrast and to provide precise settings.

Basic image manipulation

The following steps demonstrate a number of basic image manipulation steps. In this example, a children's party invitation is produced from a single digital image.

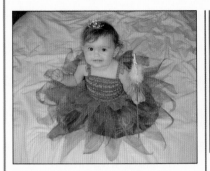

This is the original digital image. The birthday girl has been dressed as a fairy as this is the theme for her party.

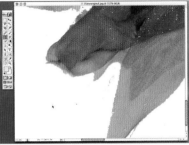

Step 2 If there are still areas of original background remaining, clean them up using the Eraser tool for large areas and the Clone tool for delicate jobs.

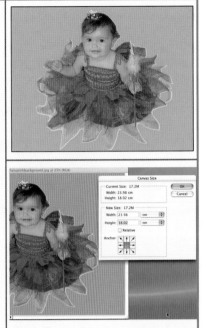

Step 4 Text needs to be added below the image, so the pink background needs to be extended. This is done by selecting Image>Canvas Size and increasing the height.

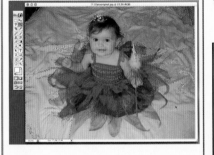

Step 1 The first step is to remove the untidy background from the frame. There are a number of ways of doing this, but in this instance, the best method is to use the magic wand, as the area to be removed is large. The selected area is shown by moving dotted lines, known as marching ants. By using the shift key, you can highlight any areas that the wand originally missed. Once you're happy, select Edit>Cut.

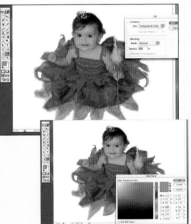

Step 3 Click on the large square on the toolbar to open the Colour Picker screen, which allows you to choose a suitable background colour. Fill the background with this colour by selecting Edit>Fill. Ensure you choose Background Colour in the pop-up window.

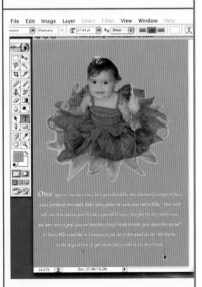

Step 5 The Text tool is used to add text. Choose the appropriate font, size and alignment, and use the Move tool to place the text where you wish. The invitation is now ready to be printed!

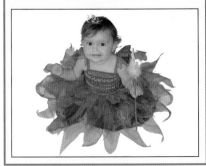

Darkrooms

The popularity of the traditional chemical darkroom may be in serious decline since the advent of digital technology, but many photographers still prefer to make traditional prints from film than from digital media.

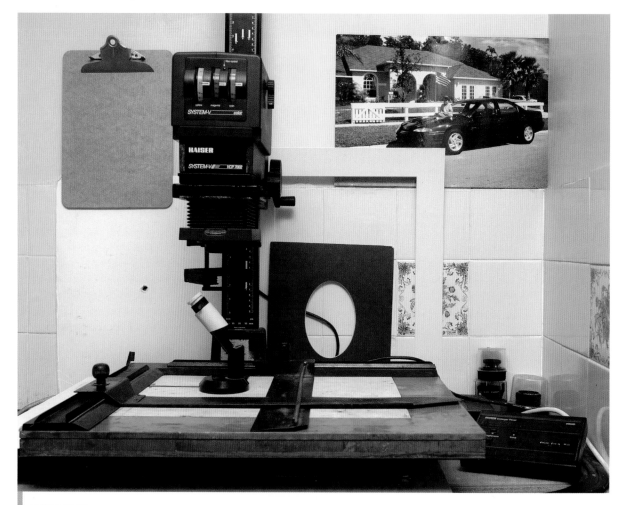

DARKROOM SET-UP
This darkroom was set up in a small room measuring 2m (6ft) square. Here, you can see the enlarger with easel, focus magnifier and timer, plus a selection of lenses.

What makes a good darkroom?

In theory, any room of the house can be used as a temporary darkroom. However, the bathroom has always been the most popular choice, for two main reasons. The first is that a bathroom usually has the fewest and smallest windows, making it the easiest to make lightproof – an essential factor for darkrooms. The second reason is that a supply of running water is required to wash developed film or prints, usually in a sink or bath.

When arranging the darkroom, it's important to ensure that the various elements are arranged methodically, so that you move from one stage to the other as easily as possible. Place the three chemical trays in order, with the last being found beside the wash receptacle (sink or bath).

Standard equipment

Making a print in a darkroom does not require a huge amount of equipment. A basic but workable darkroom requires only the following items.

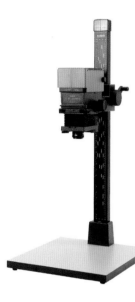

Safelights

As its name suggests, a safelight is a low-powered source of illumination that is safe to use in a darkroom when printing. The colour depends on the type of paper used, but usually it is a particular shade of red or orange, which the paper's emulsion is insensitive to and therefore cannot be fogged by, so long as the safelight is kept a safe distance away.

Enlargers

An enlarger is basically a box that uses a lamp in its housing to project light through the film onto a baseboard via a lens. By varying the duration the light is on for and the aperture of the lens, you can vary the exposure of the print.

Enlargers boasting a colour head are the best choice. These models feature integral magenta, yellow and cyan filters, used for colour printing or varying the grade of black-and-white prints made on variable-contrast papers.

TOP TIP

If you're looking to set up your first darkroom on a budget, check out starter kits, available from larger photo outlets. These offer all the accessories you need to develop your film and make prints.

Focus magnifiers

These simple accessories are used to ensure that the image on the easel is as sharply focused as possible.

Easels

These hold the paper perfectly flat and in position during the printing exposure.

Timers

The most accurate method for printing exposures is facilitated by using a timer. With the press of a button, a timer automatically starts and stops the exposure after a preset length of time.

Paper trays

These trays, or dishes, hold the chemicals used to develop the image. The size of tray is determined by the size of print.

Chemicals

There are three types of chemical used in the developing of a film or paper.

If viewed in light, an exposed film or paper would look no different to an unexposed emulsion, because the image has yet to form. This latent image is developed in the first stage of processing by the developer, which forms visible silver crystals from the previously invisible exposed silver particles. The second stage is the stopbath, which is a chemical that stops the action of the developer, to prevent further development of silver particles in the emulsion. The third and final process is the fixer.

Thermometers

These are required to ensure that the chemicals are kept at a relatively constant temperature, as the effect varies according to how hot or cold the chemicals are.

Measuring cylinders

These are required to ensure the correct dilution of the chemicals.

Tongs

Due to the risk of skin corrosion, tongs are used to handle wet prints.

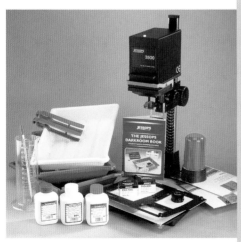

Types of developer

Different types of developer suit particular forms of development, so it's worth knowing what is available. Acutance developers are formulated to increase edge contrast and provide higher perceived sharpness, while fine-grain developers keep grain size to a minimum. One-stop developers are made to be used once only before disposal.

Film processing

If you're planning on printing in a darkroom, you will probably want to process films yourself. Developing a black-and-white film is relatively easy, and requires only a modest amount of equipment.

How to process films

The easiest method of processing films is to use a purpose-made film tank, a light-tight tub that holds the films on a spiral and allows them to be processed in daylight.

It's a relatively simple process. In darkness (a changing bag is the best option), the film canister is opened and the film leader is cut to give a straight edge. The film is then loaded onto a spiral, which winds the film on by alternate twists of each side. Once loaded, the end of the film is cut to separate it from the empty canister, and the spiral is placed into the tank. Once the funnel and lid of the tank are securely replaced, the tank is once again light-tight, so future stages can be performed with the lights on.

Developing the film is then a simple procedure of pouring in the chemicals, replacing the lid and regularly agitating the tank to ensure that fresh chemicals are kept in contact with the film surface. Once the time for each stage has elapsed, the chemicals are poured out and the next are poured in. Once all three chemical stages (developer, stopbath and fixer) are complete, the film needs to be washed, usually by placing a hose directly from the tap into the tank for around 15 minutes. Once washed, the film is hung to dry in a warm and dust-free environment.

SPIRAL
For decades, the light-proof tank loaded with spiral has been the basic equipment needed to process film.

TOP TIP
If you are limited for space, consider investing in a print slot processor, which is a tank with vertical slots for processing prints. For further details, visit www.novadarkroom.com

How to make a print

Before making a print, you must first make a test strip. This is a torn strip of paper that receives different exposures in regular steps to help you assess the best printing exposure.

To make a test strip, place the strip on the easel, then expose the whole strip for say, two seconds. Cover a small portion of the strip with card (hold the card above the strip but don't touch it), then expose for the same amount of time again. Repeat this step until you have covered the whole strip, then develop. By looking at the strip, you can determine the best exposure for the print.

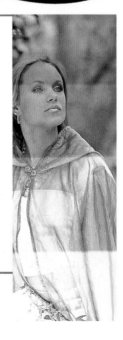

TOP TIP
If you have developed your own film, contact sheets are the best method for determining which negatives are worth printing. To make your own contact sheet, place the negatives on top of a sheet of paper, then rest a sheet of glass on top of the negatives to keep them flat.

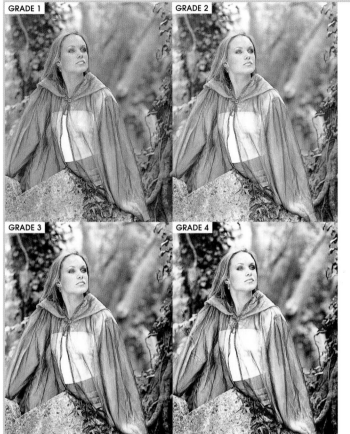

GRADE 1 GRADE 2

GRADE 3 GRADE 4

Paper

Various types of paper are available in a range of grades, paper stock and finishes. The grade of a paper reflects its contrast. Grade 2 has average contrast, grades 0–1½ are lower in contrast (softer), while higher grades (up to 5) are much harder, with far more contrast. As well as papers with fixed grades, variable-contrast papers are available. These allow the contrast to be determined by the filtration set on the enlarger head.

The actual base the paper is printed on is the next important consideration. Fibre-based paper is the preferred choice of professionals, who favour its feel and find it easier to retouch. However, resin-coated papers are easier to use, as they wash quicker and dry flat (fibre-based papers tend to curl).

The surface finish has a major effect on the final result. The two main types are gloss and matt, with semi-gloss, semi-matt, satin and pearl falling in between. Gloss is by far the most popular, giving a higher perceived sharpness and more solid blacks. However, it is more prone to surface reflections.

BURNING
This print was made at grade 4, but the face has received an extra ½-stop of exposure, and the edges and corners an extra 1½ stops. The result of burning in these areas is to place more emphasis on the subject and less on the background.

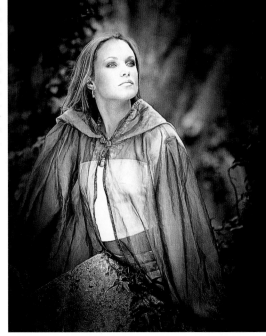

Darkroom manipulation

Don't be fooled – image manipulation started in the darkroom, not with Photoshop! There are various ways in which the darkroom printer can manipulate images. The most common is dodging and burning, which refers to two techniques that reduce or increase the amount of exposure reaching part of the print, by using objects or hands to black out parts of the print.

Manipulation can also be done when the print has been produced. The most popular is toning, where a chemical is used to add an attractive colour cast to the print. This technique can also be used to extend the archival properties of the image. Some photographers use specialist inks or dyes to hand-colour prints and add an extra creative element to images.

Basic techniques
Composition

Knowing where to place different elements in a scene is one of the fundamental aspects of photography, and should be grasped at the earliest opportunity. Successful photography comes from successful composition – the sooner you learn the basics of composition, the quicker your images will begin to show balance and shape.

You often hear photographers talk about how they can 'see' a scene, or 'picture' an image. When doing so, they are usually referring to how they would arrange the various elements within a scene; in other words, how they would compose it. Learning the fundamentals of composition should be one of the first lessons you master.

Fundamentals of composition

Creating a photographic composition is all about working out where the various elements fit into a scene to create the most pleasing result. The following aspects are key to taking successful pictures.

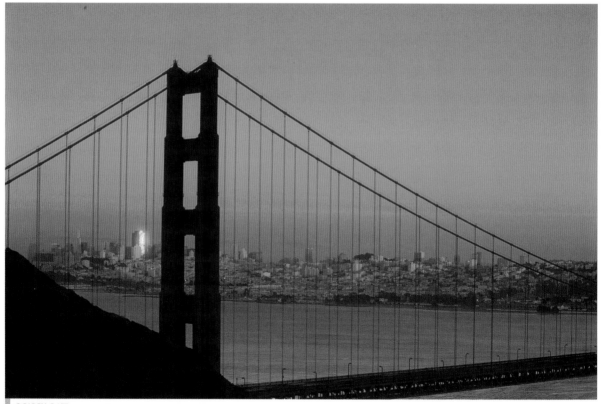

GOLDEN GATE BRIDGE
The reflections of the building, as much as the silhouette of the bridge, catch the eye in this image.

The focal point

For a picture to work, it usually requires a focal point – a place that the eye is naturally drawn to and an object that adds scale to the overall scene.

For example, take a landscape with a solitary castle in view. Without the castle, the eye would wonder around the scene and be unable to settle on any single element. Not only that, it would be difficult to determine the scale of the landscape – are you looking at a small cross-section of land here, or at a sweeping vista?

A focal point helps to brings order and sense to an image, so be sure to include at least one in the frame.

Rule of thirds

This is the perhaps the most important rule of composition. The rule of thirds (also known as the golden section) can be applied to all photographic subjects, although it is used in particular for landscape photography. The rule of thirds should be used regardless of the focal length of the lens that you are using or whether you are holding the camera in an upright or landscape format.

The rule of thirds was originally developed by painters, who would mentally grid a canvas to help achieve balance in their paintings. It is a very easy compositional aid to learn and should be the first thing that springs to your mind when you are composing an image.

When you look through the viewfinder, imagine that the scene is split into thirds – in other words, there are two horizontal and two vertical lines intersecting the frame to create nine equal-size rectangles. What you have to do now is ensure that the focal point is placed at any of the four points where the lines cross each other – this achieves the maximum visual harmony in the scene. You should also use either the upper or lower line as a guide for where to place the horizon, so that it sits along the lower or upper third of the image.

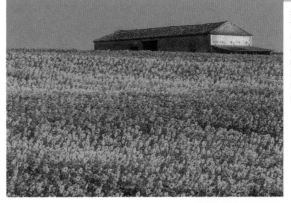

SUNFLOWER FIELD
The merits of using the rule of thirds are perfectly illustrated in this landscape image.

Framing the scene

You will often find that you can add an interesting new element to a scene by finding a frame to set it within. This can often be a hole in a wall, a gap in some trees, or an archway. The theory is that you naturally draw the eye of the viewer to look at the scene behind the frame.

If you are using a wide-angle lens, it is best to get close to the frame, otherwise the scene in the distance will be too small to recognize any detail. Using a telephoto lens means you have to stand further back and also results in making the background appear much closer to the scene than it really is.

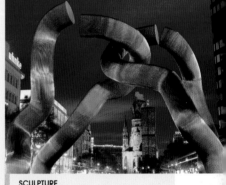

SCULPTURE
This modern sculpture provides an unusual frame for the scene in the distance.

Take a new slant

Although it's normal to keep the horizon completely level, adding a slight slant to an image can work wonders. Although this isn't a technique to try with subjects such as landscapes, there are times when doing so can add real dynamism to a scene.

Try photographing a car driving along a road normally, then tilt the camera at a slight angle and try again. All of a sudden, the picture has far more impact and the car seems to be travelling much faster.

Another interesting area to try pictures with a slant is portraits. Shot at an angle, portraits can take on added zing.

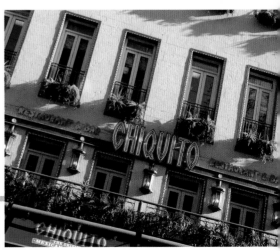

CHIQUITO
Photographing a building at a slant can provide a much stronger result than keeping the horizon level.

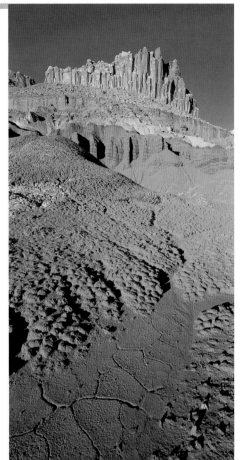

LITHIC VALLEY
The natural path in the foreground acts as foreground interest as well as being a natural line for the eye to follow into the frame.

Foreground interest

Another important aspect of composition is the foreground interest – in other words, what you include at the front of the scene. Although it's not essential to include anything in the foreground, you will find that doing so helps to add balance and scale to the scene, as well as helping to lead the eye into the frame.

Including foreground interest also gives your pictures a sense of depth and distance, especially if you angle the camera down, adopt a lower viewpoint and use a wide-angle lens to stretch perspective and make the foreground more imposing. A 28mm lens is adequate, while using even wider focal lengths will emphasize foreground subjects even more.

You can use any subject as foreground interest. For example, in landscape photography, rocks along a coast line, a wall or fence leading into the scene or even an interesting pattern on the ground, such as ripples of sand or a limestone pavement, all have potential.

Always bear the foreground in mind, as no matter how stunning the scene in the distance may be, a boring, monotonous foreground can ruin the result.

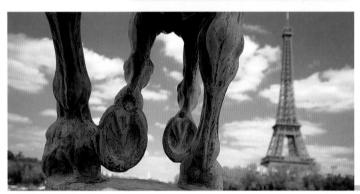

EIFFEL TOWER
Careful placement of subjects can have a dramatic effect on the perspective of a scene.

Perspective

Although pictures are two-dimensional, our brain uses the elements in the scene to determine scale, distance and depth – in other words, the perspective. Using the correct lenses and learning to arrange the elements of a scene in a particular order can help you to create and control perspective.

For instance, use a wide-angle lens to stretch perspective and make subjects in the foreground look far larger than those in the background. In a series of electricity pylons, for example, the one closer to you looks far larger than those in the distance – this phenomenon is termed diminishing perspective and can be used to emphasize depth.

Shots taken with a telephoto lens can compress perspective, making subjects that are a distance apart look as if they are pressed up against one another.

Using lines

Powerful compositions often have strong lines passing through them. Lines help lead the eye of a viewer through the scene and can also help divide the image into different components. Roads, rivers, walls and coastlines can create strong lines in an image, and their impact can vary on the direction they take through a scene.

Horizontal lines help divide up a scene – the horizon is the most obvious example, but other examples include a road traversing the scene, or a fence separating two fields. Diagonal lines add a sense of depth to the image and help to lead the eye into the frame. The strongest diagonals tend to run from bottom left to upper right in the frame. Converging lines provide an incredible sense of depth to an image. Using wide-angle lenses particularly emphasize converging lines, especially when used with subjects like roads or railway lines, which converge all the way until they create a 'vanishing point' in the distance. Finally, vertical lines are used to highlight height and direction, in particular when the camera is used in an upright position. Vertical lines work particularly well with architectural photography.

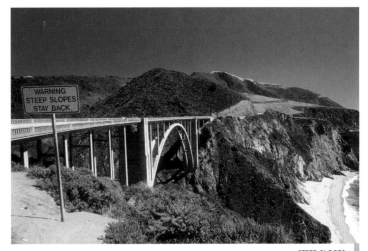

STEEP SLOPES
The bridge provides a powerful lead-in.

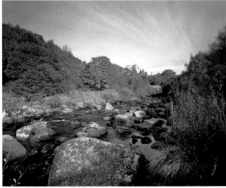

RIVER
The river leads the eye into the frame, where the building in the distance provides a sense of scale.

DAFFODILS
Adopting a new angle to a familiar subject is a great way to add impact to a scene.

A sense of scale

Although not strictly a compositional rule, it is important to always try to bring some scale to your images. Have you ever looked at a scene of something ambiguous like a waterfall, then noted a small figure of a person standing in the frame, which suddenly brings around a clear understanding of the scale of the cascading water? Although not necessarily the most important element in the frame, something that sets the scale of the rest of the scene is useful to include.

Breaking the rules

Of course, rules are made to be broken, as much in photography as in any other aspect of life. So, for example, in landscape photography, place the main subject directly in the centre of the frame rather than along a third and see if it works. Sometimes it will, sometimes it won't. With portraits, use a tight crop on the face so that you crop out one of the eyes to create an unusual composition.

Photographic rules are only a guideline to help you develop your technique – never be afraid to experiment with any of them, including composition.

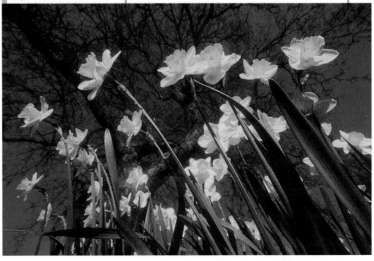

Depth of field

One of the fundamental techniques to master in photography is the control of depth of field. The amount of depth of field in a scene plays an important role on the final result – use it to render the background out of focus and make the main subject stand out, or have the whole scene appear sharp from front to back. It's important to understand how it works and how to control it, regardless of what type of camera you use.

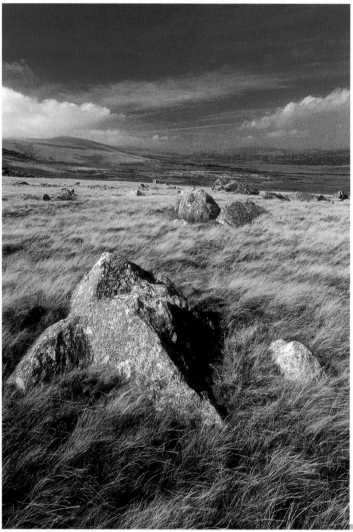

HILLTOP
Use a very small aperture to give front-to-back sharpness in your landscapes.

What is depth of field?

Depth of field is the term used to describe the amount of a scene behind and in front of the focusing point that appears sharp in the image. A lens only focuses at one point, which is the sharpest area in the image. However, using depth of field, you can control the perceived zone of sharpness to suit the type of subject you are photographing.

There are three main factors that affect the extent of depth of field: the focal length of the lens, the choice of aperture, and the focusing distance. Each has its own effect on depth of field, so for maximum control, learn to use all three whenever appropriate.

Aperture setting

The choice of aperture is the biggest single factor in controlling depth of field. The general rule is that the wider the aperture, the less depth of field produced. For instance, selecting f/3.5 will not give as much depth of field as choosing f/22.

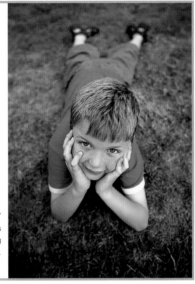

BOY
The lens's widest aperture (f/3.5) was used to deliberately throw everything out of focus except the boy's face.

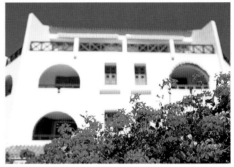

CONTROLLING DEPTH OF FIELD
In the shot above, the lens is focused on the plants in the foreground; at f/4, only the flowers are in focus. With the lens set to f/16 (below), the building in the background is also sharp.

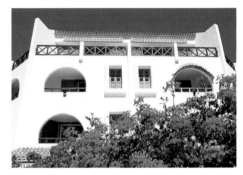

Lens focal length

A wide-angle lens gives much greater depth of field at a given aperture than a telephoto lens. For instance, a 28mm lens at f/8 provides much greater depth of field than a 300mm lens at f/8. Therefore, when using a zoom lens, consider how the choice of focal length you use will affect depth of field.

Focusing distance

The distance the lens is focused at is the final factor. For any given lens, the depth of field increases the greater the focusing distance. In other words, the further the subject is from the camera, the more depth of field will be produced.

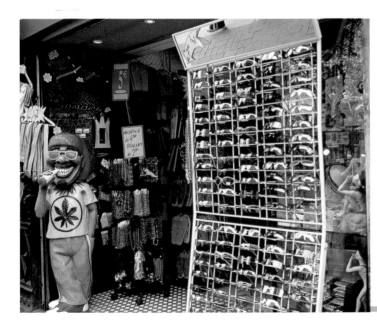

TOP TIP
Depth of field does not extend equally either side of the focused point. In most situations, it extends twice as far behind as in front. With very close distances, such as macro photography, however, depth of field on either side of the focusing point is more equal.

Depth-of-field preview

Many SLRs offer depth-of-field preview, also called the stop-down facility, which works by closing the aperture to whatever the current aperture setting is. It's a very useful facility, although some find that the darkened viewfinder image – a result of the lens stopping down to the required aperture – can be hard to view through.

RASTA
Selecting a wide aperture to provide shallow depth of field ensures the eye isn't distracted from the main subject by the sunglasses rack in the foreground.

When to use shallow depth of field

Using a very wide aperture has the effect of throwing most of the scene out of focus – only the distance focused on appears sharp. This is an excellent technique to highlight a particular element in the scene.

Portraits in particular work well where a person is isolated from their surroundings and all attention is focused on them. A shallow depth of field is also useful when photographing animals in a zoo or other enclosed environment. The shallow depth of field created by using a wide aperture in this situation helps to remove the wiring or bars from view by blurring them until they are almost unrecognizable.

TOP TIP

If you're using a compact and have very limited control over depth of field, a simple way of improving your chances of achieving front-to-back sharpness is to use a wide-angle setting and focus a third of the way into the scene; if you're shooting a landscape, try focusing around 5m (16ft) into the frame.

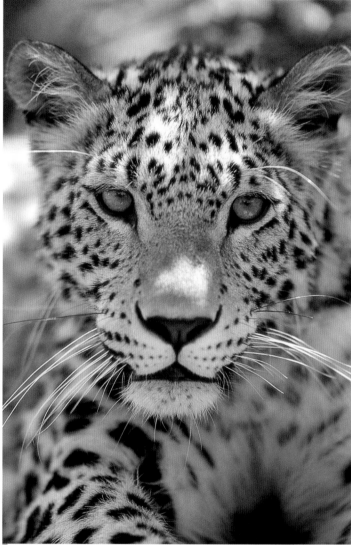

LEOPARD
To ensure that the eye contact from the animal is as strong as possible, a wide aperture ensures that any distractions are thrown out of focus.

How to control depth of field

Minimize depth of field by:
Selecting the widest aperture
Increasing the camera-to-subject distance and using the lens at the telephoto setting

Maximize depth of field by:
Selecting the smallest possible aperture
Using a wide-angle lens
Using hyperfocal focusing

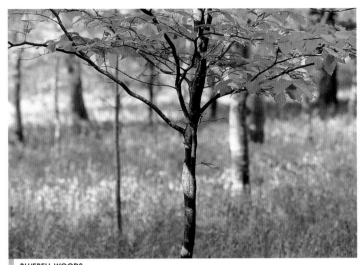

BLUEBELL WOODS
Controlling depth of field is vital to emphasize a
particular part of the scene – in this case, a solitary tree.

When to maximize depth of field

The most obvious situation for having as
much depth of field as possible is when you
want to record as much of the scene in
focus as possible. A stunning landscape is
one example of this, when you want to
keep all distances from the foreground to
the distance in focus. In a similar way,
using a wide-angle lens with a prominent
subject close-up, along with a distinctive
backdrop, also requires achieving as
much depth of field as possible.

Macro photography, which presents its
own sets of problems, is a specialist area
where depth of field is at a premium and
using every technique possible to maximize
it is required to keep as much of the
subject in focus as possible.

Hyperfocal focus

SLR users can use a technique known as
hyperfocal focusing to provide even greater
depth of field than simply using the smallest
aperture. This technique is becoming less
common, as fewer lenses feature the depth-of-
field scale on the barrel that is needed for
hyperfocal focusing. However, it's a very useful
and fairly easy technique to use. All you have to
do is focus the lens to infinity, then check the
scale to see what the nearest focus distance is
that aligns with the aperture you are using – the
hyperfocal distance. Set the focus to this
hyperfocal distance and you maximize depth of
field, which extends from half the hyperfocal
distance to infinity. Bear in mind that when using
this system, the image through the viewfinder
can look out of focus – if it does, use the depth-
of-field preview button to get a better
representation of the final result.

NIGHT SCENE
For this scene to work, the
subjects at all distances
must appear sharp. By
selecting the smallest
aperture and using
hyperfocal focusing, depth
of field is maximized.

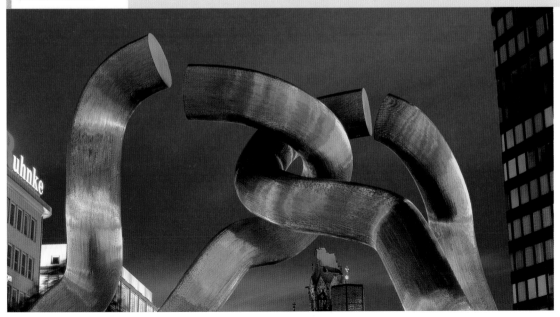

Shutter speed

Shutter speeds play a crucial role in the making of an image, working in combination with the lens aperture to give a correct exposure. They are also a vital element in creative photography, so knowing how they work and what effects they create is vital to getting the most from your photography.

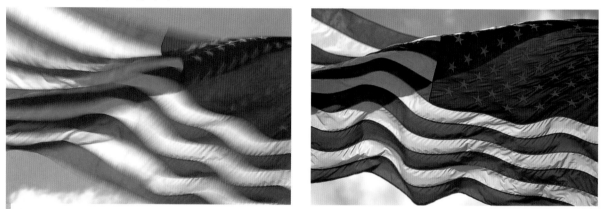

SLOW SHUTTER SPEED
Lowering the shutter speed to blur a moving subject can work well. These examples show how dropping the shutter speed to $\frac{1}{30}$sec gives a far more creative result than a 'straight' shot at $\frac{1}{500}$sec.

Most cameras, with the exception of some budget models, offer a range of shutter speeds, from fractions of a second to several seconds or even minutes. These are set via a shutter speed dial or in shutter priority mode. Although their main purpose is to ensure a correct exposure, varying the shutter speed/aperture combination can affect how subjects in the actual exposure are recorded. This in particular applies to moving subjects – adjusting the length of the exposure time determines how motion is recorded.

Bulb and Time

Bulb (B) and Time (T) are two modes designed for long exposures; both work by allowing you to control the length of the exposure. With Bulb, the shutter button (or release) is pressed to start the exposure, which ends when pressure on the shutter button (or release) is taken off.

With Time, a single press starts the exposure, and another one ends it. When using older cameras, this operation is fully mechanical, so there's no power consumption, while with many newer models, you'll find that battery power is consumed during the exposure – so use this mode with care!

CARRIAGE DRIVING
Panning a moving subject is the best method to emphasize energy and speed.

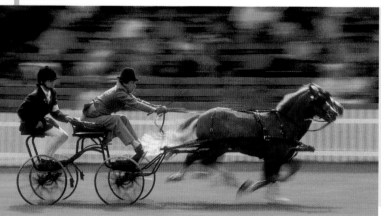

Panning

Slow shutter speeds can be used in sports photography to depict motion by blurring the background, a technique known as panning. To do this requires setting a relatively low speed, say $\frac{1}{30}$–$\frac{1}{125}$sec, then following the moving subject through the viewfinder before and during the exposure, so that the subject appears sharp but the background is blurred. A steady hand and plenty of practice are required.

Using slow shutter speeds

The most common time to use a slow shutter speed is when the shooting situation dictates it; in other words, when light levels are low, such as indoors or outdoors at night. In these conditions you need to be aware that your biggest problem is camera shake, so:

1. Support your camera on a tripod or any steady surface;
2. Use a remote release rather than the shutter button, which can cause shake when you press it;
3. If you can't use a remote, set the self-timer instead;
4. Make sure you bracket exposures.

You can use slow shutter speeds in bright conditions. When photographing fast-moving water such as streams, rivers, waves and waterfalls with a typical daylight shutter speed, such as $\frac{1}{125}$sec or $\frac{1}{250}$sec, the water will appear dull and still. Drop the shutter speed to $\frac{1}{30}$sec or lower, and the extra time means that the movement is blurred, adding a real dynamism. Stop down even further so that you're shooting in seconds, and you can blur the movement so that the water takes on an ethereal appearance.

Using slow shutter speeds to record the movement of people is another interesting technique. Set up your camera where there are large groups of people, such as at a railway station, and the motion of people will be captured as a blur, while any static subjects around them are recorded normally. Set a mid-aperture like f/8 and try a range of shutter speeds from $\frac{1}{30}$sec down to 1sec.

CROSSING
A slow shutter speed can add real dynamism to ordinary scenes, such as walking across a road.

TOP TIP
Can't reduce the shutter speed to what you need because it's too bright? Then use a slow-speed film or reduce your digital camera's ISO rating to its lowest setting. Still not slow enough? Fit a neutral density filter, which will not affect the colours but will reduce the exposure time.

Using fast shutter speeds

Selecting a fast shutter speed freezes the motion of a moving subject. This applies particularly to sports and action photography, when you may well want to capture moving subjects in sharp detail, but it can also be used for other subjects, such as water.

Although many cameras boast extremely high shutter speeds of $\frac{1}{6000}$sec and above, you'll find their use very specialized – in fact, $\frac{1}{2000}$sec or $\frac{1}{4000}$sec is good enough for most situations.

The shutter speed required to freeze moving subjects varies not only according to the speed, but also according to the direction of travel.

One thing to bear in mind that fast shutter speeds usually mean that the aperture will be very wide, so the depth of field will be very shallow. This has the benefit of making the main subject stand out from the background, but also means that you must take care with focusing.

To increase the maximum possible shutter speed, use fast film or increase the ISO rating on your digital camera.

FIREFIGHTER
Use a very fast shutter speed when you want to freeze movement – here, the spray of fire-quenching foam.

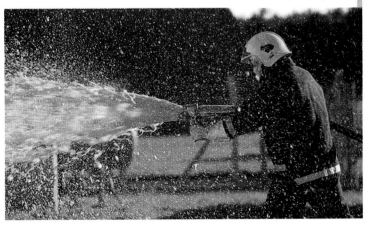

Focusing

Most modern cameras come with sophisticated autofocus systems. These have a very high success rate and can be relied upon in most situations. However, there are focusing techniques that can be used for creative purposes, and you need to know what to do when autofocus fails.

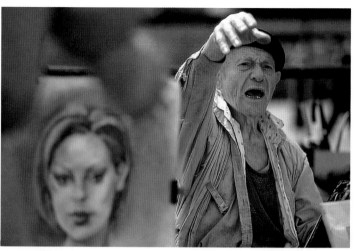

MARKET TRADER
Where the main subject is in the background, focus on an off-centre focusing point.

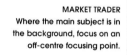

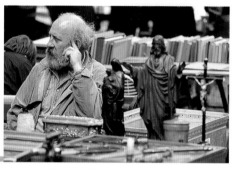

CHANGING FOCUS
The emphasis of the image is completely changed, depending on where you focus the lens.

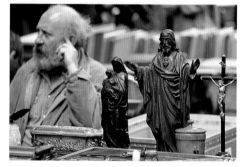

Locking focus

The standard autofocus mode detects the subject and locks the focus on it. Focus lock, as this is termed, can also aid composition – when you want the focused subject to be off-centre, for instance, such as photographing a person in front of a building. Cameras with multipoint AF systems do this automatically, but if your camera uses only a single AF sensor at its centre, you need to use the focus-lock technique. It is very simple – focus on the subject, keep the shutter button halfway depressed to lock the focus, then recompose the image and fully depress the button to take the picture.

Differential focus

This creative technique mixes precise focus with a very shallow depth of field to create an imaginative result. Differential focus is particularly favoured by portrait photographers, but can be used to enhance any subject.

For portraiture, using a wide aperture throws the background out of focus to really emphasize the main subject. You can also use differential focus to produce a tight crop of a face and put only one feature, say an eye or a nose, in focus, to give a distinctive and unusual portrait.

Because differential focus works by keeping only a narrow band of the image in focus, it isn't suited to two-dimensional objects. However, three-dimensional still-life subjects like flowers also work particularly well. By shooting at an angle and focusing at the centre of the flower, you can record the petals in the foreground and background as a blur.

Deliberate defocus

As odd as it sounds, it is sometimes worth producing a deliberately out-of-focus picture to create an artistic result. This technique can be used to create moody black-and-white abstracts or powerful colour compositions. The key is to use subjects in the frame that have very distinctive shapes, so that you can recognize them even though they are out of focus.

MOTOCROSS
Prefocusing is a good technique to use for action photography where the subjects follow a predetermined route, such as motocross.

Focus for action

Keeping moving subjects sharp in the frame is tricky, and making sure the subject is sharp at the crucial moment of exposure is even more difficult. The following tips should increase your chances of capturing sharp action pictures.

Servo/predictive autofocus

With Servo focus, the camera adjusts the focusing distance to account for movement. On many compacts and SLRs, you can engage Servo AF by selecting the sports or action mode, while most SLRs offer the option of Servo AF mode. The standard servo mode tracks the focus movement and sets the focus distance accordingly. In systems employing predictive autofocus, the camera uses the ever-changing information to predict where the subject will be at the time of exposure. It offers an advantage over Servo AF in that it takes into account erratic movement, but even this system can't always guarantee success.

Manual focus

Before the days of autofocus systems, SLR photographers manually focused the lens and developed two techniques for increasing the hit-rate for sharp pictures: follow-focus and prefocus.

Follow-focus involves the photographer making continual adjustments to the focus to keep up with the action. It demands much practice, but for erratic movement, such as in sports like boxing, football or rugby, it's a useful technique to learn.

Prefocus is a very good technique to use when photographing sports where you know the subject will pass particular points. The technique is simple: watch the path your subject takes, and focus on a point you know they will cross. Then, just before they reach the point, depress the shutter button and fire a sequence of pictures. This technique is used in fast, repetitive sports like athletics and motorsports.

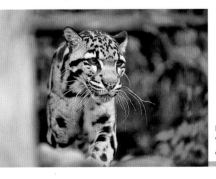

Autofocus problems

There are times when even the most sophisticated autofocus systems fail to cope with a scene. The following are the most common problems and solutions.

Low-contrast scenes
Autofocus systems work by detecting contrast on the subject. So when photographing plain objects, such as a white wall, the AF system cannot detect the subject distance.

Zoo animals
When trying to focus on an animal at a zoo, the autofocus locks onto the fence or cage.

In these two situations, the easiest solution is to manually focus, or, if this isn't possible, focus lock on a subject a similar distance away, then recompose the frame.

Low-light photography
Autofocus systems work within a particular illumination range, so once light levels fall below a particular threshold, they have problems.

Engage the AF assist beam if it has one, or use one of the options above.

Shooting through glass
Because AF systems generally try to focus on the closest subject, taking pictures through glass presents the problem that the lens focuses on the glass, rather than the subject behind it.

There are various options, the first being to focus manually. If this isn't possible, see if the camera has an infinity focus mode that sets the lens to focus at infinity. If not, get as close to the glass as possible and shoot through it at an angle.

BIG CAT
When photographing caged animals, a wide aperture ensures the barrier doesn't appear in the frame.

Using exposure

A camera's metering system might get it right nine times out of ten, but knowing when it will get it wrong is the only way to guarantee a 100 per cent success rate.

If you understand that a camera's metering system assumes the average tone of a scene is 18 per cent grey, then it becomes far easier to grasp when the exposure system can have problems.

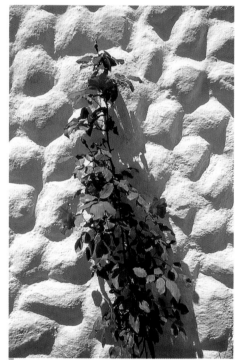

WALL AND FLOWERS
The white wall fools the camera into underexposing the main subject. Ensure that you add exposure compensation of at least one stop in similar situations.

HAND
This close-up would result in overexposure without the necessary precautions.

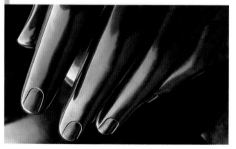

Brighter-than-average scenes

Imagine a winter wonderland where everything is covered with a thick layer of glistening white snow. You know the snow is white and want to capture the scene, but the camera averages the scene as grey and underexposes the image.

What to do:
1. Use the exposure compensation facility to shoot at +1 and +2 stops over the camera's indicated reading.
2. Place a grey card in the scene and take a meter reading from it.

Darker-than-average scenes

You're photographing a slate quarry on a dark, overcast morning. The whole scene is oppressive and dark grey. Leave the camera to its own means, and it will ruin the mood by overexposing the scene by one to two stops.

What to do:
1. Use the exposure compensation facility to shoot at -1, -1½ and -2 stops under the camera's indicated reading.
2. Place a grey card in the scene and take a meter reading from it.

Person in front of white background

You're taking a portrait of someone against a white-washed wall, such as you'd find in the Mediterranean. Unfortunately, all the light reflecting from it fools the camera into underexposing the scene and almost turning your subject into a silhouette.

What to do:
1. Use the exposure compensation facility to shoot at +1 and +1½ stops over the camera's indicated reading.
2. Have the subject hold a grey card and take a reading from it.
3. If the person is Caucasian, take a spot/partial reading from their face.

Person in front of black background

Imagine your subject is now set against a clean, black door, which dominates the scene. The camera, assuming that the door is grey, gives too much exposure, completely bleaching the detail.

What to do:
1. Use the exposure compensation facility to shoot at -1, -1½ and -2 stops under the camera's indicated reading.
2. Have the subject hold a grey card and take a reading from it.
3. If the person is Caucasian, take a spot/partial reading from their face.

Backlit subjects

A subject set against a bright backdrop, such as a sunset, is underexposed.

What to do:

1. Use the exposure compensation facility to shoot at +1 stop over the indicated reading.
2. Get the subject to hold a grey card, and take a reading from it.
3. If the person is Caucasian, take a spot/partial reading from their face.

High-contrast scene

You're in the grounds of an abbey with streams of light breaking through the trees. The scene is made up of bright highlights and dense shadows. How the camera exposes the scene is a complete guess.

What to do:

1. Take a spot or AE-Lock reading off a mid-tone (stonework is fine) and take a bracketing sequence in full stops from +2 to -2 stops.

Sunny landscape

It's a beautiful summer's day and you discover a glorious scene. You follow all the rules for landscape photography but the result is far too dark. This has occurred because the sky has influenced the meter into underexposing.

What to do:

1. Tilt the camera down and use the AE-Lock facility to lock the exposure reading.
2. Fit a neutral density graduate filter to balance the sky and the foreground.
3. Use the exposure compensation facility to shoot at +1 stop over the camera's indicated reading.

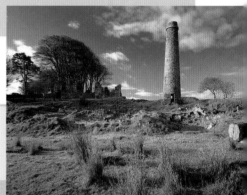

Solutions for exposure error

The following are the most common methods used to ensure a correct exposure. Regardless of the camera you use, some or all of these options are available to you.

CAMERA FEATURES

AE-Lock

This facility allows you to take a meter reading independently of the autofocus system. It is useful when you want to get close to a particular part of the scene, lock the reading and use this exposure for the final image.

Partial/spot metering

Many cameras have a facility that allows an exposure reading to be taken from a selective part of the scene. Spot and partial meters are the most common types and give accurate results so long as they are used to take a reading from a mid-tone.

Exposure compensation

With practice, you will learn how many stops to add or subtract from a scene to give the correct exposure. An exposure compensation facility is one of the most useful features a camera can possess.

TECHNIQUES

Exclude the sky

With landscapes, an easy method to prevent the sky from affecting the meter reading is to point the camera towards the ground and use this exposure reading. Be sure that the area you point the camera at is in the same lighting conditions as the rest of the landscape.

Grey card

The humble grey card is an overlooked accessory. It costs relatively little, but using it in a scene can guarantee you get the correct results if you take a meter reading from it, as it is 18 per cent grey in colour.

Bracketing

This is the term that is used to describe a series of exposures at regular steps, usually set using the exposure compensation facility.

TOWER
A typical sunny landscape shouldn't present any exposure problems so long as you meter without the sky in the frame.

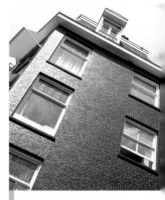

BLUE BUILDING
Subjects directly lit by sunlight can result in underexposure. Use AE-Lock from the grey pavement to avoid the problem.

Equipment techniques
Filter techniques

Learning when and where to use a particular filter can transform your photography and breathe new life into your images. Getting the most from your filters isn't a case of just slipping one in front of your lens – like any piece of equipment, each serves its own purpose and works best in certain situations.

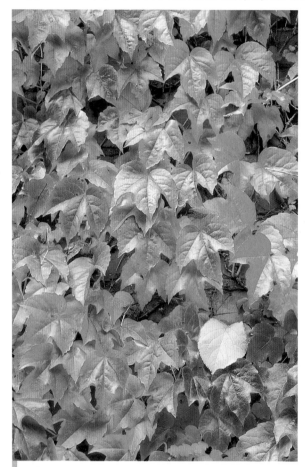
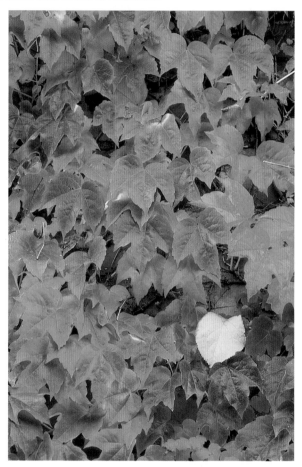

AUTUMN LEAVES
Polarizers reduce glare and reflections, and allow better saturation of colours on your subject.

Polarizing filters

The polarizer is without doubt the most useful filter that a photographer can own. Its main use is outdoors, where it is a priceless accessory for landscape photography. The main effect of using a polarizer is to increase saturation, best shown in landscape images by lush greens and deep blue skies. Polarizers also help reduce glare and reflections on shiny surfaces such as water and glass.

There are two types of polarizer: linear and circular. They look identical, but work in different ways. It's best to use the circular type, as linear polarizers can affect the camera's metering system – opt for linear only if you use a manual camera.

A polarizing filter is basically two pieces of glass with a polarizing foil sandwiched in the middle. The polarizer works by blocking particular wavelengths of light, so that only certain wavelengths pass through. This is achieved by turning a ring on the polarizing filter, which rotates the foil and changes the extent of polarization.

You can see the effect by looking through the filter and rotating the ring. This is useful on a non-SLR camera, as you can work out where to align the front ring before attaching the filter to the lens. With SLRs, you can rotate the ring with the filter attached and judge the effect through the viewfinder. Bear in mind that the fronts of many lenses rotate when they focus, so don't rotate the ring until after you have focused the lens.

For the best results, keep the sun at 90 degrees to the camera to achieve the deepest blue sky. Be careful when using a polarizer with wide-angle lenses, as you can record uneven tones in the sky, with one area much lighter than the others.

Another benefit of a polarizer is reducing glare and reflections, making it ideal for photographing water or architecture. Bear in mind that other subjects, such as foliage, can also suffer from glare, so it's worth trying out a polarizer in various shooting situations to see what benefits it can bring.

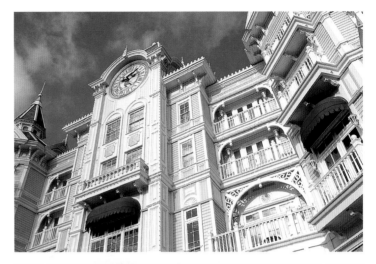

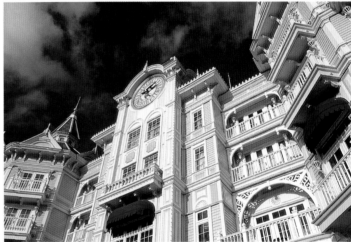

BLUE SKIES
These two images demonstrate the power of the polarizing filter for deepening a blue sky.

Filter factors

Most filters reduce the amount of light entering the lens by a particular amount, known as the filter factor. With cameras using TTL metering, this is taken account of automatically; however, with compacts, rangefinders and other cameras using non-TTL metering, you must adjust the exposure accordingly using the exposure compensation facility. The table at right indicates the filter factor of the more popular filters, as well as the amount of exposure compensation required.

Filter	Filter factor	Required exposure compensation
Diffuser	x1	None
81A, B, C	x1.3	+⅓ stop
81D, EF	x1.6	+⅔ stop
ND 0.3	x2	+1 stop
Blue 80C	x2	+1 stop
Yellow	x2	+1 stop
Polarizer	x4	+2 stops
Blue 80A	x4	+2 stops
Orange	x4	+2 stops
ND 0.6	x4	+2 stops
Green	x6	+2½ stops
Red	x8	+3 stops
ND 0.9	x8	+3 stop

A polarizer can also be used to create a special effect known as cross-polarization. See page 159.

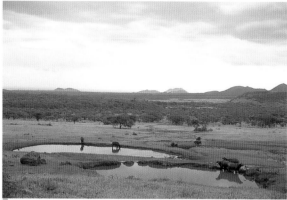

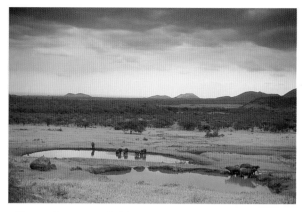

FILTERS
A neutral density graduate records detail in the sky (above).
A polarizer was used to increase colour saturation (right).

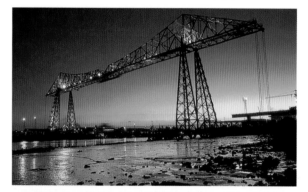

Graduated filters

A major problem faced by landscape photographers is keeping detail in the sky when exposing for the foreground. Graduated filters take care of this problem, darkening the sky while at the same time leaving the ground unaffected. There are two main types of graduated filter: the neutral density graduate, or ND grad, and the colour graduate.

The ND grad is the most popular choice and allows you to darken the sky without affecting its colour. ND grads come in different densities, with 0.3, 0.6 and 0.9 being the most common. These reduce light by 1, 2 and 3 stops respectively, and can be used in combination if required. You must take care when aligning the graduate so that the darkened area matches the horizon. This is relatively easy for SLR users, but users of compact or rangefinder cameras have to take an educated guess.

Colour grads work in much the same way, but add a strong colour cast to the sky. The result can look stunning, but care must be taken not to make the scene look too unnatural. Colour graduates are usually used at sunset or at dusk, with mauve, tobacco and orange being the most popular colours.

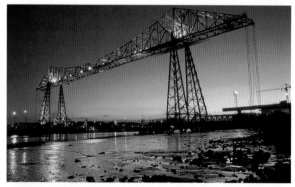

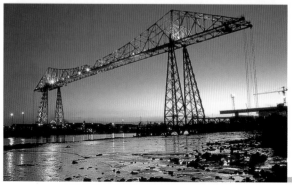

COLOUR GRADS
Colour graduates can have a dramatic effect on the backdrop to a scene. This set of images shows what can be achieved when using pink (top), tobacco (centre) and mauve (bottom) graduates.

Cool blue
The opposite to warm-ups is the 82-series of blue filters, which are used to cool down images in situations where the light is too warm. They can prove useful when you want to add an exaggerated blue cast to pictures.

Warm-up filters

The 81 series of filters, most commonly known as warm-ups, is a range of colour-balancing filters developed to enhance light when it has cool characteristics, such as in dull, overcast conditions.

Warm-up filters are amber in colour and come in a range of strengths; 81 is the weakest, 81EF is the strongest, with 81A, 81B, 81C and 81D in between. Knowing when to use a particular strength comes with experience, but there are some situations where one type is better than another.

An 81 or 81A has very limited application, so you should look to an 81B or C as your first choice. These are best suited for times when the light is slightly cool – dull weather, cool midday light and shady scenes are some examples. The aim is to add an attractive warmth to the scene without exaggerating the colours.

An 81D or EF is the choice when you want to create a very strong and obvious warm effect in your images. This could be to emphasize the colour of the sky at sunset or leaves in autumn. Bear in mind that neutral colours will also take on a colour cast, so use the filters with care, or your images will appear unnatural.

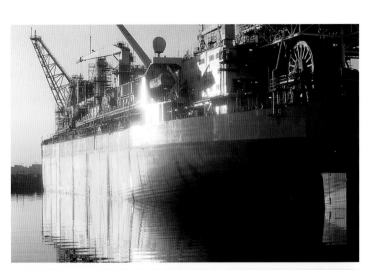

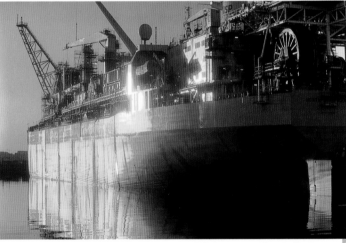

WARM-UP
A warm-up filter is a simple but effective way to add warmth to an image.

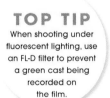

TOP TIP
When shooting under fluorescent lighting, use an FL-D filter to prevent a green cast being recorded on the film.

Colour-compensating filters
These specialist filters are used to provide accurate colour reproduction in very tricky lighting conditions. The filters come in a variety of colours (such as cyan, magenta and yellow) and strengths, and are used individually or in combination, depending on the colour temperature of the scene.

Colour-conversion filters
These filters are used when shooting on film in artificial lighting conditions (digital users only need to change the camera's white balance setting). There are two main types: the 80 and the 85 series. The 80-series are blue filters used when photographing in tungsten-lit conditions with daylight-balanced film. They range from 80A (strongest) to 80D (weakest). The orange 85 series is designed for use with tungsten-balanced film in daylight, but creative photographers often use them as a stronger option to 81-series warm-ups.

Diffusers

Often termed soft-focus filters, these are good to use when you want to add a romantic or dream-like atmosphere to your images. Soft-focus filters are suitable for a wide range of subjects; you can use them outdoors to capture scenes with an evocative mood, and use them indoors to create very moody still lifes. Diffusers are a great choice for portraits when you want to create a romantic feel to the image, which is why they are such a popular choice with wedding photographers.

Diffusers don't work by making the image unsharp – their effect is far more subtle: they blur fine detail, soften edges and blend highlights into shadows, so while pictures appear sharp, there is an obvious softening of the edges.

The effect of a diffuser varies according to the aperture you use; the wider the aperture, the stronger the diffusion. Set your lens to the widest aperture for the strongest effect – don't stop down the lens beyond a mid-aperture setting, otherwise the effect becomes barely noticeable.

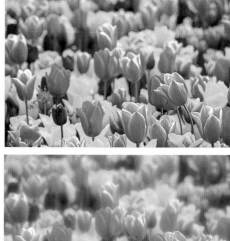

DIFFUSING FILTER
The unfiltered image of tulips (top) is an attractive image on its own. It's also an ideal opportunity to add a romantic feel to the scene (bottom) by using the diffusing filter.

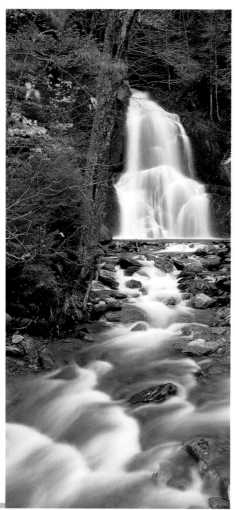

WATERFALL
On particularly bright days, achieving a slow shutter speed can be difficult. A neutral density filter is the answer. In this instance, it allowed a slow enough shutter speed to blur the water's motion.

Neutral density filters

These filters do not affect the colour balance in any way – their sole purpose is to reduce the amount of light allowed to pass through the filter into the lens. Neutral density, or ND, filters are not the type of lens you will need very often, but are worth considering if you want to take long exposures in daylight, most often when you want to record motion. Outdoor photographers use an ND filter when they photograph water, in particular rivers, streams and waterfalls, as it allows shutter speeds to be slowed down enough to record the water's movement as a blur.

ND filters come in a variety of densities, ranging from 0.1 to 4, with 0.3, 0.6 and 0.9 being the most popular.

Tricolour technique

An unusual technique to try with a red, blue and green filter is tricolour photography. This involves taking three separate exposures on the same frame, using a different filter with each. The result is that all static objects record normally, while moving subjects take on a particular colour cast. This works particularly well with water or clouds. Because you are shooting three exposures on one frame, set the exposure compensation to -1½ stops.

Colour filters for black and white

It's odd to think that colour filters such as red, green and yellow are popular with black-and-white photographers. They're used because they restrict the wavelengths of light passing through them: red only allows red light to pass through, green transmits green wavelengths only, and so on. The effect is that filtered black-and-white images can look very different from unfiltered shots, as the contrast and tonal range is affected.

Red has the most dramatic effect, as it increases contrast, while yellow causes the most subtle changes. Many photographers opt for orange as their first choice, as its effects are noticeable but not as intense as what you get with a red filter.

The effect of different colour filters on black-and-white images is shown below.

Filter	Effect
Yellow	Lightens yellows and skin tones, slightly darkens blue
Green	Lightens green, darkens red
Orange	Lightens orange, darkens red and green, reduces haze
Red	Lightens red, darkens green and blue (particularly sky); water records as almost black
Blue	Lightens green, darkens blue and red, strengthens skin tones, increases haze

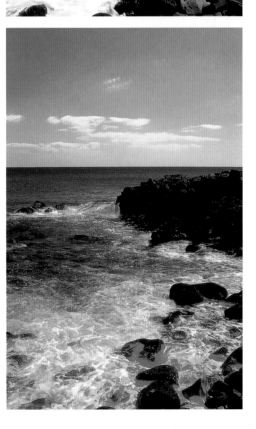

TRICOLOUR FILTER
The tricolour filter technique offers the potential to create very unusual effects.

TOP TIP
You can make your own diffuser by stretching an old pair of tights over the lens.

Lens techniques

Getting the most from your lenses comes from understanding how they capture the scene. Here we cover the essential points to consider when shooting with the two main focal lengths: wide-angle and telephoto.

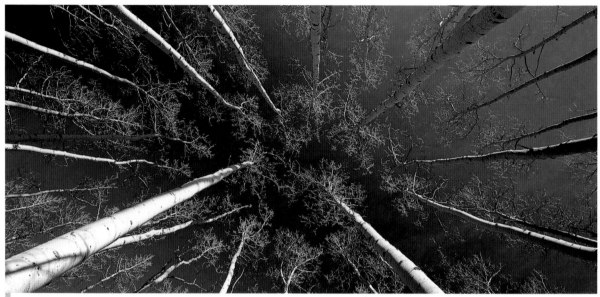

FOREST
You can't beat a wide-angle lens for creating dynamic compositions.

CHURCH
The amazing depth of field from wide-angles allows subjects from close up to far in the distance to be rendered sharp in the image.

Wide-angles

You might think that the difference in coverage between, say, a 17mm and a 24mm lens isn't that great, but you would be far from the truth. Although both are wide-angle lenses, with a focal length difference of only 7mm, the ways in which they capture a scene needs to be seen to be believed.

Wide-angle lenses have a wider field of view than the human eye, making them highly suitable for particular subjects. It also means that they should be used with care to avoid creating scenes where the interest seems a long way away.

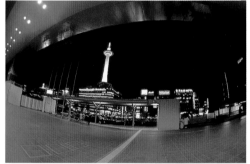

CITYSCAPE
Ultra wide-angle lenses dramatically distort straight lines.

Ultra wide-angles

Ultra wide-angle lenses covering a range of 15–21mm are capable of the most dramatic images, as they stretch perspective to an extreme. They work very well if you include subjects in the foreground, as their scale is accentuated by the lens's characteristics, which exaggerate distances and lengthen objects that stretch off into the background.

One thing to be very careful with is the foreground. With ultra wide-angle lenses, it is very easy to create a composition with a vast

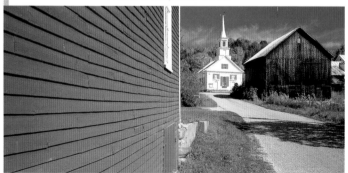

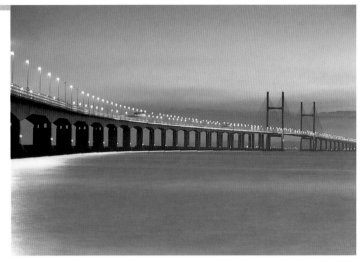

LONG BRIDGE
Wide-angles allow breathtaking vistas to be recorded.

empty space at the forefront. Always try to include interest in the foreground – if you have a field of flowers or something equally stunning, angle the camera downwards and the foreground will appear to stretch back for miles.

Ultra wide-angles produce excellent depth of field, even at relatively open apertures, making them ideal choices when you want the scene to be sharp from front to back. The lenses cause parallel lines to converge dramatically, so are an excellent choice when you want to create images with a defined vanishing point.

These lenses excel for shooting interiors, where the very wide field of view allows you to cram relatively small spaces in the frame. It also comes into its own when shooting the interiors of churches or cathedrals, as you can work at framing arches and pillars to make the most of the building's curves and straight lines.

Subjects particularly suited to ultra wide-angles include architecture and landscapes, but don't be afraid to try out the way they stretch perspective on other subjects, including portraits.

Moderate wide-angles

Moderate wide-angles, which cover focal lengths of 24–35mm, do not exaggerate perspective in the same way as ultra wide-angles, so their effect on the scene is not so dramatic. But they are better-suited to general use, in particular for landscapes. The 28mm is the favourite, as its angle of view is wide enough to fill the frame with most scenes, without distorting perspective. Its field of view means that you can include foreground detail to add scale to the scene, at the same time capturing sweeping vistas in the distance.

Because moderate wide-angles do not overly distort, they're a good choice for architecture when you want to include a large building in the frame, without exaggerating its shape. You still need to be careful of converging verticals, but the problem is less likely to occur than with wider lenses.

Wide-angles for digital SLRs

It's worth bearing in mind that the focal length of wide-angle lenses designed for film SLRs will change when used with the majority of digital SLRs, which lack full-frame sensors. This is why the current trend with lens manufacturers is to produce lenses with extremely wide focal lengths. Two examples are the Nikon 12–24mm lens and Sigma's 15–30mm.

To the right is a reference table that allows you to see the effective focal length of lenses used with particular CCD/CMOS sensors. The change varies from camera to camera, depending on the sensor size, but this table covers the majority of models. As you can see, with digital SLRs sporting a 1.6x and 1.7x increase, the need for ultra wide-angle lenses is all too clear.

Approximate effective focal length				
Lens	1.3x	1.5x	1.6x	1.7x
12mm	16mm	18mm	19.2mm	20mm
15mm	19.5mm	22.5mm	24mm	25.5mm
16mm	21mm	24mm	26mm	27mm
17mm	22mm	25.5mm	27mm	29mm
18mm	23mm	27mm	29mm	31mm
19mm	25mm	28.5mm	30mm	32mm
20mm	26mm	30mm	32mm	34mm
21mm	27mm	31.5mm	34mm	36mm
24mm	31mm	36mm	38mm	41mm
28mm	36mm	42mm	45mm	48mm
35mm	45mm	53mm	56mm	60mm

Telephotos

A lens with a focal length of over 50mm is termed a telephoto, which means that the lens has a narrower field of view than the human eye, so the subjects you see in the frame are larger than life. This focal length has its own characteristics that make it suitable for a wide range of subjects.

Short telephotos

Focal lengths of 50–135mm are termed short telephotos, because their pull power isn't great. However, this is a particularly versatile range, suitable for a large number of photographic applications.

Short telephotos, in particular 80–135mm, are an ideal choice for portraiture, as they give a flattering perspective. Before telezooms like the 70–210mm became available, no self-respecting portrait photographer would be seen without a 135mm lens in his gadget bag. Because the majority of film and digital compacts sport a zoom range that extends into the short telephoto territory, there's no excuse not to use it for taking decent portraits.

Short telephotos are also good for general close-ups of relatively small subjects, allowing you to pick out detail in architecture or photograph still lifes. Although they're not capable of macro standards, you should easily be able to fill the frame with subjects such as flowers.

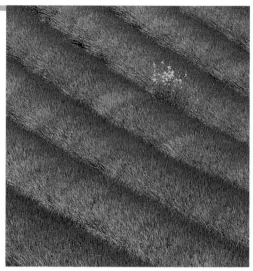

FLOWERS IN FIELD A telephoto lens has its use in landscape photography for isolating interesting elements in the scene, such as this clump of yellow flowers in a furrowed field.

TOP TIP

Increase the focal length of your telephoto lens by fitting a teleconverter. A 1.4x converter increases the focal length by 1.4x, so a 70–200mm lens becomes a 98–280mm, while a 2x converter doubles the focal length, so a 70–200mm becomes a 140–400mm lens.

LIZARD A telephoto lens allows you to capture pictures of animals that will normally disappear from sight if you get too close.

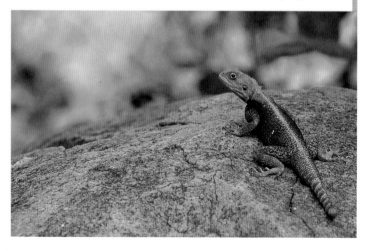

Medium and long telephotos

Medium telephoto refers to focal lengths of 135–200mm, while long telephotos cover 200–300mm. These focal lengths are perfectly suited to filling the frame with distant objects, making them a great choice for a number of very different types of photography.

Wildlife photographers swear by their telephoto lenses, which allow them to capture frame-filling images of animals that would not be possible to obtain if they had to get closer to their subjects. Candid photographers also use telephotos for a similar reason. Action and sports photographers use telezooms when they can't get close to the action, so if you're a keen sports fan and own an SLR, consider investing in a 70–300mm zoom.

Bear in mind that the shutter speed must be kept relatively high to avoid camera shake. Remember the general rule: use a shutter speed that is the reciprocal of the focal length – ½₀₀sec for a 200mm lens and so on. Also remember that depth of field is relatively shallow, even if you stop down the aperture. This is great news when you want to isolate the main subject from the background, as it makes the focal point stand out.

Although telephotos may not seem like a good choice for landscape photography, they are very good for isolating areas of a scene. They work particularly well in misty or foggy conditions, where you can use them to create more abstract images. Telephotos also have their place in architectural photography, when details of a building, rather than the whole structure, can be isolated and recorded.

Super telephotos

Telephotos that cover a range of 400mm and above are termed super telephotos. Due to the relative expense of SLR lenses that cover this range, they are sought after in the main by professionals and very keen enthusiasts. Sports and surveillance photographers in particular opt for these types of lenses, as well

Mounting a telephoto lens

Large telephoto lenses are usually supplied with a mount that features a tripod bush at its base. This allows the lens to be mounted on a tripod, rather than the camera, to provide a balanced set-up and reduce strain on the lens mount.

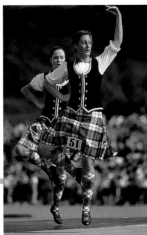

as some bird and wildlife photographers. Very few digital compacts reach this type of focal length, but there are a handful, including the Olympus Camedia C-750, which has a 10x zoom covering a range of 38–380mm.

HIGHLAND FLING
When you can't get physically close to the subject, a telephoto is the best option for frame-filling.

ROOFTOPS
Telephoto lenses compress perspective, which results in subjects at varying distances appearing much closer to each other than they really are.

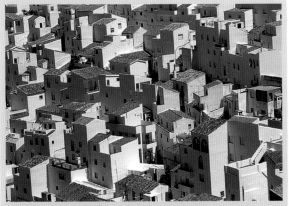

Perspective compression

A major characteristic of telephoto lenses is perspective compression, also known as foreshortened perspective, stacking or foreshortening. This effect results in elements of a scene at different distances appearing much closer to each other than they really are. The effect increases the greater the focal length, so for maximum effect with a telephoto zoom, extend the lens to its maximum setting. Perspective compression is particularly effective when you want an element in the background to impose itself on the foreground subject.

Telephotos for digital SLRs

While digital SLR users are restricted with wide-angles, the opposite is true with telephoto lenses. Because of the magnifying effect on the effective focal length caused by image sensors smaller than a film frame, telephotos designed for film SLRs are even more powerful when used on digital SLRs.

The table below provides a guide to the effective focal length of popular telephoto settings when used on digital SLRs with particular CCD/CMOS sensors.

Approximate effective focal length				
Lens	1.3x	1.5x	1.6x	1.7x
50mm	65mm	75mm	80mm	85mm
80mm	105mm	120mm	130mm	135mm
100mm	130mm	150mm	160mm	170mm
135mm	175mm	200mm	215mm	230mm
180mm	235mm	270mm	290mm	305mm
200mm	260mm	300mm	320mm	340mm
250mm	325mm	375mm	400mm	425mm
300mm	390mm	450mm	480mm	510mm
400mm	520mm	600mm	640mm	680mm
500mm	650mm	750mm	800mm	850mm
600mm	780mm	900mm	960mm	1020mm

Flash techniques

There's far more to flash photography than just pointing and shooting. Most integral flash units and external flashguns offer a wide range of features to provide sophisticated flash control capable of amazing results.

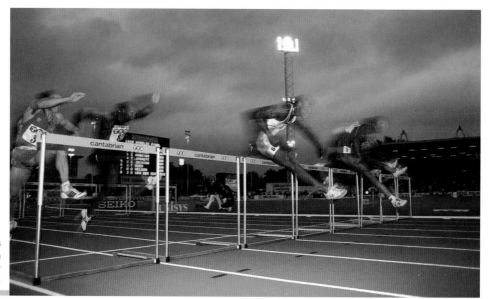

HURDLERS
Slow-sync flash is an excellent technique to try with sports photography.

Flash modes

The modern flashgun offers a variety of modes for the photographer looking to create more imaginative results than the standard autoflash is capable of achieving. The following flash techniques are relatively easy using built-in flash, as well as with external flashguns.

ALBERT MEMORIAL
A burst of flash reflecting off the railings adds an extra element to this silhouette image.

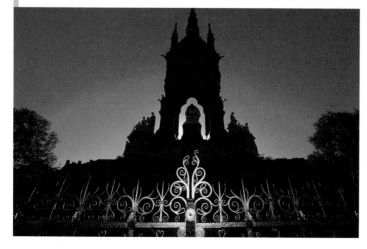

Slow sync

This is the common term for mixing a slow shutter speed with a burst of flash. On some cameras it is also termed night portrait mode. Slow synchronization (or slow sync) allows you to correctly expose a nearby subject, at the same time recording detail in the background. The burst of flash is used to illuminate the main subject, while a long shutter speed means that the background scene is also captured.

Thankfully, there's no need to calculate how to achieve this effect – the camera does it all for you. However, there are some practicalities to consider. The first is that a long shutter speed means that the camera will need to be kept steady – so use a tripod, or rest the camera on a wall, table or other stable surface. Also bear in mind that movement in the frame will be recorded as a blur. So ask your subject to remain still during the exposure, or use this effect creatively to produce an unusual result.

Second-curtain synchronization

With a normal flash exposure, the flashgun fires at the start of an exposure. Second-curtain synchronization (also know as rear-curtain sync) means that the flash fires at the end of the exposure. This provides a more natural result when using a long exposure with flash, such as in slow-sync mode. Set your flash to this feature to include movement in the image, as the flash-exposed subject appears at the end of a light trail rather than at the beginning.

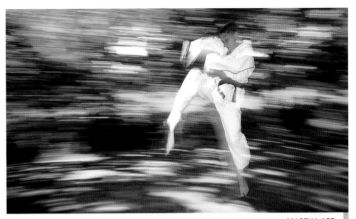

MARTIAL ART
Using second-curtain synchronization with a long shutter speed results in a powerful image.

Fill-in flash

This term relates to firing the flash in daylight portraiture to 'fill in' the subject's face. This has the effect of removing shadows from the face, while at the same time adding a catchlight in the eyes. This technique is taken for granted by modern photographers as it is all handled automatically by the camera. Before modern electronics however, the photographer needed to calculate fill-in flash manually, by balancing the flash and ambient light to give a daylight-to-flash ratio of around 1:4.

Flash accessories

Various flash accessories are available to help reduce the harsh effects of direct flash.

Flash diffusers

Flash diffusers or mini-softboxes are effective at softening direct light when bounce flash isn't an option.

HAUNTING
Combining a long shutter speed with filtered flash exposures has created this unusual image.

Filtered flash

Placing colour filters over the flash head illuminates the subject in that particular colour. Used in conjunction with a multiple exposure facility, or with a very long exposure in pitch-black conditions, it is possible to change the colour of the filters and illuminate various parts of the scene. By lighting a nearby subject with a colour-filtered flash and leaving the background lit by ambient light, you can create very unusual and interesting scenes.

Flash compensation

This feature allows you to control the balance of flash and ambient light. The exposure for the ambient light remains the same, but the amount of flash exposure can be varied to give flash more or less emphasis on the scene, with a scale of +/-2 or 3 stops, adjustable in ⅓- or ½-stop increments. Use this mode when you want the flash exposure to appear stronger or weaker in the image.

Wireless flash

Some camera and external flashgun combinations allow wireless, or slave flash. This allows multiple flash set-ups without the need for leads – the flashguns are triggered by radio or infrared. It's a very specialized area, used in the main by photographers on the move who want a portable 'studio' set-up.

Bounce flash

Using direct flash – having the flash point directly at the subject – can give harsh and unflattering results. A way around this is to use bounce flash, where an external flash is fitted to the camera and the flash head is positioned to provide indirect light on the subject. This involves bouncing the flash off a ceiling or wall so that the light is diffused and softer. Because of the longer distance the flash must travel, you need to be within a few metres or feet of the 'bouncing' surface. There's no need to worry about the exposure if you're using a dedicated flashgun.

One thing to be aware of, though, is that the bounced light will take on the colour characteristics of the surface it's bouncing off – so aim for a white wall or ceiling.

Studio flash techniques

A studio flash system offers the photographer complete control over the lighting of the subject. It's particular useful for portraiture and still lifes, with various accessories available to ensure that the subject is lit exactly how you'd like it to be.

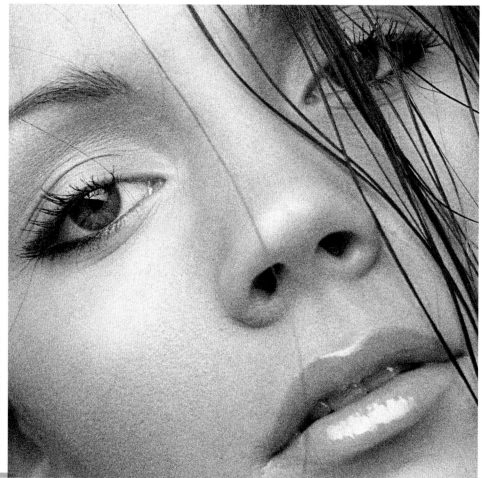

PORTRAIT
This image was used on the front cover of *Photography Monthly* magazine. Lighting was nothing more sophisticated than one light with a softbox and a triflector reflector placed beneath the chin. The image was later manipulated in Adobe Photoshop to adjust colours and add grain.

Portraits

Many photographers believe that taking studio portraits requires the use of several flash heads and a multitude of accessories. This is way off the truth – in fact, many studio photographers often work with just one or two flash heads. The fact is that you can achieve decent portraits with as little as one light and a reflector. Adding an extra light offers benefits, but isn't essential.

The key to good studio portrait lighting is making sure that the position and quality of light are flattering to the subject. The most popular lighting accessory for portraits is the softbox, which provides an even, diffuse light. Where you position the flash head is all-important: the further back from the subject it is, the softer the light. Placing the softbox high and in front of the subject provides what is termed butterfly lighting, due to the shape of the shadow that appears beneath the nose. Placing the softbox at an angle to the side lights one side of the face while casting the opposite side into shadow.

Adding a reflector is a very easy way to help fill in those shadows. By varying how close you bring the reflector to the face, you can control how much light is bounced back at the shadows. With this simple one-light, one-reflector set-up, you can achieve a wide range of results.

Often, a photographer will use extra heads, not to illuminate the subject, but to light the background. This is used especially when the background needs to be pure white. By setting the background light 2 stops higher than the subject light, the background records as pure white.

By angling a studio head towards the rear of the subject's head and using a snoot to provide a narrow, direct beam onto the head, it is possible to add an attractive highlight to hair.

The easiest way to discover studio lighting is to invest in a budget studio flash head and one reflector. Then, with the help of a notebook and a willing subject, you can try out different combinations of light/reflector arrangements and develop your studio portrait technique.

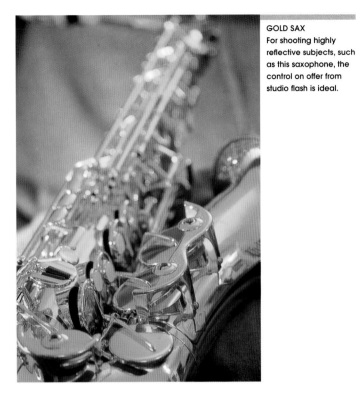

GOLD SAX
For shooting highly reflective subjects, such as this saxophone, the control on offer from studio flash is ideal.

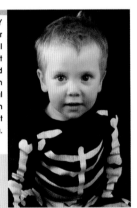

SKELETON BOY
The Cubelite is ideal for photographing small children. They fit perfectly inside and have their attention held by the unusual surrounding, which results in perfect portrait lighting.

Cubelite

Light tents have always been a regular fixture in the studio of still-life and product photographers, providing an easy method to achieve even, diffused lighting to illuminate small objects. The Cubelite has largely replaced the light tent, because its collapsible design means that it is easy to set up and pack away in a small bag, while different colour backgrounds can be clipped inside, or the rear removed to allow scenery to be included in the background. The result is a highly portable, effective method of achieving professional results.

Still lifes

Many still-life photographers prefer to use studio flash rather than daylight, as they can more readily control the power and direction of the light (as well as being able to work at night, of course).

Those dedicated to product photography invest in a white still-life cove, which is a curved background that makes it easy to shoot an object against a white background.

For most people, however, all that is required is a table top, a suitable subject and a single flash head with a softbox. For most still lifes, positioning the softbox above the subject and pointing straight down gives a nice, even illumination. Often, pointing the softbox slightly backwards means that any shadows will be directly behind the subject and out of view.

Indoor still lifes can also be taken with the softbox positioned high and to the side of the subject to mimic daylight. This works particularly well with subjects that are usually found near a window, such as a vase of flowers on a side table.

Again, using studio flash is a case of experimentation and experience. By using different lighting head accessories, such as softboxes, snoots and barn doors, and reflectors of various colours, you can create still lifes to be proud of.

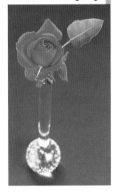

ROSE IN VASE
Many still-life photographers prefer to use studio lighting.

Subject techniques
Colour

Although colour isn't often interpreted as a particular subject in itself, it forms an integral part of photography. Knowing how best to take advantage of colours, how they affect a scene and how they work or clash with each other, is an important lesson to learn.

How we interpret colours

Everyone has a favourite colour, and it is a common belief that you reveal a part of your personality through the colours that you favour. Each colour represents a different emotion or mood, and plays different roles in pictures.

What is colour?

Colour is formed from the way in which objects absorb and reflect different wavelengths of light. An object takes on the colour of the wavelengths it reflects, so grass absorbs all wavelengths of light except green. Where more than one colour is reflected, the wavelengths combine to create other colours – for example, orange is the result of yellow and red light.

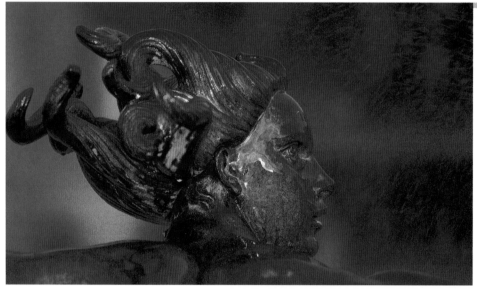

HEAD
Using a single colour adds mood to an image. The blue tone of this image suits the subject perfectly.

Red

This is the most powerful colour in photography, and can dominate a scene. Red represents danger and passion, and grabs your attention, so be careful how you include it in a scene – it can prove a distraction if you're not careful.

Green

This is a very calming colour that signifies health and life – green and lush forests, and rolling landscapes spring to mind. Green is, however, easily dominated by other colours – red in particular.

Colour combinations

When capturing scenes that feature more than one colour, it is important to know which colours clash and which work together in harmony. The colour wheel provides a quick reference guide to which colours clash and which mix well. Primary colours (red, green and blue) sit equidistant from each other and form a relationship with other colours on the wheel. Contrasting colours (also called complementary colours) sit on opposite sides of the wheel – when included in the same scene, they clash, adding impact and drama to the image.

Receding and advancing colours

Warm colours, such as red, yellow and orange, are said to advance as they stand out in a scene, while cooler colours like blue and green are said to recede. Try to include receding colours in the background and advancing colours in the foreground.

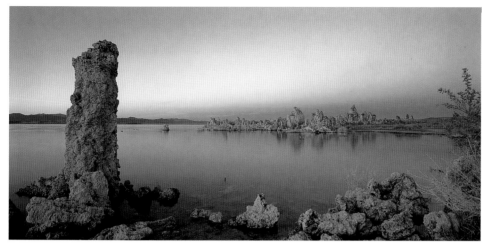

STILL LAKE
Natural colours can be simply breathtaking. The pink and blue tones of this sunrise are more important to the success of this image than the landscape itself.

Yellow

This is another strong colour that is often seen to represent nature – the sun, corn and flowers are dominated by yellow – as well as health and purity. Yellow works particularly well with blue.

Blue

This is the colour that can represent both good and bad. Blue can portray negative emotions, such as coldness, sadness and loneliness, but can also represent positive emotions, such as serenity and tranquillity.

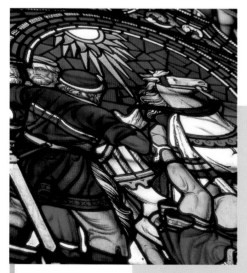

STAINED GLASS
Stained glass windows are excellent subjects for colour photographs. Use a polarizing filter to provide extra saturation.

Minimize colours

Using colours in photography isn't all about making them as bold or as brash as possible. Creating colour images with muted, weak colours can create evocative images that give the impression of peace and romanticism. Still lifes and portraits can benefit from the soothing effect of muted colours, especially when taken under very diffused lighting. Keep strong, bold colours like reds and yellows out of the frame, using shades of whites, with very weak colours like pinks or pastels. Use low-contrast films, or select low saturation on digital cameras. Very fast films, with large grain and weak colours, are also worth considering.

Maximize colours

To make your pictures really stand out, fit a polarizing filter to maximize saturation and remove reflections – a polarizer is as suitable indoors for subjects such as still lifes as it is outdoors for landscapes.

When shooting still lifes or portraits, use a bold colour backdrop to maximize impact, but bear in mind the cultural perception that we tend to associate with particular colours.

If you're using film, choose one that boasts highly saturated colours – slide film works best. Some digital cameras allow users to specify the level of colour saturation. This is also possible post-production, using image-manipulation software packages.

POPPIES
This simple but effective still-life composition is made up predominantly of only two colours – red and yellow.

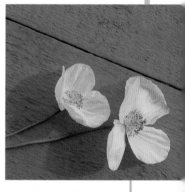

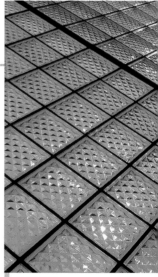

GLASS TILES
Good composition and only two colours make this picture work.

Black and white

Taking pictures in black and white is as popular now as it has ever been. Despite the arrival of colour film and, more recently, digital, monochrome remains a magical form of expression.

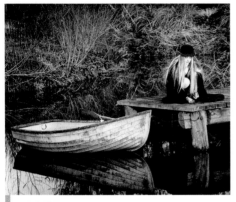

AT THE JETTY
The mood and atmosphere of monochrome make it the perfect choice for images like this.

Why shoot in monochrome?

It's a question that most photographers face at one time or another. With so much technology invested in producing colour films and CCD sensors, why would anyone want to shoot in black and white? The simple truth is that there is something about a black-and-while image: to many people, the lack of colour instantly gives the image more weight, more truth and more credit. A monochrome image is somehow more serious than a colour one. This is perhaps because by removing colour, we also take away many of the distractions that hold us from picturing the real subject. It's an ambiguous statement, but it's also a fact picked up by advertising, commercial and enthusiast photographers around the world. There is something classic about a black-and-white image, an unfathomable element that is impossible to put a finger on, but an undeniable one.

TOP TIP
Some digital compacts allow you to set the camera to black-and-white or sepia mode. However, it's recommended that you shoot in colour and manipulate images later.

What subjects suit black and white?

Any subject can be shot in black and white, although some work better than others. Portraits have traditionally been photographed in black and white, and many photographers prefer this medium over colour, as they believe that a mono image reveals more of the personality and character of a subject than a colour image could.

Landscapes look amazing in colour, but can look equally impressive in monochrome. Bad-weather pictures in particular look strong in black and white, as this medium is particularly effective at conveying mood and atmosphere. It's worth bearing in mind that black and white cannot capture the intricacies of light as colour film does – for instance, the warm light of mornings or late afternoons – but this comes down to learning to see in mono.

Mood and emotion are further aspects where black and white clearly has the advantage over colour. In particular, monochrome photography can be used to evoke strong negative emotions – images of social injustice, war and loneliness are often far more powerful when rendered in black and white.

While fine grain is usually the order of the day with colour images, using coarse grain is a popular course of action for black-and-white photographers, especially when photographing extremely poor weather conditions, such as storms. Coarse grain can also work well in portraits and still lifes. Ultimately, black-and-white photography offers as many, if not more, avenues for interesting, creative photography than colour.

WEDDING DRESS
Black-and-white images have a timeless quality and a sense of romance.

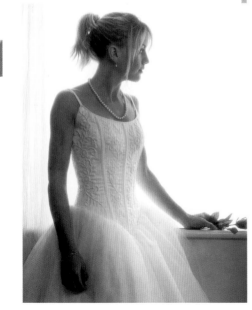

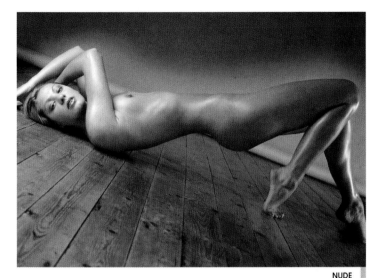

NUDE
The lack of colour means more emphasis is placed on shape and form.

Filters
Using filters with black-and-white film can radically affect the result. Colour filters such as red or yellow allow only their respective wavelength of light to pass through, significantly altering how different colours are recorded. See page 101.

Black-and-white films

There is a wide range of black-and-white films to choose from, all offering very good quality. Slow-speed films, such as Ilford Pan F Plus (ISO 50) offer high sharpness and fine grain, making them suitable for portraits, still lifes or landscapes. ISO 100–400 films produce excellent results, and the increase in grain as you move up speeds isn't so great. Fuji Neopan 1600 and Kodak TMAX 3200 are two to look at if you want your pictures to exhibit coarse grain.

Seeing in black and white

A major hurdle to overcome when shooting in black and white is learning to 'see' in monochrome. Because black-and-white film records different colours as various shades of grey, learning how colours will appear in the image takes some getting used to. Red and green, for instance, are very different colours, but record on black and white as a similar shade of grey.

The easiest way to learn is to shoot a scene in colour, then also take it in black and white. Include as many colours as you can, as this will give you a visual reference for future use. As well as the three primary colours (red, green and blue), include colours like orange, purple, yellow and brown, and also include as many shades of each of these as possible.

A technique that many photographers use is to carry around an orange filter to view through. Although looking through the filter won't provide a black-and-white image, the result is monochromatic in that it is made up of various shades of one colour (orange), which gives a relatively close interpretation of how the black-and-white image will be recorded. Another visual aid to consider is a small accessory called the monovue. This is essentially a small hooded filter, which, when held up to the eye, gives a black-and-white representation of the scene.

TOP TIPS
When shooting in artificial lighting conditions, don't worry about colour-conversion filters, as black-and-white film is unable to record colour casts.

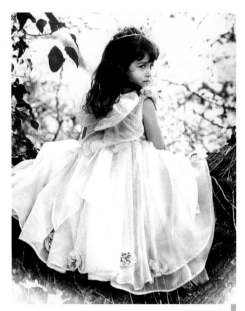

BRIDESMAID
The defined grain of fast black and white film can be used to enhance the image.

Uprating black-and-white films
Black-and-white films are very good at handling uprating. In particular, you can rate very fast films like TMAX 3200 at ridiculous settings like ISO 25,000 to create very coarse and atmospheric results.

Wildlife and nature

We live on a planet burgeoning with life. Animals and plants are found in all but the harshest of environments, so capturing them on camera is simply a case of getting out there and doing it. In this section, we cover the more popular subjects and techniques for photographing the natural world.

Keep your distance

By their nature, wild animals are nervous of people and will not hang around if they are aware of your presence. Therefore, your best chance of capturing an image is to keep your distance. A powerful telephoto lens is your best ally for capturing images of wildlife. Digital compact users with zooms offering a maximum range of 135mm or thereabouts will struggle to fill the frame with wild animals, but will find that they are well equipped for capturing close-ups of insects and flowers.

SLR cameras with telephotos or telezooms are ideally suited for wildlife, especially if they use lenses offering a focal length of at least 300mm, which can really pull in distant subjects. A macro lens is another optic that wildlife photographers should add to their collection, as there is as much variety in capturing insects, fungi and flowers as in photographing larger animals.

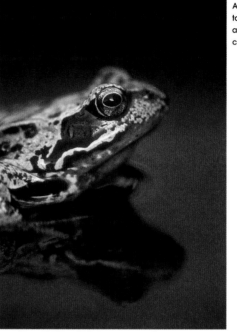

FROG
A garden pond is home to many photogenic animals, including common amphibians.

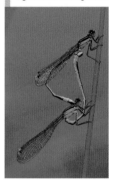

STICK INSECT
A very shallow depth of field makes the main subject stand out against the background.

Garden life

You don't have to stray far to find the right subject – there is plenty of potential to be found in your garden, where birds, small mammals, insects and flowers offer you plenty of photographic potential.

The fact that you are relatively close to garden wildlife has its advantages and disadvantages. On the plus side, being closer means it is easier to frame the subject, and because you can prepare the scenery to your own preference, you can ensure the background is uncluttered and prepare particular spots where you want the animals to visit. A good method for luring animals to a predetermined point is to leave out some food that will tempt them. Bread, nuts and fruit will attract all sorts of wildlife from birds to squirrels. If you

set yourself up inconspicuously and bide your time, you should be rewarded with some excellent opportunities. You can also attract particular birds by growing certain species of bush that produce berries, on which the birds feed.

On the downside, being so close to your subject means you need to be far more inconspicuous to ensure you don't frighten away potential subjects. Ways to get around this are to shoot from cover, such as through an open window or from a shed. If you're really keen, invest in a camouflaged hide. Whatever option you try, it is vital to remain quiet and out of view and, above all, to be patient.

Close-ups

Taking close-up pictures of small insects is a tricky business, and a macro facility is a must here. The main considerations are the composition, limitations of depth of field and camera shake, all of which are interlinked. To get as much of the subject appearing sharp you need to set as small an aperture as possible, which means a relatively slow shutter speed requiring some form of support (monopod or tripod) for the camera. Even with a small aperture, the depth of field will only extend for a few millimetres,

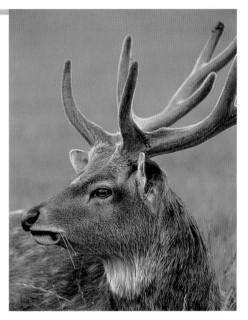

STAG
A long telephoto lens, patience and stealth are important for photographing park wildlife.

so when you compose the image, you need to keep the subject as much at right-angles to the camera as possible. In addition, try to keep the background as plain as possible – the less distraction behind the subject the better. Whether or not you use the flash depends on the subject – in some situations it works, in others available light is preferable. Experiment with and without the flash to determine which best suits the situation.

Most insects only stay on the same spot for a few seconds, so you will need to work quickly. Try to avoid moving around from one spot to another, as you will scare away your subjects – instead, remain in one spot and try to be patient.

Trees

When wandering through parks and woodland, don't ignore the trees as a potential subject. Winter may be a barren month in terms of foliage, but you can still take close-ups of the pattern of the bark. In spring and summer, try shooting intricate close-ups of leaves to reveal the patterns of veins, and capture the blossoming flowers that grow around the forest floor. Autumn proves to be the most colourful, as leaves turn various shades of red and gold – in addition to the leaves on the trees, try capturing still lifes of the layer of leaves covering the ground.

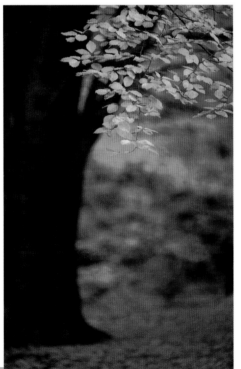

IMPRESSIONIST PARK
Be creative with your focusing to capture the trees in your local park in an imaginative and refreshing way.

Park life

Head for large parks, where you have the potential to photograph large mammals, such as deer. This is possibly as close to going on safari as many people get, and demands similar skills.

First, be prepared to get a chance to photograph animals from a distance only – you will need a lens with a minimum of 300mm to be able to record your subject in any great detail. Before leaving home, ensure you are wearing drab, neutral clothing – browns and greens are good choices – as these will help you blend into the scenery. If you spot deer, don't race straight towards them. Instead, walk slowly in a zigzag direction, stopping at intervals to look through the viewfinder and determine how much closer you need to get. If you're spotted, remain perfectly still and wait until the deer lose interest in you.

When you're close enough, you may be a little excited, but don't forget the basics. If your subject is backlit, adjust the exposure accordingly. Make sure your shutter speed is high enough for handholding, and your focusing is precise. Don't waste the opportunity by neglecting the fundamentals, and you will be rewarded with excellent images.

Birds

Apart from the garden, the best place to photograph birds is at your local park's pond or other waterways, such as streams, rivers or canals. Ducks and swans are commonplace in the summer months, and their plumage and shapes make them attractive subjects. A focal length of 135mm should be good enough to fill the frame, especially if you've enticed the birds closer with some food. Bear in mind that swans' white feathers may cause the meter to underexpose, so shoot at the indicated exposure and 1 stop over.

If you live near the coast, you can also try photographing seabirds, such as gulls, gannets and terns. You will often find these birds soaring or hovering on warm air, which makes for impressive pictures. If you are shooting a bird in flight, add 1 stop to the indicated exposure to avoid underexposure.

Birds of prey, such as eagles and owls, are incredibly photogenic, but finding these impressive birds in the wild is extremely rare. Instead, why not do a little research to find where your nearest bird of prey sanctuary is located, and head there instead. This will offer you an ideal opportunity to get close and take some brilliant images. Zoom in close on the head, and use a wide aperture to throw the background out of focus.

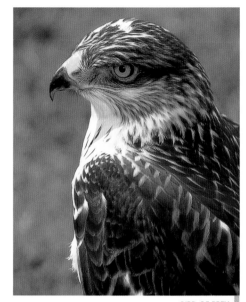

BIRD OF PREY
It is very difficult to photograph birds of prey in the wild, so visit a bird of prey sanctuary to get close to your subject.

Safaris

ON WATCH
Good safari images aren't simply a record shot of a wild animal. Instead, they reveal something about the animal's way of life and its environment.

If you are lucky enough to go on a safari, you will be presented with some fantastic photo opportunities. Large animals, such as elephants and rhinos, make superb subjects, while smaller animals, such as gazelles and zebras, are just as photogenic.

A powerful lens is in order and, because of the bright light levels, rating your digital camera at ISO 100 or 200, or using this speed film, should still give you hand-holdable shutter speeds. Avoid shooting in the middle of the day, when the sun is high and the lighting is harsh; instead, aim to get your pictures in the first and last two hours of the day, when the light has a warmer cast. At sunset, look to take silhouettes of animals against the setting sun looming large in the sky. Your local guide will know where animals are to be found during the course of the day – waterholes are often a popular retreat.

During the hottest hours in the day, animals will be at rest. Use this opportunity to capture classic images, such as big cats resting on the branches of trees or sheltering in the shade.

If you are brave enough to venture out on foot to photograph less dangerous animals such as zebra, make sure you are downwind – if not, they will catch your scent and make off in the opposite direction immediately.

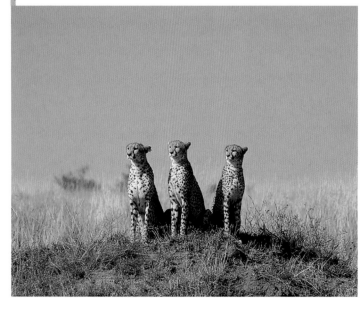

Zoos

Photographing captive animals has the advantage that you can get close to dangerous species like big cats without any danger of harm. However, the bars and fences that protect you from the animals can also prove a problem when it comes to photographing them. There are techniques that allow you to shoot through these obstructions and, in some instances, eliminate them completely.

The secret to shooting through cages or bars is to get as close as possible to the obstruction (without breaking any rules or antagonizing the animal) and set the lens aperture to its widest setting. The result is that the fence or bars are completely thrown out of focus and the shallow depth of field means that the background will be blurred, helping the animal stand out. You'll most likely find that the lens keeps focusing on the fencing or bars, so switch to manual focus if possible to avoid this problem.

Some enclosures don't have any obstructions, which should make your life easier. In these situations, your aim should be to try to make the scene look as natural as possible, so it isn't obvious that the animal is in captivity.

Shooting through glass presents the problem of reflections. You can get around this by fitting a lens hood, using a polarizing filter and getting as close to the glass as possible. You won't be able to use flash, so a tripod or camera support may be necessary.

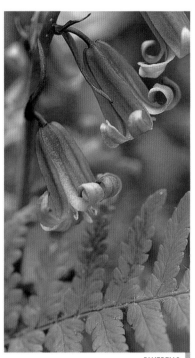

BLUEBELLS
Look to capture shapes and patterns.

TOP TIP
Find out the feeding times of animals – these are often the best chances to take pictures, as the animals are most active at these times.

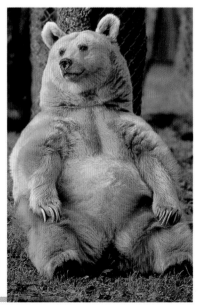

RESTING BEAR
Zoos and animal parks allow you to take great shots of animals you'd normally rarely get a chance to get close to.

Flowers

The intricate shapes and beautiful colours of flowers make them a popular subject for photographers. The relatively small size of the subject means that you need to have the equipment necessary for close-up photography.

If shooting flowers outdoors, take full advantage of days that are overcast, as the light is bright enough yet has a far softer effect than in sunny conditions.

On sunny days, look for flowers, ferns and leaves that are backlit. Keep a water spray bottle handy, and lightly spray the subject – the droplets will pick up the sparkle of sunlight and add an extra element to your images.

Colour plays a vital factor – look for pictures with strong colour clashes or several hues of the same colour. Patterns are also very attractive – look for intricate shapes in leaves, petals and ferns.

As well as close-ups of individual plants, don't forget to use a wide-angle and capture sweeping views of colourful fields. In spring, head for forests and woodlands to capture bluebells and poppies, and in summer look to create powerful compositions from bright yellow sunflowers set against a deep blue sky. Pack a polarizer, and make full use of the colours on offer.

In windy conditions, you need to be patient and take full advantage of a lull in the breeze. Alternatively, you can set up a still-life scene indoors. Consider how the colours of the subject work with the background, and try different viewpoints to find which gives the best results. Experiment with differential focus to create images that have only a small part of the subject in focus.

People

More photographs are taken of people than of any other subject. From the simple snapshot to the studio set-up, the walls and mantelpieces of homes around the world are adorned by portraits of friends and family.

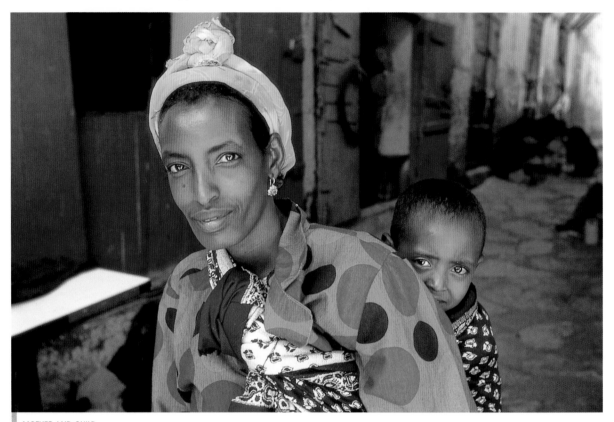

MOTHER AND CHILD
A moderate wide-angle lens allows some surroundings to be included in the frame.

The comfort zone

The key to successful portraiture is not related to a photographic skill or a piece of equipment; it is all to do with the personality that you, as a photographer, manage to bring out from the subject.

Very few people enjoy having their picture taken – whether it is by someone they know or a complete stranger, the thought of having to pose for a picture can be a frightening prospect. Unless the photographer can relax their subject and make them feel comfortable, the result will be portraits that exhibit nervousness, tension and anxiety. This is not good news at all.

Successful portrait photographers are those who can put their subject completely at ease, both before and during the photo session. The key is to make the subject feel completely comfortable and be almost unaware of having their picture taken.

Before even getting the camera out of the bag, you should sit and have a chat with your subject. Talk about their interests over a coffee, find out a little about their lives, and generally make them feel as relaxed as possible. Have some fashion or lifestyle magazines available so that you can run

Filters for portraits

The most suitable filter for portraits is the 81 series of warm-ups, which can be used to add a healthy skin-tone when shooting in cool light, or taking pictures of someone with a pale complexion.

Another filter to consider is the diffuser, which can be used to create soft, romantic-looking portraits.

through them and select poses and looks that you both like the look of – this is particularly useful if your subject isn't used to being photographed.

When you start taking the picture, act confident about what you are doing – any nerves you have will be instantly picked up and transmitted to the subject. Give them encouragement as you work – don't snap away and bark out instructions – tell them they're doing well and ask them to change poses. What you will discover is the more subjects relax and enjoy the session, the better the pictures become, as their natural expressions begin to break through and the nervous smiles and taut, tense shoulders begin to disappear.

All this may sound straightforward, but you'll find there is a skill involved in developing the relationship between photographer and subject. Master this, and you're on the road to taking great portraits.

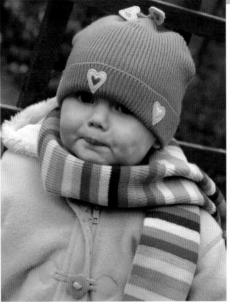

WOOLLY HAT
A telephoto zoom means that the child isn't distracted or frightened by the photographer.

Use the right film

Film users should take care which type they load in the camera. There are several films designed specifically for portraits, which offer natural colours, in particular for skin tones. Fuji Reala and the Kodak Portra series are excellent print films to try, while for slide, consider Fuji Astia or Kodak Ektachrome 100G.

Watch the background!

The most important element in a portrait is the subject, so make sure they're not having to compete with the background.

The first thing to do is make sure that the lens aperture is as wide as possible. This gives a very shallow depth of field, which throws the background out of focus.

Second, try to avoid backgrounds that are overly fussy – plain is best, as the emphasis is then placed on the subject. If there is no plain background available, try to shoot against a background made up of neutral and recessive colours, such as green or blue, rather than dominant colours, such as red and yellow.

Portrait lens choice

When shooting portraits, be careful to use the correct lens; if your camera has a zoom, set it to the appropriate focal length. Wide-angle lenses are a definite no-no if you are trying to capture a flattering image, as they will exaggerate perspective – making noses look like beaks and distorting the shape of the face. A standard focal length, such as 50mm, is better in terms of perspective, but for a tight head and shoulders shot, you will need to stand quite close to the subject, which may prove intimidating.

A short telephoto, 80–135mm, is the ideal choice. Your working distance is far enough from the subject for them to be more relaxed, while not too distant that you have to shout instructions to them. Better still, the perspective of this focal length provides a very flattering portrait by flattening the facial features.

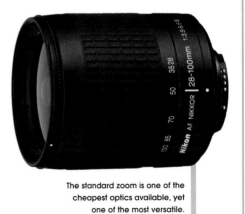

The standard zoom is one of the cheapest optics available, yet one of the most versatile.

Creating a 'look'

It's important that both you and the subject have a clear idea of how they would like to be photographed. This involves not only their expression or pose, but the location they would like to be photographed against, their clothes, make-up, hairstyle and so on. This is where having fashion magazines on hand comes in very useful. Looking through these allows both parties to get a better understanding of the pictures that will be taken, and this helps the photo session to run more smoothly.

There are not any hard and fast rules about what the subject should wear or how they should pose – this is determined in particular by how the subject wishes to look in the photographs. As the series of photographs on this page demonstrates, there are literally hundreds of different poses and styles that the person you are photographing can adopt.

One thing to be aware of is that fashions change very quickly – bear this in mind when determining the outfits your subject wears. A good guideline to adopt is always have the subject wear clothes that are timeless: casual clothing, such as jeans, T-shirts and plain woolly jumpers, usually works best.

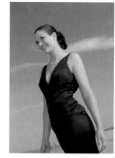
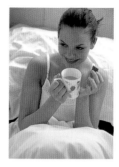
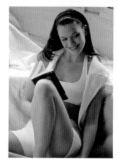
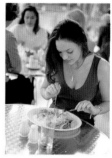

Eye contact

The general rule with portraits is that there should be strong eye contact, as this grabs the attention of the viewer. Although this is often an important aspect of portraiture, don't imagine that it is always required; this is another rule in photography that is meant to be broken. Having the subject looking away from the camera can add mood to the portrait, while obscuring an eye, perhaps with strands of hair, can invoke a sense of mystery on the subject.

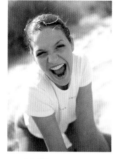
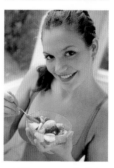
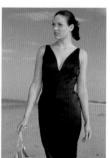

DIFFERENT LOOKS
When shooting portraits commercially, bear in mind that different markets look for different types of pictures. One person can take on very different looks, depending on how you want to market the pictures. These shots are ideal for health, lifestyle and fashion markets.

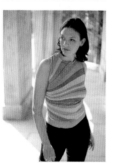
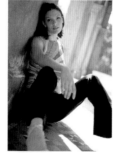
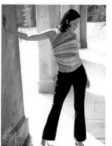
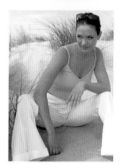

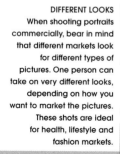
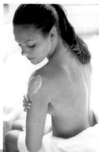
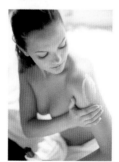
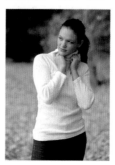
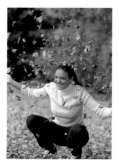

Candid photography

Because the subject is unaware that you are taking their picture, candids are a good way of capturing their natural behaviour. The best chance of success is to use a decent telephoto lens, which allows you to fill the frame with the subject, while at the same time keeping a good distance away, so that you are unnoticed by the subject. The secret to candids is to not make it obvious you have a camera, so keep it hidden until required, and work fast.

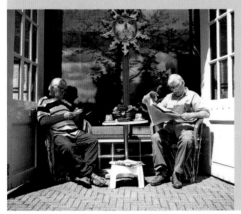

OLD FRIENDS
These men were too deeply engrossed in reading to notice their picture being taken.

Portrait style

It is generally accepted that there are two main types of portrait: formal and contemporary. Formal portraiture is the style that professionals have used for countless decades. With formal portraits, the sitting is very well planned out, Studio flash is used, the photographer has a set regime of poses for the subject to adopt, and the backdrop is usually a part of the home, such as a fireplace or a mottled background. For timeless portraits, this approach works well and remains popular today.

However, a newer, fresher style of portraiture has become increasingly popular since around the 1980s; that of contemporary portraiture. As the title suggests, this is a far more relaxed approach for both the subject and the photographer, and aims to add a contemporary, 'lifestyle' feel to the portrait. Unlike formal portraits, where the camera is usually mounted on a tripod, studio lights are used and the whole exercise is planned, contemporary portrait photographers have the opposite approach, choosing to handhold the camera and foregoing studio flash completely for available light, or possibly a flashgun. In addition, the location is less planned, with almost any location inside the home or outside being suitable. The result is that portraits are far more relaxed and informal, mainly because everyone has more fun doing them. Contemporary portraiture is certainly a method you should attempt to adopt, as the results are far more modern and justifiably popular.

One area where contemporary photography has become very popular is for weddings, where the photographs take on a far more relaxed style than you would find in a traditional wedding portfolio. Gone are the formal group shots, to be replaced by candids of the wedding couple, guests and bridesmaids. The result is a far more informal set of pictures that can record the emotions of the special day far better than traditional images do.

Environmental portraits

Often the best way to reveal part of the character and personality of a subject is by photographing them in their favourite surroundings; this is known as environmental portraiture. This could be at their place of work or in their home – the location depends on where the subject feels most comfortable. For instance, if you know the subject is a keen gardener, you could shoot them in their garden or shed; if they run a market stall, photograph them at work. Use a wide-angle lens to fill the frame, and make sure that the subject looks natural and relaxed.

The important thing to remember is that, in this instance, the surroundings become as important as the person, so be sure that you take this into account in the composition.

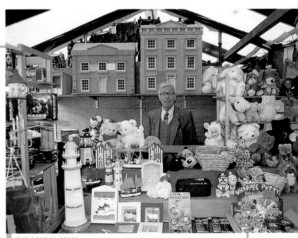

THE MODEL MAN
Environmental portraiture is all about revealing an aspect of the subject's life.

Lighting for portraits

Lighting plays a vital element in all types of photography, but is particularly important in portraiture, as how a subject is lit will completely determine their appearance. Both natural and artificial lighting are suitable for portraiture; the essential factor is that you know how to control and use lighting.

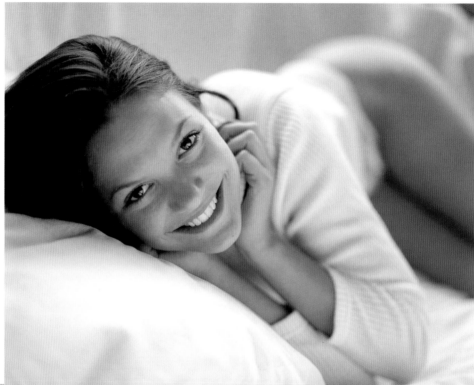

NATURAL LIGHT
Large patio/french doors or large windows can be more than adequate for provide perfect indoor portrait lighting.

Using reflectors and diffusers

These are vital accessories for controlling available light, and should be high on your shopping list for portraits.

When to use reflectors

Reflectors allow you to bounce light back onto a subject. Place them on the opposite side of the subject to bounce light back on to the subject. With sunlight, the chin and neck may be in shadow, so place a reflector at waist height to even up the lighting. If the light source is behind the subject, place a reflector between the subject and camera (making sure it is out of view) to bounce light back on to the subject. Bear in mind that you can also use elements in your environment, such as white walls and lightly coloured sand, as reflectors.

When to use diffusers

Place the diffuser between the light source and the subject to produce a much softer light. In strong sunlight, for instance, the diffuser needs to be above the subject. Diffusers work well with reflectors, so be ready to use them together for the same image.

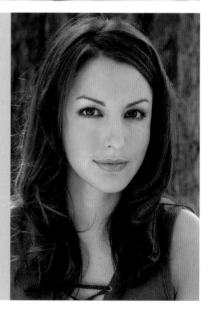

DIFFUSED LIGHT
This shot was taken on a sunny day. However, a diffuser placed above the model's head meant lighting was diffused, while a reflector to the side added some highlights to the hair.

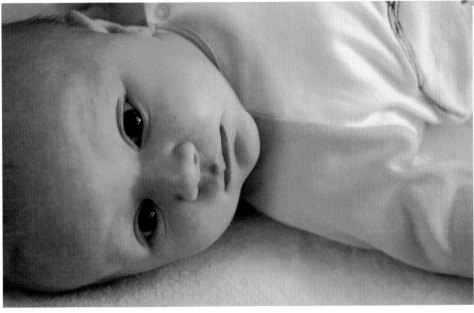

SOFT LIGHT
Soft lighting through net curtains perfectly suited this shot of a baby.

Daylight portraits

Many photographers regard daylight as the best way of lighting portraits, as they feel that studio flash can't match their ability to create a natural feel to the portrait. Learning how to master daylight won't come quickly and easily – even professional photographers claim they have much to learn about using available light! This may have something to do with the fact that the characteristics of daylight are different not only from one country to another, but from one day to the next, and from hour to hour. Therefore, learning how to use daylight comes from experience and practice.

The first thing to understand is that the weather conditions that suit portrait photography aren't what you would normally expect. Overcast conditions may be a hindrance for the landscape lover, but are ideal for the portrait photographer. When the sky is filled with cloud, the light becomes soft and diffuse, which is perfect for portraits. Although the sun is obscured, the light during overcast conditions changes during the day, with the best times being mid-morning and mid-afternoon.

Bright, sunny days give a harsh light for portraits and cause the subject to squint, which never looks good. Diffusers and reflectors can be used, although the light is more difficult, and sitting the subject in the shade works well – although it does limit your choice of locations.

Using daylight means that you are at the mercy of the weather, and should it be too wet or windy to be taking pictures outdoors, another option is to shoot indoors. This may sound like a poor alternative, but so long as there is a reasonable amount of light to work with, you should still be able to take great portraits using window light. If you set up the picture properly, it needn't be obvious that the portrait is taken indoors – if the lighting is good, a nondescript background will not give the location away.

Alternatively, you could use the surroundings to your advantage and incorporate them into your picture – for instance, have the subject looking out through the window.

Incidentally, using window light should not be restricted to when the weather is bad outside; this is also a good option when the light is particularly bright, as you can set the subject against the window and bounce light back on them to create romantic portraits with a soft light and perhaps a pure white backdrop.

TOP TIP
By using reflectors and diffusers, you can increase or decrease the amount of light on your subject, but leave the background unaffected. This is a creative technique known as key shifting.

For details on using studio flash for portraits, see page 108.

Children

Never work with kids? Rubbish! Photographing children can be fun and highly rewarding.
It can also be very tiring and frustrating, so make sure you go about it the right way.

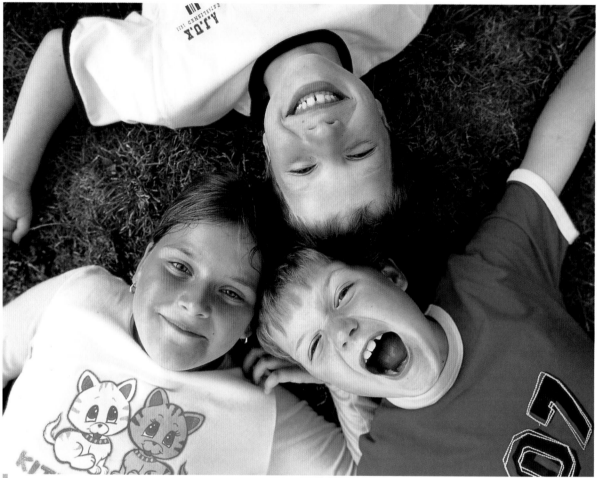

FRIENDS
You won't hold a child's interest for long, so catch kids while they're playing with friends, for natural, lively portraits.

TOP TIP
Always ask permission of a parent before photographing any child.

Babies, along with puppies and kittens, win every cutie contest, so be sure to capture lots of pictures of them. Newborns are too young to do anything particularly interesting, but their frailty alone makes them lovely subjects to capture. Include a parent in the picture to add a sense of scale to the image. From six months on, babies start to make expressions and react to sounds, so take advantage of this and capture some great shots.

The first thing to remember is that children have a very short attention span, so you need to work fast and keep them interested for as long as possible.

Digital users have a real advantage when photographing children – they can show the kids the pictures straight away on the back of the camera. The result of this is that a group of reluctant young grumps almost invariably becomes a boisterous bunch of buddies, all clambering to be the next to be photographed. Use their enthusiasm and excitement to your advantage while you hold their attention.

The next thing to bear in mind is that kids rarely do what you want them to do. Ask them to sit and they stand, request a smile and you're rewarded with a frown. Rather than get annoyed, keep taking pictures –

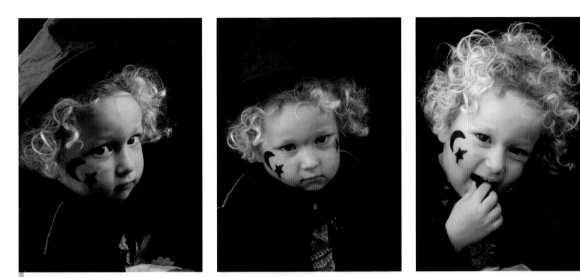

LITTLE WITCH
Most children go through a range of emotions in a very short space of time. Each of
these images works well, even though the girl is displaying three very different moods.

BIG NOSE
Kids like having fun, so take bizarre portraits –
here the photographer used a fish-eye lens.

you might not be getting what you want,
but they will still be great shots!

Make sure you have plenty of toys to
hand, as they will keep the kids occupied.
Frame a picture, call their name and grab
the shot when they look up.

Because they rarely sit still, you will have
to work on your feet. Zoom lenses come in
really useful in these situations, as they allow
you to shoot a group of kids playing with
the wide-angle setting, then zoom in tight
to capture an individual's expression.

Clothing for children is usually brightly
coloured and full of patterns, so make full
use of this to create colourful compositions.
Kids look incredibly cute in coats and hats,
so take them outside and grab some
pictures of them in the garden.

Finally, it's worth remembering that
a child's mood can change in a split-
second, so keep the camera ready at
all times – a sad-looking child can make
a poignant image.

Props

Adding simple props can transform a portrait.
Get the child to prop sunglasses on their head,
mix and match jewellery, wear a hat or hold
a flower. Sometimes it works, sometimes it
doesn't – but it is always good fun.

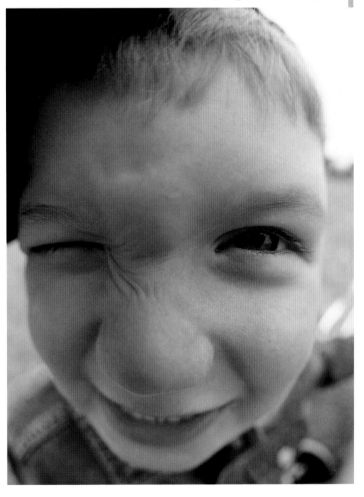

Landscapes

Taking pictures of landscapes is a favourite choice of a great number of enthusiast photographers. Every country – and in most cases, every region of every country – has a countryside with its own unique identity. No matter how many countries you visit, you will always find a different landscape to capture – ranging from the beautiful greens of the English Lake District to the island paradise of a Caribbean coastline.

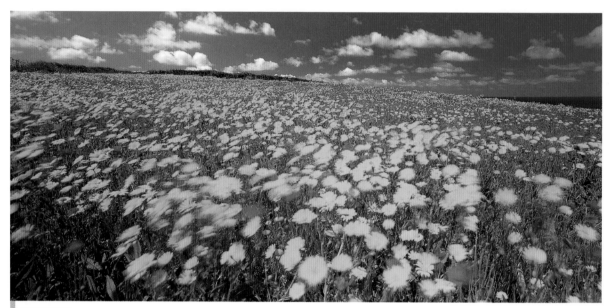

FLOWER FIELD
This stunning landscape is the result of deeply saturated colours, aided by a polarizing filter. A small aperture ensures front-to-back sharpness, while slow shutter speed records an attractive blur in the flowers.

Gear checklist

If you're heading into the great outdoors, you want to ensure that you have everything you need, as you won't be able to pop back home to stock up. However, as you will be trekking over relatively long distances, you won't want to take unnecessary items with you. So before setting out, decide carefully what you need.

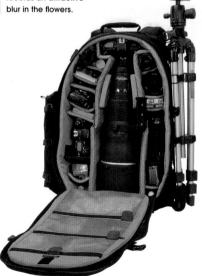

Spare batteries: Are the batteries loaded inside your camera (and other items such as a flashgun) fresh? Do you have a spare set?

Lens choice: For landscapes, the focal length of choice is a wide-angle. SLR users may also want to pack an ultra-wide zoom and possibly a short telephoto zoom.

Filters: Essential for taking premium landscape images – see pages 128–129.

Tripod: You'll be setting a small aperture to give plenty of depth of field, so a tripod is essential to cope with the long shutter speeds. A lightweight model makes the most sense, as you will be carrying it over long distances.

Remote release: Ensure you minimize the risk of camera shake by firing the shutter remotely.

Landscape composition

Composition is discussed in detail on pages 82–85, but it is worth highlighting here the most important aspects in relation to landscape photography.

The first is the rule of thirds, which regards where important elements of the scene should fall in the frame to provide a balanced result. This rule not only relates to individual elements, such as a tree or a farmhouse, but also to lines running through the frame. The most common of these is the horizon, which should be placed along the upper or lower third of the frame. Other common lines include rivers, walls or boundaries of fields. The lines need not only run horizontally – vertical and diagonal lines also work well, the latter in particular leading the eye into the frame.

Watch where the sun is in relation to the camera. Having it to the side is preferable, as it will cast nice shadows in the scene from objects like trees, fences and hills. With the sun behind you, the shadows are hidden from view, while shooting into the light (contre-jour) creates strong silhouettes but runs the risk of lens flare.

Foreground interest

Taking pictures with the camera in the upright position can result in very strong images, in particular where there is good foreground detail. While landscape-format shots can show off foreground interest, the extra depth created by an upright image can provide a sense of distance and scale to the scene.

By using a wide-angle lens, getting very close to the foreground subjects and adopting a low viewpoint, you can accentuate these elements and give them a prominent, larger-than-life appearance that dominates the image. Ideal subjects to use as foreground interest include rocks, fences, flowers and boats.

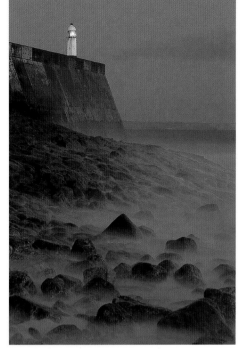

Shooting in bad weather

Landscape photography isn't all about taking pictures in brilliant sunshine – shooting in bad conditions can result in strong, moody images. In particular, the onset of a storm can produce the most dramatic clouds. Skies filled with dark grey clouds provide a fantastic backdrop to a landscape. If you're lucky – and prepared – you may be blessed with a parting in the clouds that allows a golden streak of sun to break through and provides a split-second opportunity to capture a dazzling scene.

Taking great bad-weather pictures is a waiting game. You never quite know what the elements will do – one minute the scene may be dull and lifeless, while the next could result in a brilliant image. Capturing a magical moment requires dedication, patience and preparation. If you're willing to make the time, the rewards can be amazing.

LIGHTHOUSE
Rocky coastlines make for dramatic landscapes. An exposure of 30sec at f/16 ensures excellent depth of field and a beautifully blurred sea.

TOP TIP
Keep an eye on the weather forecast. When a storm is predicted, head to your location with time to spare, to allow for proper preparation.

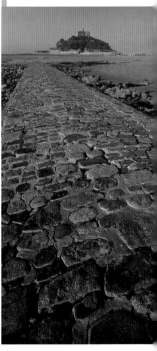

ST MICHAEL'S MOUNT
The viewpoint adopted here means your eye can't help but be led into the distance by the stony pavement.

Breaking the rules
Once you've learned all the rules, don't be afraid to break them. Photography isn't a science, so rules can be broken yet give a pleasing result. If you find a scene that you think merits, for instance, placing the subject in the centre of the frame, don't be afraid to try it.

Filters

Perhaps with landscape photography more than any other subject, knowing when to use the appropriate filter can turn a good image into a fantastic one. Although there are dozens of suitable filters, below is the essential shortlist.

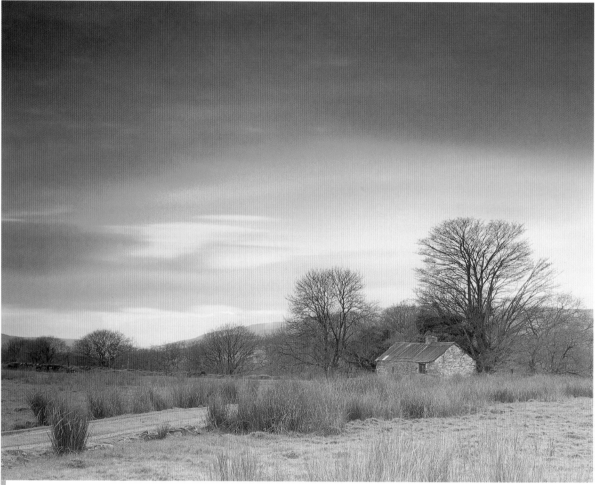

BARN
A 1.2 ND grad filter was used with an 81C warm-up to provide a deep, warm brown sky that perfectly complements the colour of the landscape.

Polarizer

A must-have for landscape photography, the polarizer increases colour saturation, bringing out the greens of foliage and grass, as well as providing a deep blue sky as a backdrop. A polarizer also helps with water, as it minimizes reflections off the surface.

Warm-up

When the light is a little cool and needs warming, use the 81 series warm-up filter to inject a soft golden glow into the scene. The warm-up is also a good choice for enhancing the colours of sunrise or sunset.

Neutral density graduate

Although specialist landscape photographers won't leave home without it, many photographers have yet to grasp the importance of the humble neutral density graduate (ND grad). Bland, pale skies are a thing of the past with the ND grad, which darkens the sky while leaving the foreground unaffected.

Optimum sharpness

For a sweeping landscape scene to work best, the image should be sharp from the foreground to the furthest reaches of the frame. To do this, the depth of field must be as deep as possible. Setting a very small aperture is one way of increasing depth of field, while for SLR users, using hyperfocal focusing is another.

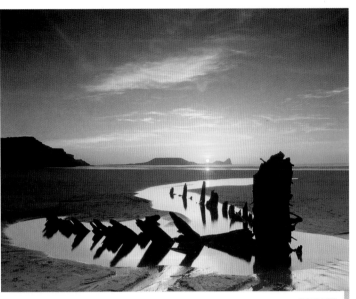

BOAT RIBS
To maximize front-to-back sharpness, use hyperfocal focus and a small aperture.

Time of day

The characteristics of a landscape vary radically over the course of a day as the characteristics of light change. Around sunrise and sunset, the light has a very strong warmth that looks extremely attractive, so these are very good times to be shooting landscapes.

During the colder seasons, the sun doesn't rise fully into the sky, so you can shoot all day long – weather permitting – as the light never becomes particularly harsh. This isn't the case during the warmer periods of the year, in particular in summer, where the hours from midday to early afternoon see strong, harsh light that isn't particularly good for capturing attractive landscape scenes.

Mornings are also particularly good for landscape photography in valleys and sheltered areas, where ground mist forms into a blanket over the ground. You need to work fast, as the rising sun will quickly make the mist evaporate.

Exposure advice

With most landscape scenes, much of the frame is filled with sky, so there is a risk of underexposure. Using an ND grad filter (see opposite) can overcome this. Another way is to take an exposure reading from the grass and lock this setting. Greens in a landscape are a good mid-tone from which to take a spot-meter reading or make an autoexposure lock (AE-L).

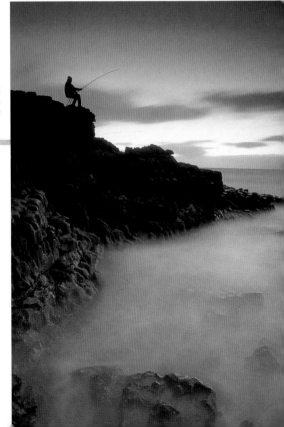

ANGLER
Including a person in the frame adds a sense of scale to the landscape.

Which film?

Film users should consider that colour films are made to give either over-the-top colours and strong saturation, or more muted, realistic colours. For strong colours, Fuji Velvia is a favourite with colour slide users. Kodak Elite Chrome 100 Extra Colour is also a popular slide film for punchy landscapes. For realistic results, use Fuji Astia or Kodak Ektachrome 100G. For colour print film, Agfa Ultra 100 and Fuji Superia 100 deliver strong results, while Fuji Reala 100 provides a very natural colour reproduction.

You are spoilt for choice with black-and-white film, as all emulsions are suitable for landscape photography. Choose your film depending on what film speed you prefer. If you want really moody mono images, try the faster emulsions, such as Fuji Neopan 1600 or Kodak TMax 3200.

The four seasons

In temperate climates, such as in the United Kingdom, the change of seasons completely alters the landscape. The same scene looks completely different, depending on the time of year. Each season has its own unique characteristics that make outdoor photography an all-year-round proposition.

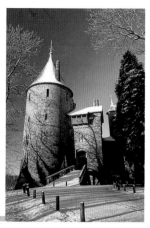

GATE TOWER
As well as adding a deep blue backdrop, a polarizer removes any coolness in the colour temperature.

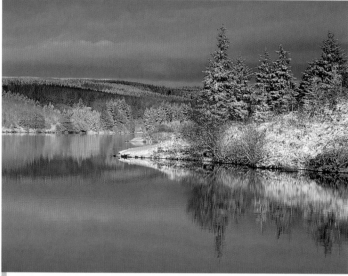

WINTER LAKE
Landscapes take on a completely different look when covered in snow.

Winter

Winter is often perceived as a barren period, but there is still plenty of scope for photography. This is particularly true when there is a sequence of winter days and nights with little cloud, as this brings with it various natural elements that make great pictures and demand you get up early to spend the whole day capturing them.

Winter mornings bring plenty of opportunity to capture misty landscapes. Head for the hills and use a telephoto lens to isolate ghostly trees, or seek the shore of a lake or river and use the colours of sunrise to mix with the mist over the reflections on water to create an ethereal result. As the day brightens, seek out leaves and vegetation covered in frost, as these make great natural still lifes. Use a telephoto lens to isolate leaves and try close-up techniques for frosty leaves in fine detail.

If you're really lucky and it has been snowing, you could be blessed with a winter wonderland. If you're early enough, the landscape should be free from human footprints and the snow will not have melted from the branches of trees, allowing you to capture incredible winter scenes.

Use a polarizing filter not only to deepen blue skies but also to reduce the glare and reflection from snow. Some photographers also like to use a very light warm-up filter (81A) to remove some of the coolness from the snow without creating an unnatural warm cast on the snow.

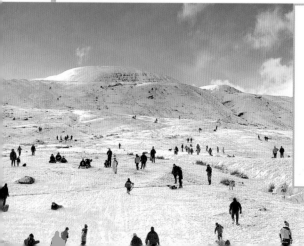

SLEDGES
Make the effort to capture seasonal activities, such as tobogganing or sledging.

Exposing for snow

Correctly exposing a winter scene can be a nightmare if you're unsure of what to do. The predominance of white in the scene fools camera meters into underexposing the scene. There are various ways around this:

1. Leave the camera in automatic but bracket over the indicated reading by +1, +1½ and +2 stops.
2. Set the camera to snow & sand mode if it has it.
3. Take a handheld meter reading. Bracket by +½ to be sure.
4. Take a spot meter reading from a mid-tone, such as green vegetation.

Spring

An explosion of colour greets us in spring, when plants, flowers and trees, that have been lying dormant during the winter months, emerge in a glorious multicoloured invasion of life to announce the arrival of a new season. The spring season provides nothing short of a metamorphosis in the landscape, making it a dream season for photographers, particularly those looking to exploit colour.

Spring days are longer than winter ones, which is great news, as is the fact that the days tend to be filled with more blue skies and less cloud. Saying that, spring is prone to bursts of rainfall (hence the phrase 'April showers'), but this is in itself a good thing as you've a good opportunity to capture rainbows, which are most common in this season. With rain also comes dew, so look to capture dewy still lifes in the morning – spider's webs are a favourite with many photographers. You'll need a camera/lens capable of close-ups to get the best result. In addition to webs, look for beads of dew on grass and leaves, shooting so that the subject is backlit, which will add a lovely sparkle to the dewdrops.

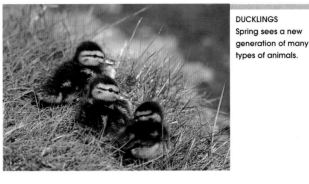

DUCKLINGS
Spring sees a new generation of many types of animals.

A drive through most rural areas should reveal potential scenes. Fields will be filled with flowers, be they poppies, buttercups or tulips. Woodland will also have its own vegetation springing up, such as snowdrops and daffodils. Use a wide-angle lens to include wide expanses of scenery, as well as for getting in low and close to blossoming flowers to emphasize their colours and blooms.

To bring out the colours of flowers, the lushness of green vegetation and the blues of a spring sky, you need – you guessed it – a polarizer. Although colours will probably look great without it, using a polarizer will add that little extra saturation to make your pictures stand out.

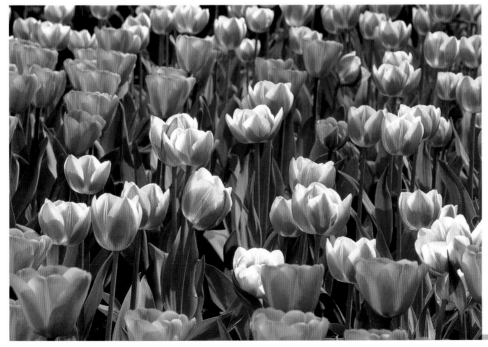

TULIP FIELD
Spring is the best season to capture flowers in bloom. When photographing flowers, it's worth researching where they are grown, to maximize your picture-taking potential.

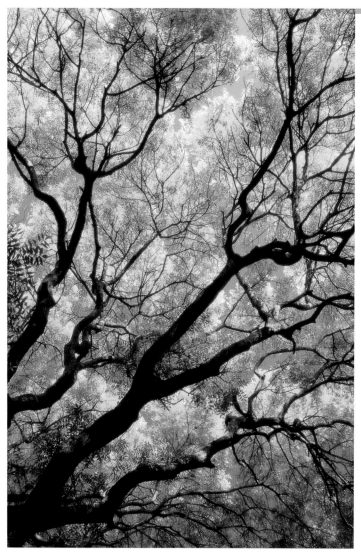

SKY THROUGH BRANCHES
Green and blue work well in photographs, and a polarizer helps to saturate colours.

Summer

For most landscape photographers, summer is the season to go out and take pictures. The weather is at its finest and most predictable, the days are at their longest, and the whole countryside is teeming with life and colour.

The polarizer comes into its own in this season and should become a semi-permanent fixture on the front of your lens. The summer is an excellent time to fill up your album with landscapes – the grass will never be greener and thicker, and the trees are at their glorious peak. As well as general landscapes, look for fields of colour – try to locate a field of sunflowers, as the bright yellow of their petals contrasts brilliantly with a clear blue sky.

In summer, the middle part of the day, when the sun is highest in the sky, isn't usually the best time for landscapes, so use this time to shoot still lifes and other subjects, and save your landscapes for the earlier and later parts of the day.

BEACH SCENE
Summer provides a great opportunity for candids on the beach or any other typical summer activity.

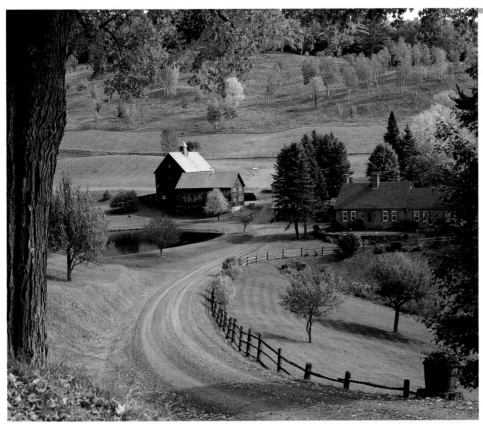

AUTUMN IN THE COUNTRY
In early autumn, you can capture the mix of the sumptuous greens of summer with the gorgeous gold of autumn leaves.

AUTUMN LEAVES
A diffusing filter blurs the highlights and adds an extra sparkle to the result.

Autumn

The prelude to winter is met with an amazing burst of colour as the landscape changes from green to gold. Autumn is a favourite season with many landscape photographers, who use the relatively short time when autumn's golden glory is evident to capture images worth their weight in gold. Although the autumn season lasts the same as any other, the actual time that the glorious colours of the changing leaves remains on trees and plants is very short – sometimes only a couple of weeks. So keep your eyes peeled on the changing colour of the landscape and join in with the gold rush.

In the UK, the best time to capture autumn is from mid-October to mid-November. At these times, you should aim to visit areas of natural beauty that are home to deciduous trees and vegetation, as these are the types that change colour. The actual technique to photographing them is the same as for shooting landscapes at other times of year, but because you have less time to work, you should plan ahead and be prepared.

The warm glow that is associated with shooting in the early morning or late afternoon is even more accentuated in the autumn, when the warm light adds further colour to the reds and gold of the autumn foliage. The long shadows cast by a low sun work well in wooded areas, so be sure to head into woodland as well as shooting it from the periphery.

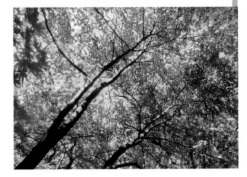

Although the colours will already be warm, consider using a warm-up filter now and again, as well as the trusty polarizer, which adds a complementary deep blue background to the scene.

This season more than any other, the vegetation that has fallen off the trees is as important as that remaining on it. The bed of golden leaves that you will encounter in woodland makes its own images – shoot natural still lifes of leaves carpeting the ground, as well as other objects, such as chestnuts and acorns.

Water

We live on the blue planet, with two-thirds of its surface covered by water, so we shouldn't really have any trouble finding suitably wet subjects to photograph. The options available are possibly even better than you originally thought.

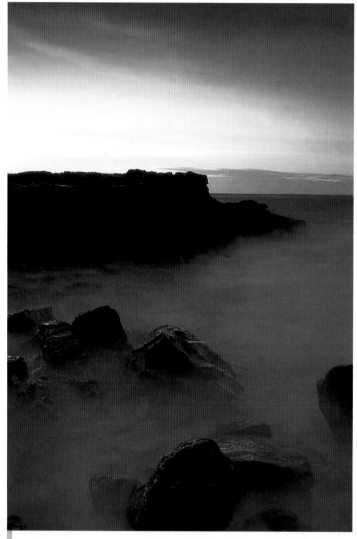

MOVING WATER
Using a very long exposure allows water's motion to be blurred to resemble mist.

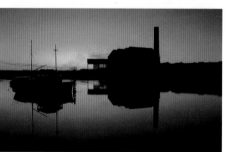

SUNSET
In tranquil weather, the stillness of water makes for the perfect reflective surface. Sunset is ideal for capturing reflections.

Water in the landscape

You shouldn't have to travel far to find water in landscapes. In the countryside you can find streams and rivers meandering through the scene, while in mountainous or hilly areas, waterfalls are fairly common. All of these subjects can be used as an important element in a scene, or, by getting closer, can become the main subject.

Even in urban areas, you should be able to find suitable subjects – in addition to rivers, many towns and cities have canals, while fountains are also commonly seen.

Rain can be a great subject for photography, and once a rainfall has died down or stopped, abstract images can be taken of subjects reflected in puddles. The impact of reflections in water shouldn't be ignored – scenes with lakes, rivers or other large water bodies gain an extra dimension through reflections, especially when strong colours are evident, such as during sunsets.

Coastlines arguably provide the photographer with the largest number of options, as the sea can be used as a backdrop to a sandy beach or a rugged, cliff-filled coastline. The sea looks even more dramatic in rough, stormy weather, when crashing waves can bring turbulent life and energy to the scene.

No matter where you live, or whatever the time of year, look out for the potential of the earth's greatest resource as the subject of your photography.

TOP TIP
A polarizing filter is very useful for photographing water, as it can be used to remove surface reflections.

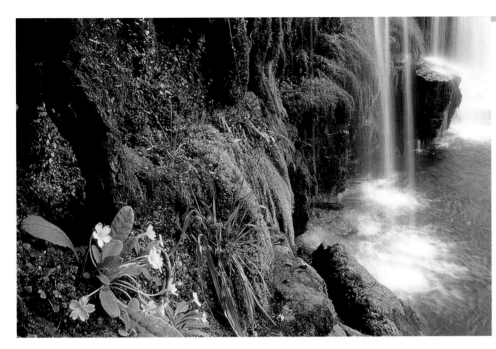

WATERFALL
An exposure of ¼sec was enough to blur the movement of the water.

Water in close-up

You don't need huge volumes of water for great shots – a single droplet of water can create an interesting close-up image. You can also use a water spray to create a multitude of droplets on a surface. After a rainfall, head out into the garden in search of rain droplets dripping from leaves or flower stalks, which can also make gorgeous close-up images.

Freeze it

Many photographers have discovered that freezing a subject in water can produce very interesting results. It's a simple process – place a recognizable small object in a bowl or tray of water and freeze it. Then take the chunk of ice out of its container, wait for the outer surface to defrost enough to reveal the subject, and photograph it.

Shutter speeds

The choice of shutter speed can have a major impact on how water appears in your images. A fast shutter speed can freeze movement – useful if you want to record individual droplets. Use a slow shutter speed, and the movement of water will be recorded as a blur – this can result in water taking on an ethereal appearance similar to fog or mist. A neutral density filter is a useful accessory if you want to use slow shutter speeds in bright light.

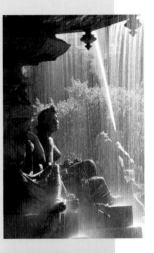

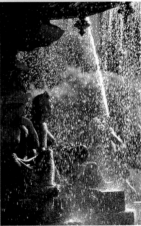

FOUNTAIN
These two images demonstrate the different effects that are possible by using a slow (top) or fast (bottom) shutter speed.

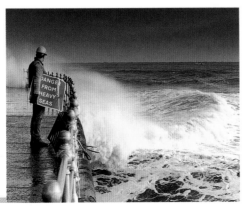

ROUGH SEA
In windy conditions, head for the coast to capture dramatic images.

Action

One of the hardest techniques to master is photographing a moving subject. Taking great shots of sport and action demands patience, skill and a small degree of luck.

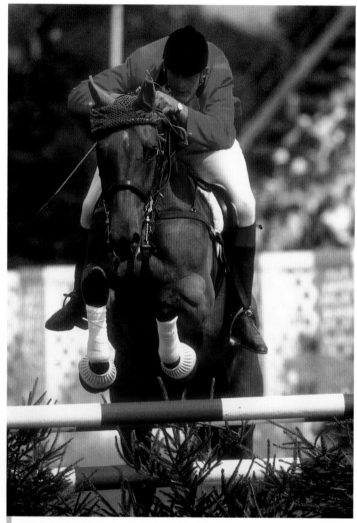

SHOW JUMPING
Prefocusing is a useful technique when subjects take a particular course. Here, prefocusing on the jump meant the photographer could concentrate on timing the exposure.

The key is timing

Whether taking pictures at a major sporting event or the local park, or of family and friends at play, the key to capturing a fast and frenetic moment comes down to mastering one key skill: timing. While some subjects, like landscapes or portraits, require the photographer to work relatively slowly, action photography demands fast thinking and fast working. The perfect moment may last for only a fraction of a second, so being ready to grab the moment is vital.

Mastering timing technique comes with practice and experience: you need to get the vital elements of exposure, focusing and composition working together for that split-second opportunity. It's not easy, but with practice you can greatly increase your rate of success.

Shutter speed techniques for action

How you capture action in an image depends in particular on the shutter speed you set. You must decide whether you want to freeze the action, in which case select a fast shutter speed, or intentionally use a slow shutter speed in order to create more of a sense of movement in the image by adding blur to the subject, the background, or both of them.

Get equipped for action

You will probably be some distance away from the subject, so use a camera that either has an integral lens with a good telephoto setting or fit a telephoto lens – a good choice is the versatile 70–300mm zoom.

Always leave some space in the frame around the subject, otherwise you run the risk of cropping them should they move erratically. Take a careful note of the shutter speed, to ensure that pictures aren't ruined by camera shake. You can increase the shutter speed with a fast film, such as ISO 400 or 800, or, in the case of digital cameras, uprate the ISO setting.

The success rate for action photography is relatively low, but you can increase your chances by shooting a sequence of images. Use a continuous shooting mode if you have one. SLR users can also fit an optional motordrive to boost the speed of the motordrive.

Freezing action

Freezing movement is the easiest technique to master, as essentially all you have to do is set a fast enough time to freeze any movement. Make sure that your camera or film has a high enough ISO rating to handle the conditions. The table at right provides examples of what shutter speeds you should set for particular subjects, depending on whether they are travelling across the frame or towards the camera.

Recommended shutter speeds		
Subject	Across frame	Towards camera
Runner	$\frac{1}{250}$sec	$\frac{1}{125}$sec
Trotting horse	$\frac{1}{250}$sec	$\frac{1}{125}$sec
Sprinter	$\frac{1}{500}$sec	$\frac{1}{250}$sec
Galloping horse	$\frac{1}{1000}$sec	$\frac{1}{250}$sec
Car (60mph)	$\frac{1}{1000}$sec	$\frac{1}{250}$sec
Motorsports	$\frac{1}{1000}$sec	$\frac{1}{500}$sec

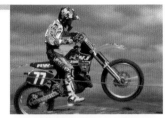

WHEELIE
Practise panning with a telephoto lens to capture images like this.

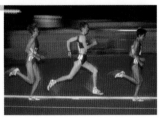

RUNNERS
Panning works well with slow-sync flash.

Using flash in action

For subjects that are relatively close to you, it's worth experimenting with adding flash to your images. By combining slow-sync flash with panning, you can create very dynamic images where the subject leaps out of the frame due to the extra exposure. This technique is widely used in cycling and motocross photography, and is well worth considering. Take care not to startle your subjects when using it, though!

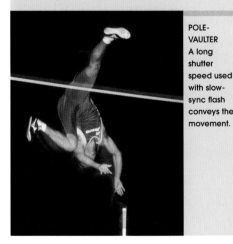

POLE-VAULTER
A long shutter speed used with slow-sync flash conveys the movement.

Panning

The other technique worth trying is to set a slower shutter speed and capture a real sense of movement. This is far more difficult, but is well worth persevering with, as the results can be very dynamic and exciting.

Panning involves keeping the moving subject in the frame, following its movement in the viewfinder, then firing the shutter release while continuing to track the subject. Get it right, and your image will show a sharp subject set against a blurred background. Even with relatively slow-moving subjects, the result can look extremely effective. The secret is to have a very smooth panning movement, so that the direction and speed you move the camera match that of the subject. For motorsports, try speeds of $\frac{1}{125}$–$\frac{1}{500}$sec. For athletics, anywhere from $\frac{1}{60}$sec for long-distance runners to $\frac{1}{125}$sec for sprinters is a good starting point.

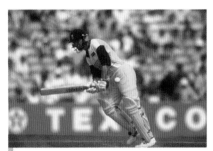

BATSMAN
Use a wide aperture to throw distracting backgrounds out of focus.

SPORTS

Motorsports
For maximum impact, always shoot cars or bikes coming towards you, rather than going away from you.

Tennis
Players usually have a style of play that means they tend to stick to particular parts of the court, such as the baseline. Exploit this by prefocusing on these areas.

Athletics
Rather than try to keep up with the action, prefocus on a particular part of the track and press the shutter release just before the subject reaches it.

Football
This is very difficult to photograph, so take advantage of set pieces like corners or free-kicks, when the action is less frenetic.

Still lifes

This term refers to photographs of static objects, usually arranged. Success is as much in the preparation of the subject as it is in the technical merits of the photographer. Form, shape and colour are key ingredients to still-life photography, but a keen eye to spot potential subjects is very important.

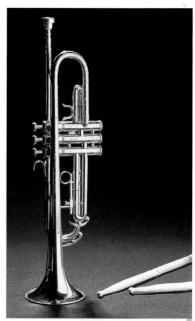

TRUMPET AND DRUMSTICKS
In this simple composition, everything, from the subject placement, to the choice of background and the lighting, have been planned to perfection.

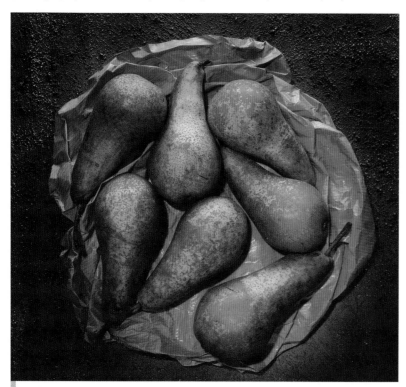

PEARS
Household items make great still lifes. The painting with light technique (see pages 160–61) makes a fantastic image.

Colour or black and white
The vast majority of still lifes are shot in colour. While shape and form are important, the contrast of colours between subjects can be very effective.

That said, monochrome images can also look very powerful, especially if they are made to look deliberately nostalgic – such as a shot of old toys – or if they feature subjects with strong textures.

What subjects are good for still lifes?
You don't need to look far for inspiration; every home is filled with objects which, when made the sole ingredient in a scene or mixed with other items, can create very interesting still-life images.

The kitchen is often a great place to start. Fruit and vegetables offer huge scope. You can arrange a group of identical fruits or mix and match them. Experiment to find potential images.

Almost any household item can be used to create a still life – bottles and jars are promising subjects, whether full or empty – while standard tools, such as a hammer, some old paint brushes or a pair of scissors, can work if you work with them imaginatively.

Step into the garden, and another assortment of subjects presents itself. Flowers are particularly popular, thanks to the many shapes and colours they come in: shoot one individual flower or set up a bunch in a jar – the options are endless. Rummaging around in the undergrowth can reap rewards, as leaves, acorns, chestnuts and berries all present themselves as ideal subjects.

When you start to think of what's available for the still-life photographer, it becomes clear that the creative options are endless. And because you can try this type of photography indoors, it's a good topic to try on cold or wet days when venturing outside is an unattractive option.

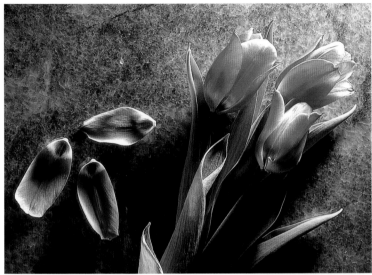

Backgrounds

The background of a still life plays a major part in its success. Keep it simple wherever possible, or use a background that complements the subject.

FLOWERS AND PETALS
Flowers make a popular still-life subject. Take time composing and lighting the scene, to create an imaginative and attractive result.

Found still lifes

This term refers to still-life images that are created using subjects that have been found, rather than set up. It's a more difficult discipline to master, as finding suitable subjects with appropriate lighting isn't easy, but it's worth testing yourself to see what you can achieve.

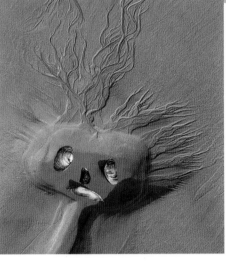

SAND FACE
Don't be afraid to have fun with photography. Here, natural patterns in the sand and a few well-placed shells create a humorous still life.

Still-life equipment tips

● A macro lens/facility is ideal for still-life photography, as it is invaluable for close compositions of smaller still-life objects, such as flowers, fruit and so on. That said, the range of a standard zoom is good enough for a wide variety of still lifes.

● More often than not, you will shoot still lifes indoors, so a tripod is a good idea, as shutter speeds will be relatively slow. While setting up a still life, check your composition through the viewfinder, knowing that the composition will not change. This is particularly useful when working with an intricate table-top arrangement.

● Window light is ideal, but studio lights are more controllable and always available, so it's worth thinking about investing in a one- or two-light outfit. You don't need anything powerful, so look at budget heads on offer.

BADGE
Look for detail shots of larger subjects.

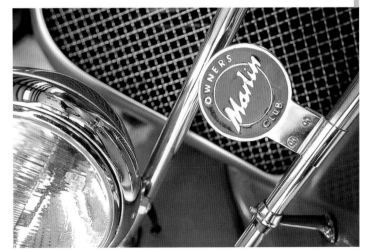

Fine art

Is photography an art form or a science? This argument rages on and on. One thing's for sure – photography can be a fine art.

Any picture that is taken as a creative exercise can be said to be an art form, in the same way that any painting or drawing can be classed as such. However, although it is impossible to define fine art, it is possible to point out subtle differences that allow some pictures to be clearly categorized as fine art. The first is that, invariably, fine-art pictures aim to be displayed and sold. The second is that fine-art images are very creative pieces of work that usually have a distinctive style, developed by the photographer. Finally, the production values of a fine-art picture are high, and the costs reflect the effort the photographer has put into creating the result.

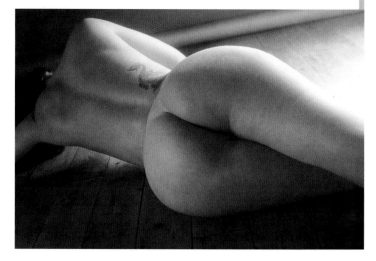

NUDE WITH TATTOO
Photographs that show the shape and form of the human body are a very popular subject.

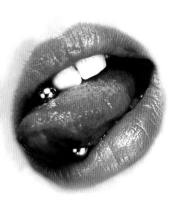

MOUTH
Successful fine-art photography often succeeds because it draws a reaction from the viewer. This simple but sexy shot is one example of an image that is pretty well guaranteed to receive different reactions.

Developing a style

As with any art form, developing your own style is crucial. There is nothing wrong with looking at the work of photographers you admire and adopting their style as a way to develop your own approach, but if you want to become a fine-art photographer in your own right, you must develop your own style. This could be in your choice of subject matter; how you compose, light or print your images; or how you decide to present your work. The key factor is that, to be recognized as a fine-art photographer, you must be confident in your own style – if your heart is really in what you are doing, the chances of success are higher.

Look for a particular theme and work around this, rather than trying to cover many different subjects. Decide whether you want to take a very classic approach or create your own abstract way of working. The key to success in fine art is to be individual and unique in your approach. You also need to be aware that your style may not be universally popular and so not commercially successful, but so long as you are satisfied with your work, you have achieved your aim.

What subjects suit fine art?

Any subject you can photograph has the potential to be a fine-art image. Your imagination and creativity are what will ultimately determine the standard of your fine-art work, not the actual subject matter. The most common subjects in the past have been portraits, nudes and still lifes, but you should not be afraid to experiment – by doing so, you will discover where you are strongest.

Digital or darkroom?

Traditionally, fine-art photographers also had a major part to play in the darkroom – in fact, some saw printing an image as more important to the final result than actually taking the photograph. In recent years, producing exhibition-quality prints from inkjet printers has become possible. The advantage to the photographer is that once the image has been digitally manipulated, the final print is much easier to achieve. From a collector's point of view, prints produced in the darkroom still hold more value, as each is unique.

Something that is very important to remember is that fine-art prints have traditionally been produced to be archival in quality – in other words to last more than a lifetime. While some inkjet prints claim to have archival properties, evidence suggests that chemically produced prints still have a longer lifespan.

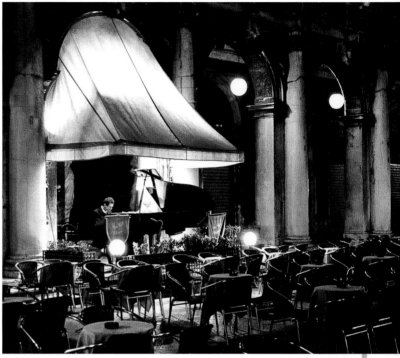

PIANIST
The mood and atmosphere created by monochrome make this medium a favourite. This image, by Bjorn Thomassen, was voted Fine Art Image of the Year 2003 by the British Institute of Professional Photography.

Colour or black and white?

Fine-art photography was for a long time the reserve of black-and-white prints, but colour work is becoming increasingly popular, in particular in the abstract market. Choosing between colour or black-and-white work is the prerogative of the photographer, and should be determined by the style and approach of the photography and the subject matter.

Selling your work

Some fine-art photographers take pictures with commercial interests in mind; for others, making money from their art is a secondary consideration. If you wish to pursue a career in fine-art photography, or simply wish to make extra money from your work, there are some considerations to be aware of.

Having an exhibition of your work is a little like the chicken-and-egg scenario: to be exhibited, your work needs to be well-known and respected, but to become well-known and respected, your work has to be exhibited.

Having your work displayed in a gallery is the ultimate exhibition. However, there are other ways to have your work seen by a larger audience. One tried and tested method is to send your work to a specialist photography magazine. Titles like UK-based *Photography*

Monthly showcase the work of aspiring, as well as established, photographers in every issue. Sending your work to a magazine is also a good way of gauging the standard of your work, as only the very best is published.

A relatively modern method is to set up your own website and exhibit your work on the Internet. Once it has been set up, a website is relatively easy to maintain and update – getting potential customers to visit your site in the first place is a different matter, but it's a good credential to own.

Finally, for your work to receive any form of praise, it must always be presented at the highest standard. The quality of the print and how it is mounted and framed are all crucial elements. If you neglect these areas, all the hard work and effort you spent on producing the image will be wasted.

Documentary photography

Some of the most recognized names in photography have been associated with the field of documentary photography or its associated discipline of photojournalism. In almost all cases, they worked exclusively in black and white.

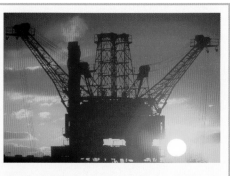

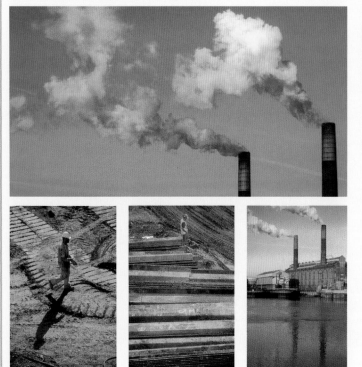

Photo story

Good documentary photography usually comes not from one image, but from an entire series. It's worth bearing this in mind and thinking about what theme to take. It could be something as simple as photographing people at your local market over a period of time, or even capturing life in your own household over the course of a year. A good photo story works by having a strong link between the pictures – be it a central character, a certain location or a particular ideology.

THEMES
Choose a theme on an aspect of local life. Here the theme is industry and its effect on the local environment.

If there was ever a need to demonstrate the merits of black-and-white photography, it would have to be documentary photography. Almost without exception, photographers throughout the decades have captured true-life moments of our lives through the medium of monochrome. Black and white is the perfect medium, because it tears away any distractions that might be imposed by colour and leaves us with the basic ingredients of the scene.

Documentary photography is one of the hardest disciplines to master, as you need to have a good eye for observation as well as composition – you need to be very aware of what is happening around you. Most people go about their daily business without paying too much attention to what is happening around them.

A good exercise to test your observation skills is to sketch your street. What shapes are the windows? How many cars are parked outside? Are there any lampposts, chimneys, pillarboxes or trees? When you start to think about it, it becomes clear that we see only what we need to see to get from A to B. To be a documentary photographer, you need to be aware of everything that is going on around you.

Another reason why documentary photography is not for the faint-hearted or impatient is the amount of effort you need to be prepared to go through to achieve great results. This isn't the type of photography you can do in a day, a week or even a month. Documenting life takes time, so any projects that you undertake will need to last some time.

In addition, because you will usually be photographing strangers, you need to be prepared for some people expressing their dislike of having their picture taken.

If you are willing to make these sacrifices, particularly with regards to the time required to cover a theme properly, then you have the potential to be a good documentary photographer.

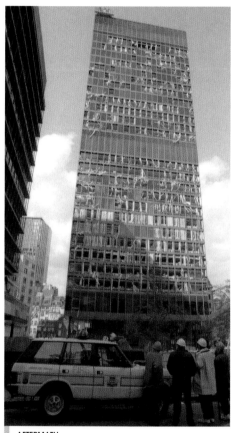

AFTERMATH
Major incidents are the bread and butter of the photojournalist. This image was taken in central London after a bomb explosion.

'The decisive moment'
This term is associated with legendary French photojournalist Henri Cartier-Bresson, who coined the phrase to describe capturing a particular moment in time.

Equipment for documentary photography
You need to work quickly in documentary photography, which is why many photographers over the years have used the Leica rangefinder camera. Most pictures include people in a scene, which makes a wide-angle lens the best choice. Because of its excellent depth of field, you can leave the lens preset at around 5m (16ft) and, so long as you have set an aperture of at least f/8 or f/11, you don't need to worry about sharpness.

Needless to say, black-and-white film is the order of the day for this type of photography. Use ISO 400 film, which will help keep your shutter speeds handholdable.

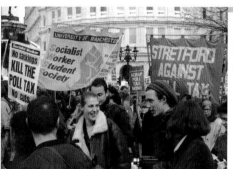

MARCH
Political marches are always worth covering, as the chance to capture historic protests is not to be missed.

Popular themes for documentary photography
Any sphere of life is suitable for documentary, but there are some themes that are particularly popular. They usually centre around people and how they interact with others.

Local life is a good starting point. Many photographers have documented their street or local area over a period in time to illustrate the local characters and their way of life. This is an interesting exercise, especially if you return to the same scene over a number of years, as you can build up a strong picture of how the society and environment changes over time.

Great documentary photography often stems from moments in time that are particularly terrifying or exciting. Political unrest, which results in rallies and protests, is ideal for the photojournalist to document, while capturing excitement or disappointment on faces watching a major sporting event is another classic observational moment. Be aware of when your subjects are likely to do something out of the ordinary, and be prepared to exploit it.

Although social documentary can be rather depressing, there is often a lot of humour to be found too. This may involve spotting quirky or mismatched and incongruous subjects, such as a small person walking a Great Dane, or a scruffy tramp looking at expensive suits in a shop window. As with other types of documentary photography, observation and working quickly, as well as a sharp sense of humour, are vital.

Architecture

Although buildings are constructed to serve a functional purpose, architects try to create as attractive a design as possible for both the interior and exterior. Old and new, big and small, industrial and residential – buildings come in many forms, each offering the photographer their own personality to capture. Taking pictures of buildings, or more specifically architecture, is an easy practice for most photographers to take up; and because buildings are static, you can take as long as you like to photograph them and return at your convenience to record their changing face during the course of the day.

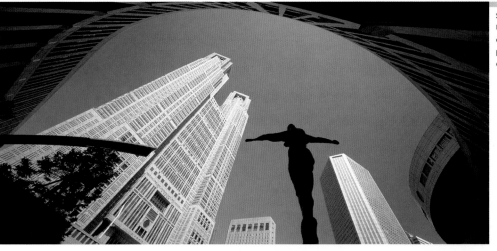

SKYSCRAPER
Use one structure as a frame when photographing other buildings.

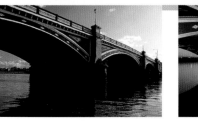 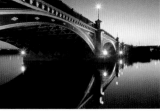

DAY AND NIGHT
What may appear ordinary during the day can take on a new lease of life after dark.

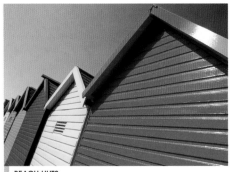

BEACH HUTS
Use shape and colour to good effect whenever possible.

TOP TIP
Churches and cathedrals make strong subjects, particularly when floodlit at night.

Day and night

The most important point to remember about photographing architecture is how the appearance of buildings changes over 24 hours. During the course of the day, the changing light not only means that the scene looks warmer at some times than at others, but also affects the direction and length of shadows. Depending on which direction a building faces, it could be in shade from neighbouring buildings for many hours of the day; east-facing buildings receive light in the morning, west-facing in the afternoon. When a building receives direct sunlight, you need to observe how the shadows cast by balconies, structural protrusions and other features help or hinder the scene.

At night, the scene takes on a completely different appearance. Streetlamps, light shining through windows and other forms of artificial lighting – in particular floodlighting – all help to provide a completely different look to a familiar structure.

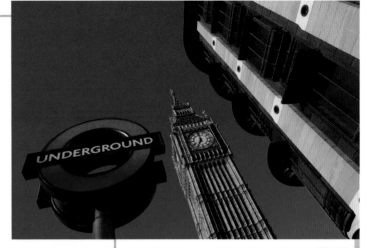

Converging verticals

This is used to describe how a building appears to be falling backwards in a picture, with the verticals converging towards the top, due to tilting the camera upwards when shooting.

Converging verticals can add drama to an image, but you can minimize the problem. Standing back and using a telephoto setting works well with strong foreground interest. Shooting from a higher viewpoint reduces how much you need to tilt the camera. Large-format cameras offer lens movements to correct this problem, while some SLR lenses offer perspective control, providing a similar solution. Some software can correct converging verticals on-screen.

BIG BEN
Point an ultra-wide-angle lens up to make buildings lean inwards.

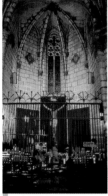

CHURCH
When shooting interiors, try to rely on the ambient light, rather than flash, as results are more natural and attractive.

Interiors

The interior of buildings can also make great photographs. With churches, the interiors make for stunning images, while he character of older buildings can be captured by a keen eye. If the location is artificially lit, you may need a filter; digital users should adjust the white balance. Due to limitations of space, the wider the focal length of the lens, the better.

Filters

Some filters can improve architectural images.
Polarizer: This reduces reflections in windows and increases colour saturation – dark blue skies make good backdrops.
Warm-up filter: Can lift the way brickwork is recorded by adding warmth.
80A (Blue): Use with daylight-balanced film when shooting interiors lit by tungsten lighting, unless you want a warm cast to your images.

Details

It's not only the entire building that you should consider photographing; take a look at architectural details, too. The arrangement of windows, pillars, arches, staircases and brickwork can all be used to form strong photographic compositions. While a wide-angle lens is more suited to capturing whole buildings, you will find that the telephoto end, along with a close-up facility, opens up new possibilities.

Take care!

Never photograph government-owned buildings or sensitive areas like airports without asking for permission first. In some countries, you can be imprisoned for doing so.

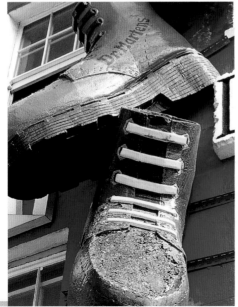

DMs
Look for unique or unusual details that could make an interesting image.

Night photography

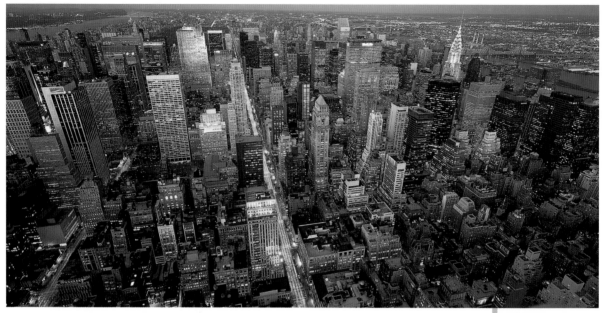

They say that the fun really begins after dark. The world takes on a different dimension when night falls, so be sure you know how to exploit it.

Night photography requires a different set of skills, as well as the right photo equipment, to perfectly capture its mood. Familiar scenes can take on a whole new feel and dimension at night, when artificial light sources mix with what little natural light is left to create some unusual and dazzling results. The long exposures that result from shooting in such low light conditions bring with them their own challenges, but if you are prepared for what's required, you'll be able to bring the night to life.

NEW YORK
Shooting at dusk has allowed the ambient light to be recorded so that it almost looks like a daytime shot. The lights on the buildings and the traffic trails give away at what time this picture was taken.

What to shoot at night?

Although rural localities offer great scope for photographers during daylight hours, it's urban areas that hold the most potential for taking night pictures. Buildings take on a completely different appearance at night, with artificial light creating bright, colourful images. Floodlit buildings can look very impressive at night. Other forms of artificial lighting that can make great images are neon signs: these will present you with a dazzling display of reds, blues and greens. It's a good idea to head anywhere that has large expanses of water, such as rivers, ponds or lakes – the reflections of night lights can add an extra dimension to such images.

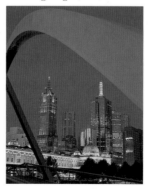

Essential night gear

Tripod
Due to very long exposure times, use a sturdy model that isn't going to shake in the wind or when heavy traffic passes nearby.

Remote release
Pressing the shutter release with your finger can result in slight (but potentially disastrous) camera shake at the start of the exposure. A remote release prevents this problem.

Torch
It may be difficult to see the controls at night, so keep a small torch in your gadget bag.

Warm clothing
Night brings with it a drop in temperature. Make sure to wrap up warm.

Night techniques

The most important thing you need to bear in mind is that you are going to be working with long exposures – we're talking several seconds here – so you need to ensure that the camera remains completely still while the shutter is open.

As for the exposure, if you're using a camera with an automatic flash, make sure it is switched off or the effect will be ruined. You can leave the camera to work out the exposure, but bracket it by +1 and +2 stops as it is a very difficult lighting situation for the camera to handle. Better still is to work in aperture priority mode. Set a mid-aperture such as f/8 or f/11 for optimum sharpness, then let the camera take care of the shutter speed. Again, use the exposure compensation facility and shoot extra frames at +1 and +2 stops.

With film, stick to slower speeds like ISO 50 or 100 for quality results. Don't worry about compensating for the colour casts from the artificial lights – these create the unusual colours you're looking for.

Finally, don't ignore the backdrop of the picture. If you shoot shortly after dusk, when there is still some colour left in the sky, this will appear on the image.

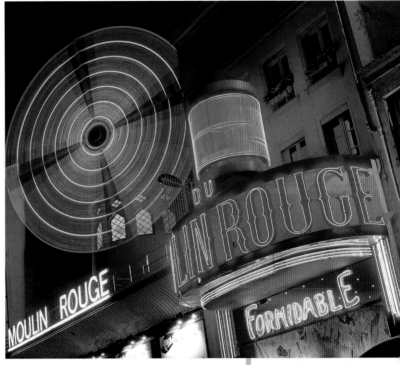

NEON LIGHTS
The Moulin Rouge is brought to life by giving the shot an exposure of several seconds.

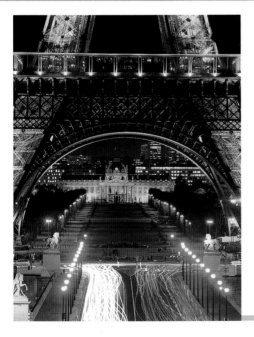

THROUGH THE TOWER
Even familiar landmarks can take on a completely different appearance at night. Here, the base of the Eiffel Tower frames a wonderful traffic trail beneath. This shot required an exposure of 30sec at f/13.

Traffic trails

The trails of light that emanate from car headlamps and rear lights can be used to add an extra creative element to night photography. Traffic trails are relatively easy to achieve: all you have to do is to ensure that you include a road or two in the frame. The longer the exposure, the longer the trails will be, and the more traffic there is, the more trails that will be recorded. Follow the technique guidelines you'd use for a normal night shot, but bear in mind that you will need to take up a decent viewpoint to capture the trails well.

A high viewpoint always works well, so look for a building, hill or bridge that you can shoot from. Whenever possible, have the traffic running into the frame, as opposed to across it, as the trails will be more defined this way.

Close-ups

Get into close-up photography, and you will discover a world within a world. Familiar objects take on a completely different appearance, while new, undiscovered subjects are revealed. Close-up photography is an area where having the proper equipment for the job is more important than ever.

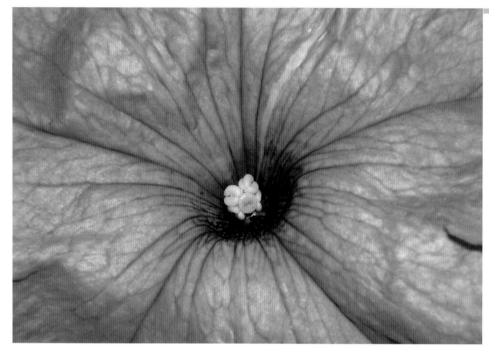

FLOWER CENTRE
The macro facilities of even modest digital compacts allow for very close focusing indeed.

Macro photography

Macro photography involves recording an image at least life-size. In this way, a coin that has a diameter of 10mm (⅜in) will appear on the film/sensor as the identical size in diameter. The reproduction ratio refers to how the subject's size on the image relates to its true size. A 1:1 ratio means life-size; 1:2 means half life-size; 1:4 a quarter life-size, and so on.

What subjects make good close-ups?

Almost anything is suitable. Close-ups of familiar subjects can reveal textures, patterns and shapes you wouldn't normally notice. Try natural objects like flowers, wood or leaves; small animals like insects; or close-ups of small parts of larger subjects, such as fruit or feathers.

Which SLR macro lens?

Many lenses boast a macro setting, but their reproduction ratios fall far short of life-size. True macro lenses have at worst a 1:2 reproduction ratio. The 105mm is the most common, with 50mm and 180mm lenses also being popular.

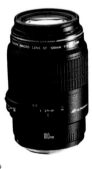

There are a small number of zooms, such as the Sigma 70–300mm, that offer a 1:2 ratio. These won't match a true macro lens for quality, but are a worthwhile consideration if you have a small budget.

Although different focal lengths may give the same reproduction ratio, they do offer one major difference: their working distance. This refers to the distance required to give the maximum reproduction ratio, referred to as the minimum focusing distance or working distance. The general rule is that the greater the working distance (in other words, the further the lens is from the subject to achieve the maximum reproduction ratio), the better. There are two main reasons for this. The first is that, when photographing small insects, the further away you are, the less likely you are to frighten them away. The second is that you are less likely to obscure the subject from the light or to cast a shadow across it.

Close-up techniques

Depth of field is far more limited in close-up work than in general shooting conditions, so focusing and the correct choice of aperture are vital.

Autofocus systems can struggle with the very short focusing distances involved, so if the option is available, set your camera to manual focus or single-point AF. Confirm the camera has focused by checking the AF confirmation (usually a green circle in the viewfinder).

If you can choose the aperture setting, choose the smallest f/number to maximize depth of field. Even this may only provide a tiny zone of sharpness, which will result in a slow shutter speed, so set the camera on a tripod or monopod. If shooting subjects like flowers outdoors, try to shield them from wind, as any movement will blur the result.

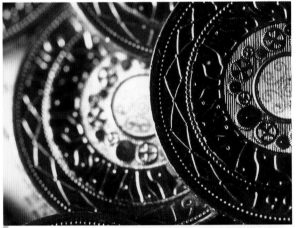

COINS
If you want to record small objects at high magnification, you'll need a dedicated macro facility or lens.

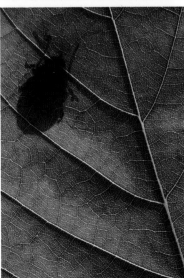

BEETLE ON LEAF
A little imagination and perfect composition can go a long way in close-up photography.

Close-up accessories

Various accessories are available to photographers to increase the close-up capabilities of their outfits. The main types are listed here.

Extension tubes

These tubes fit between a lens and the SLR body. By increasing the distance between the lens and the film/sensor, the result is an increase in magnification. This is a relatively low-cost option, with more expensive tubes offering electronic links to retain full communication between lens and camera.

Close-up filters

These screw to the thread of a lens and serve to increase the lens magnification. Various strengths are available, with the most popular being +1, +2 and +3. Close-up filters can be used together to combine their magnifying power.

Bellows

These are not so popular as they were a few decades ago, due to their size and limited features, but offer even higher magnification than extension tubes can manage.

Reversing rings

These rings allow lenses to be fitted back to front to provide high-magnification photography. The lack of communication between lens and camera gives the rings limited appeal.

Ring-flash

Due to the small working distances involved in close-up photography, lighting presents a major problem. Integral or hotshoe-mounted flashguns aren't suitable, so specialized flashguns, with tubes that circle the lens, have been developed. Similar models boast independent bulbs that can be positioned to provide precise directional light.

Patterns

The world is full of patterns, and you can find them everywhere you look. Some may take a little more searching for than others, but with a trained eye, you'll soon be able to spot them with ease and use them in your photography. Broadly speaking, you can divide patterns into two main types: the manmade and the natural.

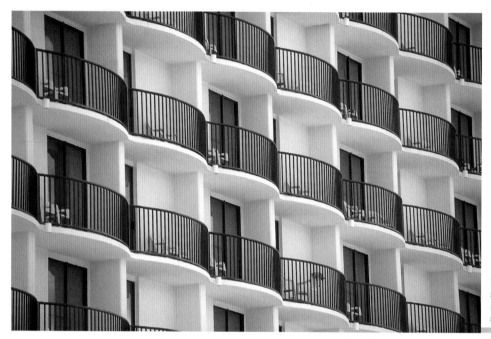

BALCONIES
Shooting from an angle reveals the curves of this series of hotel balconies.

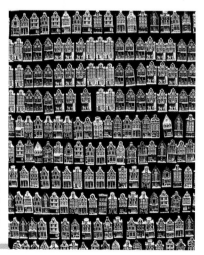

LITTLE DUTCH HOUSES
Look out for patterns everywhere you go – even fridge magnets on a market stall offer possibilities.

Is there a best lens for patterns?
Because patterns come in all shapes and sizes, there's no one particular lens of choice. However, a macro lens is a good option if you want to exploit the smaller patterns, such as a flower's petals. For more on close-up techniques, see pages 148-9.

Manmade patterns
Symmetry dominates the manmade world. Don't believe me? Then just have a look down your street. Are the buildings similar in size and shape? Has each got a symmetrical set of windows and doors? Looking even closer; are all the bricks put together on a symmetrical basis? Of course they are. And it doesn't stop there. Go inside a building and you'll see many patterns there too – the tiles on a floor, for example, the spiral of a staircase, or the arches of a cathedral roof.

Visit a market and you'll see patterns in fruit and vegetables; take a close look at a bouquet of flowers and you'll see some more. View a town or a village from high on a hill, and you'll see that the streets conform to a pattern. Even the cars in a car park conform to a tidy arrangement. The manmade world is full of patterns – you just need to identify them.

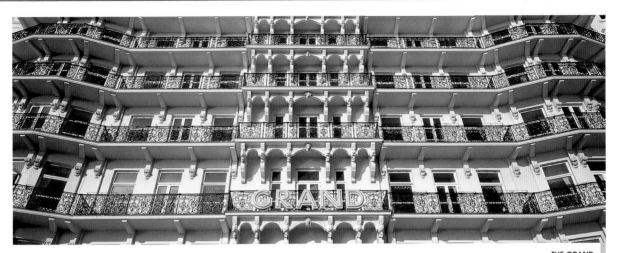

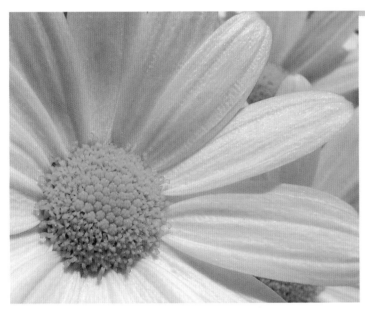

POLLEN
All flowers are the
source of many
natural patterns.

THE GRAND
The panoramic format
offered by the Hasselblad
XPan shows the majestic
patterns of a famous hotel in
Brighton, England.

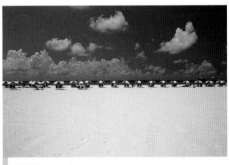

BEACH
This scene is filled with patterns, from the footprints in
the sand, through to the arrangement of blue and
white umbrellas and the puffy white clouds in the sky.

Natural patterns

Nature follows symmetry too, so you won't be short of subjects to photograph in the natural world. Usually, you need to get in close to a specific subject before the patterns become apparent. Take a flower like a gerbera, for instance – its petals form a uniform circle around its centre – there's one pattern for you to exploit. Pick up a leaf and examine it – can you see the intricate series of veins that run through it? There, you have another pattern to photograph.

As for a wider view of the natural world – you won't go short of patterns there. Visit a sandy beach, and you'll find ripples in the sand; visit a forest, and you've a pattern of trees to capture; a field full of poppies has its own colourful arrangement for you to enjoy, while every pond or lake has its own collection of ripples.

One additional pattern to consider is that created by shadows. Whenever strong side-lighting is evident in a scene, watch for the shadows that appear, as these can be used to form another interesting composition.

We're truly spoilt for choice when it comes to patterns, so start looking for them and you can build up a portfolio of patterns to enjoy.

Create your own patterns

The next time it's raining outside or a blizzard has snowed you in, use the time on your hands to create your own pattern pictures. Slice up some fruit, for instance, and photograph the pieces on a lightbox, or look around the home for anything you have a collection of that could form a pattern, such as coloured pencils or matchsticks.

Sunsets

The few minutes when day turns to night present photographers with an ideal opportunity to capture some of nature's most beautiful moments: sunsets.

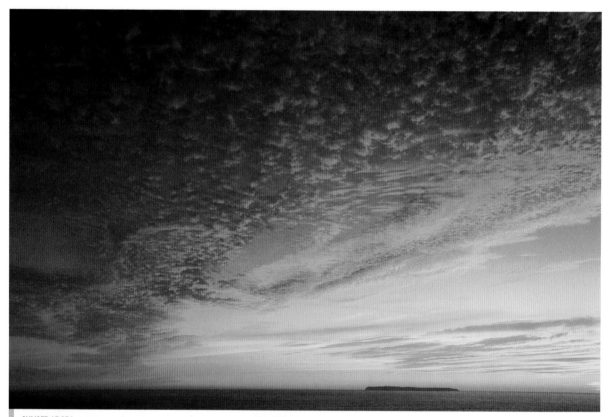

SUNSET AT SEA
Try to capture strong cloud formations at sunset, when they are transformed by the setting sun.

Shooting sunsets

There is very little to match a glorious sunset for sheer colour impact. When nature gets it right, the splendour of a sky filled with golden hues is hard to equal.

The secret to taking great sunset images is to plan them well in advance and to be set up ready to go well before the sun starts its final descent in the sky. First, you should find the right location: coastlines or any areas with large expanses of water, such as lakes and rivers, are ideal as they allow an unobstructed view of the sky and horizon, and also provide the added bonus of reflections on the water's surface.

Good foreground interest is important. A frame-filling sunset is attractive, but will look even more spectacular if it forms the backdrop to fantastic scenery, such as a village or coastline. You will often find that because you are exposing for the relatively bright backdrop, the foreground will tend to record relatively dark, so it is important to choose subjects that have distinctive shapes that work well as silhouettes – boats, rocks and churches are good options. You can get around this by using a graduate filter (see page 98).

Bear in mind that you will only see the sun sink below the horizon in flat areas or at the coastline – shoot inland and it's likely that the sun will disappear behind a hill long before it reaches the horizon.

Once you've decided on the location, you should find out at what time the sunset takes place. Most national and local newspapers will provide information on sunset times for your area.

Equipment

Any type of camera can be used to photograph sunsets. You are likely to want to include a fair amount of scenery in the frame, so you will need to use a wide-angle lens to capture some foreground details as well as large expanses of sky. If you are using an SLR, you will have the advantage of being able to fit filters to the lens, but this is not always essential.

Because the exposure will be quite slow, handholding the camera presents the risk of camera shake, so you should take along a tripod or other camera support to provide a steady platform to work from.

If you're using film, you should choose a slow-speed film that can record stronger, saturated colours to do full justice to the scene. Fuji Velvia and Kodak Elite Chrome Extra Colour are good choices for slide film, while Fuji Superia 100 or Agfa Ultra are recommended for prints.

Exposures

Sunsets can present problems for exposure systems, due to the wide range of contrast between the bright sky and dark foreground, but there are various ways to ensure that you have the correct exposure. If you're shooting digitally, you can check the screen, but this isn't completely foolproof, so try out the following methods.

The first technique is to shoot at the camera's recommended exposure and then bracket in 1EV-increments 1 and 2 stops over. If your camera has a partial or spot-meter facility, you can get an accurate exposure by taking a reading from a mid-tone in the scene.

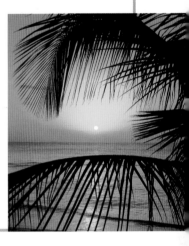

Look to take your reading from an area of the sky that falls midway in brightness between the area closest to the sun and the darkest part. If you're still unsure, take an exposure reading of the brightest and darkest areas and shoot at the average of the two. You could also use a reading from the foreground, although you should use a graduate filter to prevent the sky from burning out in the frame.

Filter choice

Two or three filters can be considered for photographing sunsets. A warm-up (81 series) or even an orange filter can be used when the colours in the sunset are weak. Some manufacturers produce an orange graduate sunset filter, as well as a range of colour graduates aimed at intensifying the colours in the sky.

If colours are naturally strong, a grey graduate can be used. It's a good choice if you lock the meter reading from the foreground, otherwise the exposure will result in a pale or burned-out sky due to overexposure.

Finally, a diffuser can help to add a soft and romantic feel to sunsets. It can be used on its own or alongside another filter.

The weather conditions will dictate the intensity of the sunset and determine whether or not you should use a filter to enhance the colours. If the sky is naturally rich in golden hues, it's best not to overdo things by using a filter. If you decide to do so, always take an unfiltered shot, just in case.

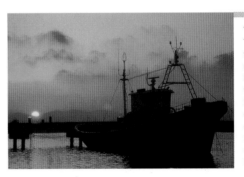

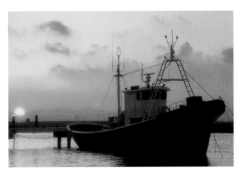

TRAWLER
These two pictures show the difference a filter makes. The image below left is unfiltered, and while the sunset in the backdrop is pleasant, the colours are weak. Using a Cokin orange filter, as in the image on the left, adds a boost to the scene giving it far more impact.

TOP TIP
Search engines such as www.google.com can be used to find sites that offer sunrise/sunset times for most areas around the world.

Travel

Visiting new locations, be they in the same country that you live in or abroad, offers an exciting potential for capturing new images. Because you may visit some places only once, be ready to take advantage of what is a once-in-a-lifetime opportunity.

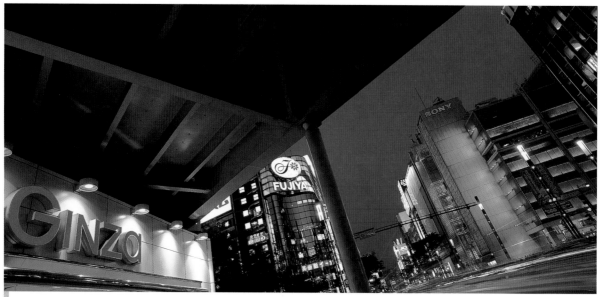

TOKYO
Architecture reflects a country's culture. Make sure you capture its distinctive style.

TOP TIP
A great space-saving tip for film users is to seal two slide boxes together with tape and place films inside.

Research

Good travel photographers plan much of what they will photograph well in advance of the trip. This can involve guide books, such as the *Lonely Planet*, *Rough Guide* or *Blue Guide* series, which are excellent for finding out the locations that offer the best opportunities. The Internet, with its potential for information resource, is another port of call for gathering information on places that you plan to visit.

In addition to researching locations, check to see whether any special events are taking place when you travel. Festivals and fairs offer enormous potential for photography, so don't miss out on these colourful and lively occasions.

Travel gear

Only take what you need. Be very disciplined on what photo kit you take abroad with you. It's pointless packing your entire outfit when you are only going to use 20 per cent of it on your trip.

Camera: An obvious inclusion, but before you travel, make sure it is working properly and you have packed spare batteries.

Film/memory cards: Have you packed enough for your trip? You might be able to buy more supplies abroad, but is it worth the risk when they take up only a small space in your luggage?

Filters: Another accessory that takes up hardly any room and weighs next to nothing. The minimum should be a polarizer and a warm-up filter.

Tripod: It's worth packing a very lightweight or table-top tripod, which will allow you to shoot night scenes.

Photo backpack: Invest in a small backpack, which provides protection for your gear and holds items like maps and snacks. The Lowepro Orion Trekker is an ideal choice.

Lenses: Zooms are best. Packing an ultra wide-angle and a telezoom covers most focal lengths. A macro lens is also useful.

Lens hood: SLR users should not travel without an appropriate hood for each lens.

Clear plastic bags: Pack your gear in these to prevent condensation forming on equipment.

Capture the culture

The best travel pictures are those that reveal the culture of the areas that you visit. The three key subjects you should try to capture on camera are landscapes, architecture and people.

Landscapes offer the best potential when you visit a climate unlike what you are used to at home. It's unlikely that you have large expanses of desert or a Caribbean beach with overhanging palms around the corner, so make sure you make an effort to capture the landscape of the country you visit.

Architecture can reveal much about the history of the location. Churches and other places of worship are excellent places to practise your architectural skills. After shooting the exterior, head inside – but make sure you gain permission first, and leave a donation as a gesture of thanks. Famous landmarks are obvious subjects to photograph. Take a look at postcards to find the best angles to shoot from, then try to be different and look for unusual ways of capturing a familiar scene. Break off from the beaten track and take long walks through the quieter streets – here you'll find the real character of local architecture.

As well as using a wide-angle to include the whole building in a scene, use a telephoto to pick out details, such as intricate statuettes outside a temple, or use perspective compression to make buildings appear stacked against each other.

Nothing exudes the culture of a race more than its people, from the differences in skin tones, hair colour and eye shape, to the variety of clothes and costumes. Look to capture people in traditional outfits – some are happy to pose if you ask them; others request money, which seems a fair trade if you get a decent picture. Visiting local markets provides enormous potential for colourful compositions, candids and environmental portraits, as do ports and harbours, where you can look for fishermen emptying nets and traders bartering over produce.

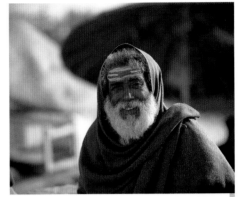

SADDHU
A true travel portrait includes the subject's culture, such as religious or tribal facial markings, clothes and jewellery.

X-ray machines

X-ray machines are a concern for both film and digital users, but in reality, the risk to either medium is low. Storage cards are least at risk – accounts by travel photographers state that X-rays do no harm to the cards. Film users should take a little more care and pack films in hand luggage. In fact, only high-speed emulsions (ISO 1600+) run any risk of fogging, and even then, the chances are very slim.

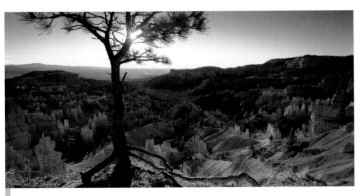

BRYCE CANYON
Some places have a unique landscape, making them ideal for travel pictures.

Use your time wisely

Planning what you will photograph during the course of each day ensures that you make full use of every available hour.

Mornings and late afternoons usually have the best light, so use the opportunities to photograph landscapes or wander around the area you are staying in and capture the architecture.

During the middle of the day, when the light is at its least attractive, look to capture details in the landscape or photograph the locals. While you're out and about, look around for ideal locations to shoot sunsets – areas with large bodies of water, such as coastlines, are ideal.

Special effects

Like them or loathe them, special effects are here to stay. In fact, with image-manipulation software so readily available, special effects have never been so popular. This section looks at what special effects are available to the photographer using the camera, as opposed to the image manipulator on their computer.

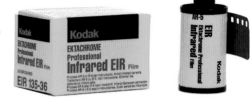

Infrared film

While most films record light in the visible spectrum, some films break convention and are also able to record infrared light. Infrared film is available in both colour and black-and-white forms, both of which are capable of incredible results.

As you'd expect, using this type of film isn't straightforward. First, it has no film speed rating, as its sensitivity varies according to the amount of infrared radiation. Also, to get the best results, you need to fit a filter to exclude light from the visible spectrum. Another point to bear in mind is that camera meters cannot be relied upon, as they cannot measure infrared radiation. Finally, infrared light focuses at a different point to visible light, so you have to take this into consideration, too.

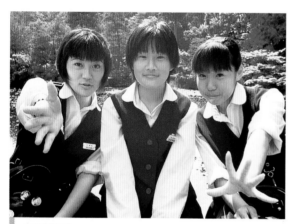

GIRLFRIENDS
Colour infrared isn't for shooting flattering portraits, but is an interesting film to try if you're after a wacky effect.

Focusing with infrared film

Infrared radiation is longer in wavelength than visible radiation, so it focuses at a different plane to visible light. If you are using a wide-angle lens with the aperture at a mid or small setting, say f/8–f/16, the depth of field is sufficient. However, if you are shooting with a telephoto lens, focus at a slightly further focusing point than is recommended.

Colour infrared

If you want to try out colour infrared, you're limited to a choice of only one film: Kodak Ektachrome Infrared slide film, or EIR for short. It is a very specialist emulsion, so stores won't generally stock it. If you need any, you will have to order it well in advance. Also bear in mind that it is expensive – normally around two to three times what you would expect to pay for a colour slide film. However, the results that can be achieved from the film are amazing.

Most photographers using colour infrared film set the camera to ISO 200 as a starting point, and then shoot a sequence at +1 and +2 stops.

Personal preference will teach you which filters you prefer, but the most popular are red, orange, yellow and sepia. Shoot without a filter, and your slides will exhibit a strong green cast; use a red and the skies take on a dark blue colour, while foliage appears red.

Ektachrome film is processed in standard E-6 chemistry, but ensure that the film is unloaded from the camera in complete darkness and remains in the tub at all times. Also make sure the processing lab knows how to handle it.

Warning – handle with care!
Take an infrared film canister out of the light-tight tub that it is supplied in, and it's ruined. This type of film is extremely sensitive to infrared radiation; so much so that it can be loaded into a camera only in complete darkness. Even dim light can fog the film, so your best bet is to invest in a film-changing bag, which allows you to load a camera in daylight without fogging it.

TOP TIP
For comprehensive details on Kodak infrared film, including further details on exposure, filters and how to develop the film, visit www.kodak.com

Infrared films

In addition to the two Kodak films, infrared emulsions are available from Konica and Ilford. Konica 750 Infrared has a recommended speed of ISO 32 and finer grain than the Kodak, but with sensitivity only up to 900 nanometres, the results are not as strong. Ilford SFX is an ISO 200 black-and-white film with an extended red sensitivity. Its results fall far short of the Kodak in terms of infrared sensitivity.

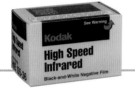

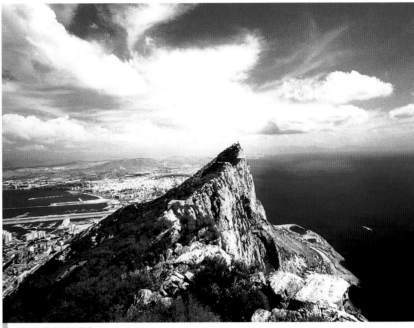

ROCK OF GIBRALTAR
Colour infrared gives distinctive results that can be very dramatic in the right circumstances.

Black-and-white infrared

For ethereal results, there is nothing to touch black-and-white infrared images: foliage records as a ghostly white, skies become a foreboding black mass, and skin tones take on a pallid grey tone. There is more of a choice when it comes to mono infrared, but the clear favourite is another Kodak emulsion – High Speed Infrared – which is sensitive to 900 nanometres, well into the infrared range.

Although there is no ISO rating, most photographers rate the film at values between ISO 10 and ISO 200. As a starting point, set the camera to ISO 50. Use a red filter and you have the advantage that this enables you to use the viewfinder to compose, as it allows red light, as well as infrared, to pass through. You can also use the camera's meter, although you should take extra exposures at +1, +2 and +3 stops. If you want the strongest possible infrared effect on your pictures, you need to use an opaque filter, such as a Kodak Wratten 87C or 89B. The disadvantage of this type of filter is that you will not be able to view the scene with it in place, so you need to compose the image first, and then attach the filter.

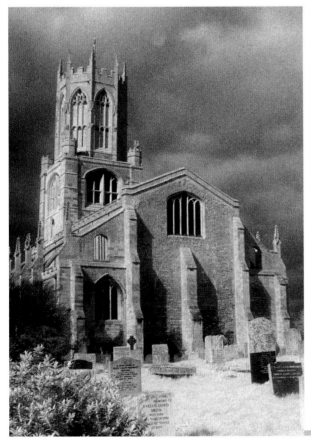

GRAVEYARD
Although not as straightforward to use as conventional film, the unusual characteristics of mono infrared make it worth the effort.

Multiple exposures

Many cameras offer a multiple-exposure facility, which allows you to shoot more than one exposure on the same frame by disengaging the film transport system. With many cameras, you can shoot up to nine exposures on one frame, although it is doubtful that you would require more than two exposures on a frame.

Multiple exposures offer endless possibilities, especially if you use a camera with interchangeable lenses. For instance, you could use a telephoto to capture a magnified image of the moon, then superimpose this with a wide-angle shot of a landscape. Alternatively, you could photograph someone on one side of the frame, then capture them on the other.

If you are shooting with film, bear in mind that you will be exposing the same frame more than once. For a double exposure, you should set the exposure compensation to +1 stop.

Multiple exposures may be easy to do in-camera, but facilities like Layers in Photoshop make them simpler to achieve using image-manipulation techniques.

MULTIPLE EXPOSURES
When shot on the same frame, the image of the moon is superimposed on to the image of the landscape.

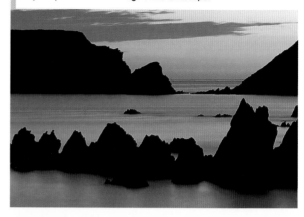

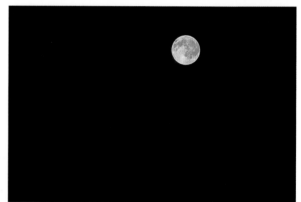

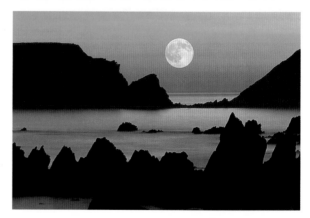

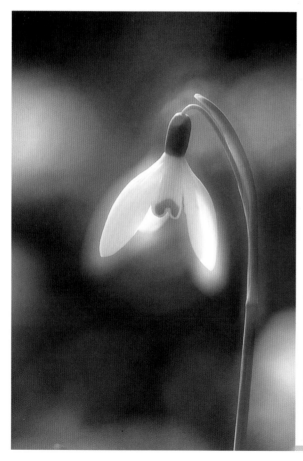

SNOWDROP
Shooting two exposures on the same frame, one in focus, the other out of focus, can yield very interesting results.

TOP TIP
Most high-street labs will not cross-process film – check your local phone directory for a pro lab, which is more likely to offer this service.

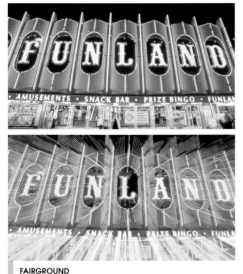

FAIRGROUND
These images were shot on a 35–80mm zoom, the top one normally, the bottom one by zooming the lens.

Zoom burst

Dramatic images are possible by zooming the lens during an exposure. This is only possible with SLRs, as compacts do not allow their zooms to change focal length during an exposure.

The basic technique is relatively easy to learn. First set the camera to a relatively long exposure that will allow you enough time to zoom from one extreme of the range to the other – an exposure of around ⅛sec is a good place to start – then try longer exposure to vary the results. A tripod or other camera support is recommended to keep the camera steady and free up your hands, so that your zoom movement is as smooth as possible.

Standard zooms of 28–90mm are a good choice, as they offer a decent range from wide-angle to short telephoto. Try a zoom burst from one end of the range to the other, and then work in the opposite direction – the results are very different.

Look for colourful subjects, but don't choose a scene that's too busy, especially when you start. Static subjects, such as buildings, signs and flowers, are good choices.

Cross-polarization

Some beautiful effects are hidden from the human eye but become visible when a simple technique is applied. In the case of cross-polarization, using polarizing material (such as filters) in the right way reveals the stress patterns inherent in plastic objects.

To try out this technique, you need a camera, a polarizing filter, a sheet of polarizing gel (available from major camera dealers) and a lightbox. Place the polarizing gel on the lightbox and carefully arrange the plastic objects on it. Attach a polarizing filter to the lens, set the camera on a tripod and compose the frame so that the objects are positioned where you'd like them to be. Switch the lightbox on and the room lights off, then look through the viewfinder and rotate the polarizer until you achieve the desired effect.

Suitable objects include CD cases, school geometry sets and anything else made of clear plastic. Because of the relatively small size, a lens with a decent close focus, such as a macro lens, is recommended.

Cross-processing

This technique involves deliberately processing your film in the wrong chemistry to produce unusual colour characteristics in your image. This means having your print film developed in E-6 slide chemistry to produce slides, or putting your slide film through the C-41 process to produce colour negatives for prints.

Processing print film to make slides generally produces muted colours, so it is better to shoot slide film and have it processed in C-41 chemistry. This can result in prints with high contrast and strong colour saturation, as well as more evident grain. Cross-processing has gained popularity in recent years, in particular with fashion photographers. The effect varies from film to film, and even using different processing labs can mean differing results, so experimentation is required. Films worth trying are Fuji Velvia, Kodak Elite Chrome 100 Extra Colour and Agfa RSXII 100.

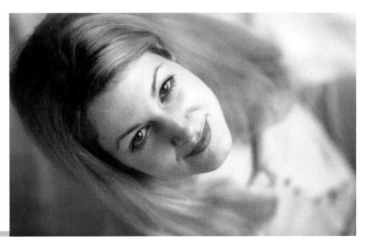

ANGLED PORTRAIT
Cross-processing film can radically alter the colour characteristics of your subject. Fashion and portrait photographers often favour this technique.

Painting with light

Techniques don't come much more surreal than painting with light, a method of using a long exposure with an artificial light source to create amazing results.

The theory behind painting with light is very simple – you take pictures in near or total darkness, set a very long exposure – we're talking times of 30sec to several minutes – and move an artificial light source (such as a torch or flashgun) around to illuminate a scene. The result is an image that has a surreal feel to it, caused by the uneven illumination of the artificial light source, often combined with any ambient light.

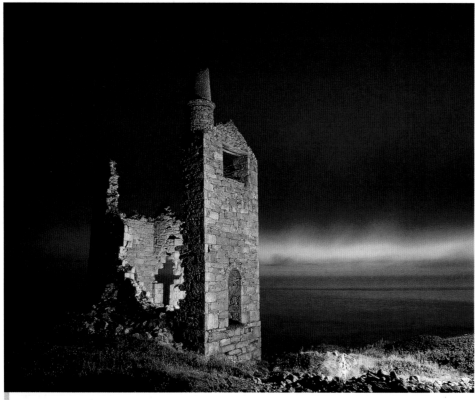

RUINED HOUSE
For large structures, you need to set an exposure of a few minutes to give you enough time to light up the scene. Shoot not too long after sundown to record detail in the backdrop.

How to paint with light

As bizarre as the technique sounds, the results are well worth the effort, as the images shown here clearly illustrate. The good news is that painting by light isn't too difficult to attempt; it is simply a case of trial and error. Fortunately, digital cameras allow you to check each exposure in turn, so that you can see what you are doing right and where you are going wrong.

The way you shoot varies slightly depending on whether you are taking pictures of small objects with a torch or large subjects with a flashgun; however, some factors remain the same. You need to set the camera to a long exposure. Start with a shutter speed of 30sec, then one minute, then two minutes. Alternatively, set the camera to its Bulb or Time facility, if it has one.

Mount the camera on a very sturdy tripod, set a mid-aperture such as f/8 or f/11, and focus manually to ensure sharp results.

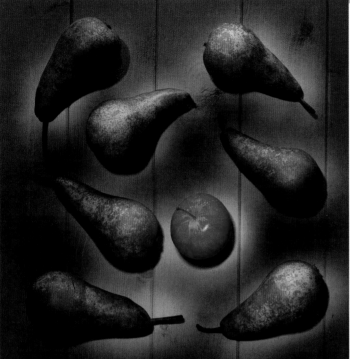

PEARS AND APPLE
You can draw attention to particular areas of a scene by keeping the light source on it for longer than others – here, the apple has been highlighted.

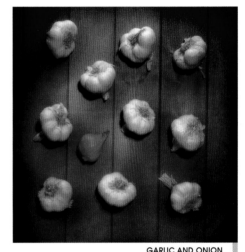

GARLIC AND ONION
You don't need anything fancy to try out painting with light – a standard camera kit, a torch and a few household items are all that is required.

If using a torch to paint small subjects, practise the routine in daylight so that when you work in darkness you have a better idea of how to paint your entire subject. Remember that you want to illuminate the whole scene and give particular emphasis to certain areas by painting them more than once. Use a slow, smooth movement to ensure the subjects are well-illuminated. If shooting subjects like fruit, circle the outlines to emphasize their form.

If working with flashguns outdoors, you will need to fire the flash far more times than you think necessary to get a decent exposure. Make sure you give emphasis to certain areas by giving them multiple flashes. Keep moving, or you risk recording yourself if you stand still. If you've a lot of ground to cover, ask friends to help.

The whole process behind painting with light is a hit-and-miss affair. Practising the technique will teach you what exposures work best and how you should light the scene, but you will never get the same result twice, so it's a great technique to return to.

Advanced techniques

As you become more proficient in this technique, try advanced techniques, such as mixing light sources or using filters. For instance, with still-life subjects, you could give a low-power burst of flash at the start of the exposure and use the torch for the remaining time to create different effects. With filters, by firing a flash through a colour filter, you can add an extra dimension to how your subject is illuminated. Remember, there are no hard and fast rules – experimentation will reveal its own rewards.

Light painting tips

Keep a notebook handy and record all your exposure details, so when you return to shoot similar scenes, you have a far better understanding of where to begin.

When photographing close-ups, bear in mind that the nearer the light source is to the subject, or the longer you illuminate it, the brighter it will appear on the final exposure.

If using a torch, fit a snoot made from white card around the head of the torch to give a more direct direction to the beam; this will give more defined light trails on the exposure.

When shooting large subjects, such as buildings, have more than one flashgun handy so that there is no delay while you wait for each one to recharge.

After the photo
Photo clinic

Have you looked through your pictures and spotted something that shouldn't be there?

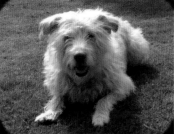

◄Vignetting

Very dark or black edges signify something encroaching on the periphery of the lens. This problem predominantly occurs with wide-angle lenses, especially when set to the widest or smallest apertures.

Solution: Make sure you use the recommended lens hood. Avoid using a wide or small aperture – sticking to f/8 or f/11 usually avoids the problem. Stop using a combination of filters at the same time.

Flare ►

Bright streaks or spots in the image.
Solution: The result of light bouncing around in the lens. Best avoided by using a lens hood or shielding the lens with your hand, to help keep the light source out of the frame.

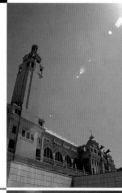

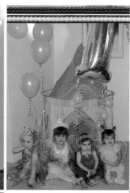

◄Corrupted digital images

Part or all of the image appears as a messy pattern of noise.
Solution: Reshoot the scene.

Fogging ►

A bleached white or red patch appears across part or all of the image.
Solution: Load film in low light, or with infrared film, in a light-tight changing bag.

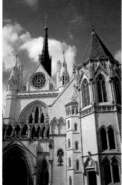

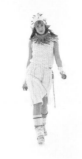

◄ Overexposure

The image appears too light.
Solution: Reduce the exposure compensation, or take a selective reading from a mid-tone.

Underexposure ►

The image appears too dark.
Solution:
Add exposure compensation or take a selective reading from a mid-tone.

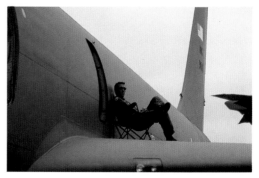

▼ Image exhibits colour cast due to artificial lighting

Film users: Use appropriate film or filters.
Digital users: Use appropriate white balance setting or filters.

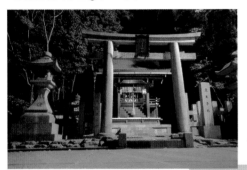

Camera clinic: looking after your camera gear

- If you're not planning to use your gear for a while, remove batteries and store cameras, lenses and flashguns in see-through polythene bags to protect them from moisture – this is also useful when travelling.
- Only clean lenses with a suitable lens cloth.
- Avoid getting sand or water on the camera. If sea spray showers your camera, wipe it with a slightly dampened tissue, which will absorb any salt.
- Keep camera kit in a well-padded bag, and avoid bumps and knocks.
- Always keep optics protected by fitting a cap over exposed elements.

Camera shake ▶

The image appears blurred, as if the whole scene has moved during the exposure.
Solution: Use a faster shutter speed, rest the camera on a steady surface, or switch on the flash.

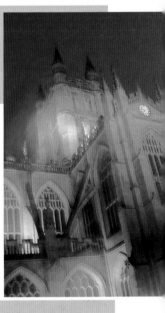

▼ Poor focus

The subject appears unsharp.
Solution: Make sure the autofocus is engaged and working properly. Use manual focus if AF falters.

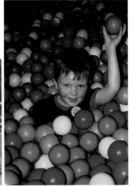

◀ Dark flash exposures

Flash exposures make subject/scene appear dark.
Solution: This is usually the result of the subject being too far from the flash. Move closer, or fit the camera on a tripod (or steady surface) and use slow-sync mode.

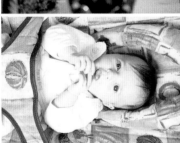

◀ Distortion

Using a wide-angle lens, the subject is distorted, with straight lines appearing to be curved.
Solution: Move away from the subject, and/or stop using a wide-angle and employ a focal length of 50mm or more.

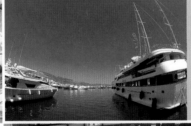

▲ Bleached flash exposure

Flash exposures make subject appear bleached white.
Solution: This is usually the result of the subject being too close to the flash, so increase the subject-to-flash distance.

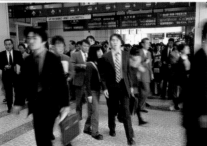

◀ Blurred subject

Moving subjects appeared blurred.
Solution: Use a faster shutter speed to freeze subject movement.

Storing and displaying pictures

After spending time, money and effort on taking decent pictures, it seems a shame to leave them in a drawer or on a hard disk, never to see the light of day again. There are now many wonderful ways in which to exhibit your work.

Photo lab services

The two most popular traditional photo services are reprints and enlargements. Most high street and mail-order labs have offered these services for decades. Many now offer a service that accepts damaged or faded prints, and uses digital manipulation to correct colour casts, tears, scratches and stains.

The Picture CD service has become increasingly popular. Along with a set of prints, the pictures from the film are scanned and stored on a CD-ROM. There are usually at least two folders featuring the images at different resolutions – low-resolution for sending with emails, high-resolution for future reprints.

Personalized products

Most labs offering processing services often have ranges of various personalized products. These range from having your pictures placed on T-shirts, mouse mats, greetings cards and jigsaws. In the UK, you can also have Smilers stamps issued, which feature a picture of your choice.

Picture storage and archiving

Photographs should be stored in particular conditions to maximize their life span.

The two biggest dangers to film emulsion are light and moisture, which can cause irreparable damage. A very simple procedure to minimize harm is to store slides, negatives and prints in a cool, dark and damp-free environment – a drawer or cabinet is ideal.

Direct sunlight will fade colours in prints, so if you have exhibited in frames, bear this in mind when working out where to place them.

When placing pictures in albums or slides in sleeves, look for products with a corrosion-free label. Some plastics, such as PVC, contain acids that can damage the emulsion over a number of years. Negative and slide sleeves made from acid-free polypropylene are the best choices.

You should always back your images onto two CD-ROMs. Work from one and keep the other as a master. Tests have discovered that CD-ROMs can become unreliable after a number of years, with cheaper makes proving most susceptible to failure. Therefore, try to use well-known and reliable brands of CD-ROM.

Personalized art

The advent of digital photography has brought with it many creative options on how pictures can be exhibited. In particular, there is now a vast number of personalized art services that allow you to turn an image into something far more spectacular than a photo in a frame. The following are some of the most popular types of photo art, along with an appropriate website link.

Photo handbags

Images can be placed on the sides of handbags, washbags and even purses.
www.digiprintz.com/bagsoflove

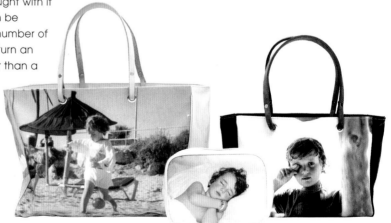

Canvas blocks

Canvas art blocks have been very popular in the last few years and now photo canvas blocks are available. These are canvas prints that are stretched over a wooden frame so that they are ready to hang. Canvas blocks are the most popular type of personalized art form, available in a range of sizes and shapes. Most places that handle canvas blocks can also print them onto wood blocks.

www.digiprintz.com/bagsoflove/photo_canvas.asp
www.willinspire.com
www.55max.com

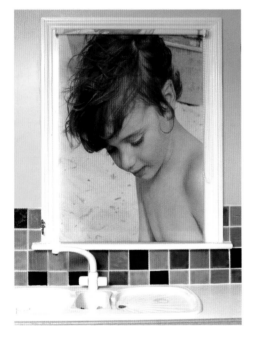

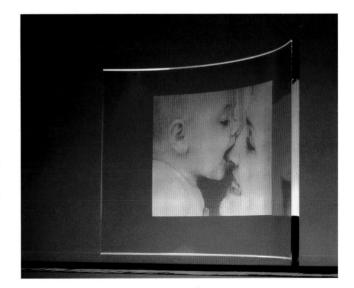

Window blinds

Add a really personalized feel to your home by introducing photo roller blinds, which can be made to measure to fit most windows. These are particularly appealing when the view from the room isn't too scenic!

www.digiprintz.com/bagsoflove/photo_blinds.asp

Engraved glass

Having images etched on to glass is the latest innovation in personalized art. The image is created by a laser, which makes thousands of tiny, but visible, fracture points in the glass. Engraved glass products include plaques, keyrings, tumblers and jewellery.

www.skydesign.biz

Making money from your pictures

A dream for many amateur photographers is to make money from their hobby. If your photographs are produced to a high enough standard, then there is a wealth of opportunities to make some spare cash, or even to earn a living, from your photography.

Commercial strategy

There are many photographers already making a good living from their craft, so breaking into the market is not going to be easy. On their side is an established reputation for delivering the goods, so whatever direction you take, making a name for yourself and building up a reputation is vital.

Your best bet is to begin small – in other words, test your market in your local area; then if you're relatively successful and your sales grow, you can consider trying to break into a nationwide (and eventually even an international) market.

Becoming established is a very difficult task to achieve, as is becoming well-known for your photographic skills. The various options that are outlined on these pages are just some to consider on how to make money from your pictures.

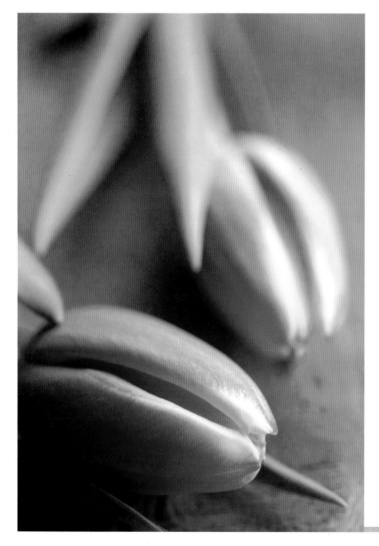

What to charge?

Determining how much to charge for an image or a service depends on your location, experience and competition. There is no set rate, but there are a few guidelines to consider. Charge too much, and you will frighten away potential customers; charge too little, and you will never make a profit. The best option is to look at the competition and find out their rates. Slightly undercut them to begin with, then charge more as demand increases.

Photography as a profession

There is no easy route to becoming a full-time photographer. Speak to the pros and you discover that some studied first; others worked as a photographer's assistant for a time; and some became a pro after years when photography was just a hobby. The biggest asset you can have, apart from natural talent, is a determination to succeed. With a few lucky breaks along the way, you might be able to make a living from photography.

TULIPS
Artistic images of subjects such as flowers have the potential to make money from greetings cards.

Magazine submissions

Photography magazines thrive on pictures, and most of them are open to submissions from their readers. If you have a good selection of images, it is worth sending them to magazines for consideration. If they are used, you will generally receive a fee – for instance, the UK-based magazine *Photography Monthly* pays up to £100 per image.

Photography competitions

Whatever the time of year, there are always one or two photography competitions worth entering. Photography magazines are usually a good bet, as well as national newspapers and general-interest magazines. As well as the potential to win big prizes, entering competitions can be used as a discipline to help you take more care of your pictures. If unsuccessful, study the winning images and try to adopt some of the techniques that the winning photographers have used.

Website

The old phrase 'Let your pictures do the talking' is a wise one. How better to show off your skills than using the images themselves? Setting up your own website, or having someone do it for you, is a relatively simple way of allowing an audience of millions around the world to view your work. Of course, the real struggle is getting people to view your website – using key words like 'photography' in the web address can help, but the website will receive more visits as your reputation grows.

Public exhibitions

An exhibition is a good way to have your images seen by the general public. Your local hall or art centre may not sound like a particularly exciting place to kick off your career, but it will allow future potential clients to view the standard of your work.

And don't discount your local market. Find out if there's a market stall selling art prints or paintings, and if so, are they willing to display and sell your work for a commission? This is a good way of gauging the popularity of your images.

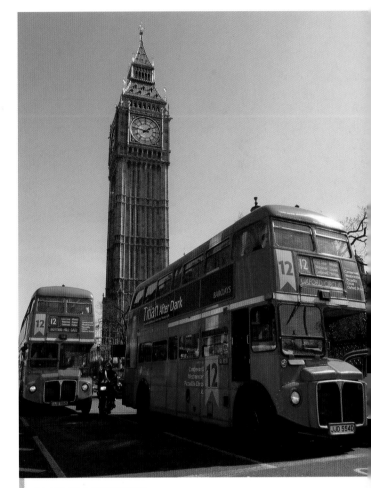

BIG BEN AND DOUBLE DECKERS
Pictures with famous landmarks and sights are potentially big sellers as postcards and calendars.

Stock pictures

Many photographers have their pictures with a stock library. The advantage is that the library can offer the pictures out to a far wider market than an individual could. The disadvantage is that the library takes a large chunk of the commission – usually around 50 per cent. You won't be able to submit individual images: libraries look to hold hundreds, if not thousands, of images from the same photographer, and expect regular supplies of new stock.

Historic moments in photography

What are the most important events in photography since its birth in the early 19th century? The following does not aim to cover every significant moment, but instead provides an easy reference guide to the people, products and images that influenced photography.

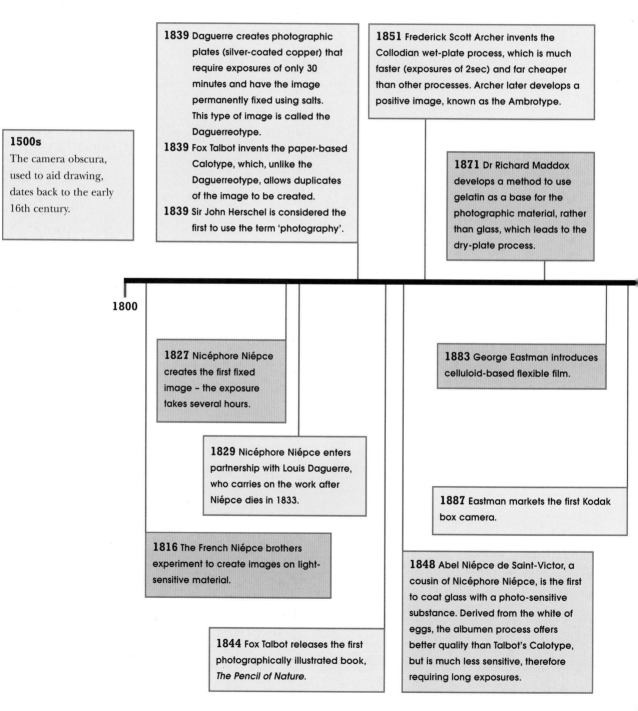

1500s
The camera obscura, used to aid drawing, dates back to the early 16th century.

1839 Daguerre creates photographic plates (silver-coated copper) that require exposures of only 30 minutes and have the image permanently fixed using salts. This type of image is called the Daguerreotype.

1839 Fox Talbot invents the paper-based Calotype, which, unlike the Daguerreotype, allows duplicates of the image to be created.

1839 Sir John Herschel is considered the first to use the term 'photography'.

1851 Frederick Scott Archer invents the Collodian wet-plate process, which is much faster (exposures of 2sec) and far cheaper than other processes. Archer later develops a positive image, known as the Ambrotype.

1871 Dr Richard Maddox develops a method to use gelatin as a base for the photographic material, rather than glass, which leads to the dry-plate process.

1800

1827 Nicéphore Niépce creates the first fixed image – the exposure takes several hours.

1829 Nicéphore Niépce enters partnership with Louis Daguerre, who carries on the work after Niépce dies in 1833.

1816 The French Niépce brothers experiment to create images on light-sensitive material.

1883 George Eastman introduces celluloid-based flexible film.

1887 Eastman markets the first Kodak box camera.

1848 Abel Niépce de Saint-Victor, a cousin of Nicéphore Niépce, is the first to coat glass with a photo-sensitive substance. Derived from the white of eggs, the albumen process offers better quality than Talbot's Calotype, but is much less sensitive, therefore requiring long exposures.

1844 Fox Talbot releases the first photographically illustrated book, *The Pencil of Nature*.

1904 The Lumière brothers reveal Autochrome plates for colour images.

1921 Man Ray creates Rayographs.

1924 Leica 35mm cameras are introduced.

1925 The first Leica camera, based on the body developed by Oskar Barnack and lenses by Max Berek, is introduced. It is called the Leica I. 'Leica' is derived from 'Leitz Camera'.

1925 The flash bulb is developed.

1928 The Eastman Kodak Company releases colour film for 16mm movie cameras.

1928 The Rolleiflex is introduced.

1913 Oskar Barnack produces the Ur-Leitz prototype, which provides the basis of future 35mm cameras.

1944 The Eastman Kodak Company introduces Kodacolor negative film.

1947 The Polaroid Land Camera, which produces a sepia print in 60sec, is marketed.

1947 The Magnum agency is formed.

1948 Hasselblad introduces its first 6 x 6cm-format SLR, the 1600F.

1948 Nikon introduces its first 35mm camera, the Nikon I rangefinder.

1948 Ansel Adams publishes his Zone System.

1944 The Eastman Kodak Company introduces Tri-X black-and-white negative film, still available today.

1964 Introduction of the Cibachrome process, for making prints from slides.

1964 The Pentax Spotmatic is the first SLR to feature a through the lens (TTL) meter.

1981 Pentax introduces the ME-F SLR, the forerunner to modern autofocus SLRs. Nikon follows in 1983 with its F3 AF, while Canon markets the T80 in 1985.

1982 Sony introduces the electronic digital stills camera.

1985 The Minolta 7000 is the world's first autofocus 35mm SLR.

1987 The Canon EOS 650 is the first 35mm autofocus SLR in what is now the world's best-selling AF SLR range.

2003 Canon introduces the EOS 300D, the first 6-mega-pixel AF SLR to become available within the price range of the consumer.

1900

2000

1932 The photoelectric cell light meter is introduced.

1932 The f64 group is founded by some of the most influential photographers of the time – Ansel Adams, Imogen Cunningham, Willard Van Dyke, Edward Weston, Sonya Noskowiak and John Paul Edwards. The aim is to promote 'straight' or 'pure' photography. The term 'f64' referred to the smallest aperture on many large-format camera lenses.

1934 Canon, or Kwanon as it is then known, introduces its first prototype camera, a 35mm rangefinder.

1936 Kodachrome film, in 35mm and 120 roll-film formats, is introduced a year after the emulsion is available for film cameras.

1936 Canon's first production camera, the Hansa Canon 35mm rangefinder, is based on the Kwanon prototype, and incorporates a Nikon lens.

1939 The stroboscopic flash head is announced.

1952 Pentax markets the Asahiflex I, Japan's first 35mm SLR.

1957 The Asahi Pentax is the first SLR using a pentaprism. 'Pentax' is a derivative of 'PENTAprism refleX'.

1959 Nikon introduces its first 35mm SLR, the Nikon F.

1959 Canon markets its first 35mm SLR, the Canon Flex.

1991 Kodak introduces digital version of Nikon F3 camera, with 1.3-megapixel sensor.

1995 The Nikon F5 is the first SLR to incorporate a metering sensor that uses colour to work out the exposure.

1996 The Advanced Photo System (APS) is introduced.

1999 Nikon announces the D1 digital SLR aimed at professionals. It sports a 2.74-megapixel SLR.

1971 The Pentax ES offers the world's first TTL automatic exposure system, with aperture priority AE as well as manual.

1972 Olympus introduces its M-1 (later renamed the OM-1) 35mm SLR, which becomes an instant classic.

1972 Developed for the 1972 Munich Olympics, the Canon F1 boasts a static pellicle mirror and motordrive, giving a top speed of nine frames per second.

1975 Mamiya introduces the world's first 6 x 4.5cm SLR, the Mamiya 645.

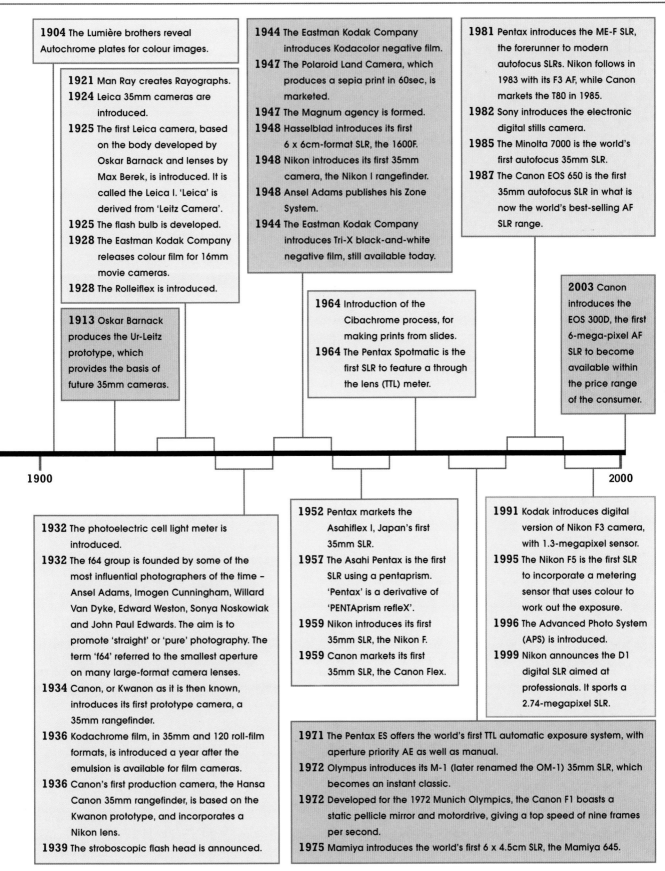

Glossary

A

Aberration
Term used to describe an optical defect in a lens.

AE-L
Autoexposure lock. Facility to lock the exposure independently of the autofocus.

Aperture
The opening in a lens, which determines how much light passes through the lens.

APS
Advanced Photo System. The most recent film format, launched in 1996.

Archive
Process by which images are treated or stored for long-term life expectancy.

Artefact
Unwanted information in a digital image – usually evident in images showing high compression, such as JPEGs.

Autoexposure
This is the system where the exposure is calculated automatically by the camera.

Autofocus
The system whereby the lens focus is controlled by the camera so that the subject is automatically brought into focus.

B

Back-up
Security measure where a copy of an image, document or entire hard disk is made in case the original is damaged or lost.

Bit
The basic unit of a digital image or file, made up of a 0 or a 1.

Bracket
A sequence of identical shots taken at slightly different exposures.

Brush
A tool used in image-manipulation packages to apply effects such as blurring or dodging.

Burning
A technique used in the darkroom and digitally to increase exposure in specific areas of an image.

Byte
A standard unit in computing terms, a byte is made up of eight bits.

Bulb
Exposure mode that allows the user to set very long exposure times.

C

C-41
Popular process for developing colour print film.

CCD
Charge-coupled device. One of the most common types of image sensor used in digital cameras.

Chromogenic film
Black-and-white print film that can be processed in C-41 standard colour print chemistry.

Cloning
A technique in image-manipulation software where a clone tool is used to replace certain areas with a clone from another area.

CMOS
Complementary metal oxide semiconductor. An increasingly popular type of image sensor in digital cameras.

Colour cast
A poorly calibrated white balance, or use of the wrong type of film to suit particular lighting conditions, can result in the whole image exhibiting an unwanted colour tone.

Colour temperature
The measurement of the colour of light, usually expressed in degrees Kelvin (K).

Compression
Digital process where an image is reduced in size when stored. Depending on the process, this may or may not result in a loss in image quality.

Contrast
Describes the difference in brightness from the darkest to the lightest points in an image.

CMYK
Cyan Magenta Yellow Black. The four inks used in colour printing.

Crop
The removal of unwanted areas of a frame.

Cross-processing
The development of a film in an alternate chemistry for creative purposes, for instance, C-41 film in E-6 chemistry or E-6 film in C-41 chemistry.

D

Depth of field
The amount of a scene (from the nearest point to the furthest) that appears sharply focused. This varies according to several factors, including focal length, focusing distance and aperture.

Depth of focus
Distance in front of and behind the film plane that will retain sharp focus of the image.

Dodging
Darkroom technique used to reduce the amount of exposure in particular areas of a print.

DPI
Dots per inch. Measurement for printer and scanner resolution.

DX-coding
System that uses a black and silver grid on a 35mm film canister to inform a camera of the film speed and type.

Dye sublimation
Printer that produces very high-quality colour prints.

E

E-6
The most popular chemistry used for processing colour slide film.

Exposure compensation
System used to override the camera's indicated exposure and add or subtract a preset value.

Exposure latitude
Tolerance of a film to over- and underexposure. Print film has the widest latitude; slide film the least.

F

f/number
Common term used to describe aperture setting, such as f/4 or f/8.

File format
Term used to describe how a digital file is stored. Common examples include JPEG, GIF and TIFF.

Filter
Optical glass/resin used with lens to provide creative options. Also used to describe digital effects with some image-manipulation software.

FireWire
Common type of computer connection. Also known as IEEE1394.

Fixed focus
A lens where the focus is fixed at a particular distance and image sharpness is determined by depth of field.

Fixed lens
A lens that does not change focal length, such as a 28mm wide-angle or 400mm telephoto.

Flare
Non-image forming light that passes through the lens. Usually the result of a bright light source in or just outside the frame.

Flash
Artificial light source that provides a strong, brief burst of light to aid exposure.

Fogging
Non-image exposure of photographic emulsion that can partly or completely ruin the image.

G

GIF
Graphic Interchange Format. A digital file format commonly used on the Web.

Grain
Visible clumps of silver halide in an image. The faster the film speed, the more evident the grain.

Guide number (GN)
Used to determine a flashgun's power. GN = subject distance x aperture.

H

Histogram
Graphical representation of aspects of an image such as contrast and tonal range.

Hyperfocal focusing
Technique used to determine the hyperfocal distance and consequently maximize depth of field.

I

Infinity lock
Feature on many digital and film compacts for fixing the focus of the lens to infinity when shooting through glass.

Inkjet printer
Most common type of home printer, which works by spraying tiny dots of ink onto the paper.

Interpolation
Artificial method for increasing image size/resolution by adding pixels.

ISO
International Standards Organization. Rating used to determine film speed.

J

JPEG
Joint Photographic Expert Group. Popular file format as it reduces file size, albeit with loss in image quality.

L

Layer
Important feature on some image-manipulation programs, allowing sophisticated adjustments to be made to the image.

LCD
Liquid Crystal Display. Found on most cameras and flashguns, and used to provide important functional information.

LCD monitor
Screen on the back of digital cameras that allows images to be composed or reviewed.

LED
Light-Emitting Diode. Coloured lamp used to provide warning or confirmation.

Lossless compression
Image file compressed without loss of information.

Lossy compression
Image file compressed with loss of information, so the image quality is degraded.

M

Megapixel
A shortened term for 1,000,000 pixels.

Memory card
Removable and reusable card for storing digital images and files. Various types available, in different capacities. CompactFlash, SD, xD and MemoryStick are the most popular types.

Metering pattern
The system used by the camera to calculate the

exposure. Patterns can range from the relatively basic centre-weighted average to sophisticated multizone patterns.

Monochrome
Image made up of grey tones from black to white.

P

Parallax error
The difference between the viewfinder image and that recorded by the lens.

Pixel
Short for picture element. The smallest unit in the formation of an image.

R

Red-eye
Direct flash photography often results in blood vessels in the retina being recorded on the image, providing subjects with red pupils, or red-eye.

Resolution
The level of quality and detail recorded in an image. The higher the resolution, the finer the detail.

S

Saturation
Refers to the intensity of colours in an image.

Scanner
Device used to convert physical images (film and print) and documents into a digital file.

Self-timer
System that provides a delay before the shutter is triggered and the exposure is taken.

Shutter speed
This determines the duration of an exposure.

Silver halide
Light-sensitive particles used in film and print emulsion.

Single-use camera
Also widely known as disposable, this is a film (and more recently digital) cameras that are only used once, then processed.

SLR
Single lens reflex. Camera that provides a through-the-lens view in the finder for accurate composition when taking pictures.

T

Telephoto
A lens that offers a shorter field of view and increased magnification than that of the human eye.

TIFF
Tagged Image File Format. Image format offering very high quality at the expense of a relatively large file size.

Unsharp Mask
Effective sharpening tool in many image-manipulation software packages.

USB
Universal Serial Bus. Standard connection found on most digital cameras, peripherals and computers.

V

Viewfinder
Window through which the image is composed on compact and rangefinder cameras.

Vignetting
Darkening of the corners of the frame, due to an obstruction – usually a lens hood or filter.

Z

Zoom
Lens that allows the focal length to be changed, such as a 28–70mm.

Acknowledgments

Thanks to contributors Bjorn Thomassen, Billy Stock, Derek Horlock, Chris Rout, Jon Hicks, Lee Pengelly and Simon Stafford for allowing use of your wonderful images in the book. I'd also like to thank the various photo manufacturers who supplied essential images and information, in particular Canon, Epson, Minolta, Nikon, Olympus, Pentax and Sigma.

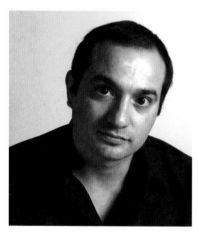

About the author

Daniel Lezano is editor of *Photography Monthly* magazine, one of the UK's fastest growing photo titles and Archant Magazine of the Year 2003. Previously technical editor at *Practical Photography* magazine, Daniel is widely acknowledged as one of the country's leading photography writers, regularly interviewing some of the world's best-known photographers, testing the latest cameras and equipment and appearing in the national press and radio. For examples of his photography and magazine articles, visit www.lezano.com

Index (**bold** page numbers refer to significant coverage)